A publication of the

CENTER FOR RESEARCH AND DEVELOPMENT
IN HIGHER EDUCATION
University of California, Berkeley

LELAND L. MEDSKER, *Director*

CONFORMITY

WARREN BRYAN MARTIN

conformity

standards
and
change
in
higher
education

Jossey-Bass Inc., Publishers
615 Montgomery Street • San Francisco • 1969

THE JOSSEY-BASS SERIES IN HIGHER EDUCATION

General Editors

JOSEPH AXELROD *and* MERVIN B. FREEDMAN
San Francisco State College

PREFACE

The biblical admonition, "Beware when all men speak well of you" need not be applied to educational researchers. They have never had the privilege of being threatened by universal adulation. The biological and physical scientists may require such a warning, but seven decades of educational research have produced an impressive mass of data matched only by the complaints raised against it.

When Guy T. Buswell, T. R. McConnell, Ann Heiss, and Dorothy Knoell of the Center for the Study of Higher Education, University of California, Berkeley, presented their report of 1966 entitled "Training for Educational Research," they began by stating certain problems in educational research that are the basis for persistent criticisms of the field. Research, they said, is often "fragmentary and small-scale," "of relatively unimaginative and uncomplicated design," and "the climate which nurtures research has too often been missing. . . ."[1]

---

[1] Guy Buswell et al., *Training for Educational Research* (Berkeley: Center for the Study of Higher Education, 1966), p. 1.

Other writers, some of them researchers and some not, have developed these and other themes. Lewis Mayhew of Stanford writes: ". . . many institutional and educational studies end with inconclusive findings"; ". . . although there are many instruments available for institutional research, there are few which can get at the refined data current questions demand"; ". . . results have not been well-communicated"; ". . . there exists no general theoretical design into which various studies can fit and contribute to the significance of each other."[2] Francis A. J. Ianni, U.S. Office of Education, comments: ". . . educational research has failed to catch the political and public imagination because it has been unimaginative . . ."; "the most common form of educational research is still the small, easily managed research project"; ". . . we have yet to show an innovative, creative vigor matching our counterparts in medicine, science, agriculture and industry."[3]

A point of significance, yet one not often recognized, is that these criticisms are not new. They are, in fact, reiterations of what has been said throughout the history of the educational research movement. In 1927, G. M. Whipple, in an article called "The Improvement of Educational Research," argued that many investigations failed to yield significant results because of the superficial and sporadic character of the problems selected for investigation.[4] Writing in the next year, Walter S. Monroe expanded Whipple's criticism and concluded by saying that "much of the material published appears to be subject to such serious limitations that it cannot be credited with much value."[5]

V. A. C. Henmon, discussing the function, value, and future of research in colleges and universities, claimed in 1934 that one of the great defects of research in higher education was that it had

[2] Lewis Mayhew, "Educational Research, Its Capabilities and Limitations." *Research in Higher Education* (New York: College Entrance Examination Board, 1964), p. 6.

[3] Francis A. J. Ianni, "Federal Concern for Research in Education." *Research in Higher Education* (New York: College Entrance Examination Board, 1964), p. 63.

[4] G. M. Whipple, "The Improvement of Educational Research," *School and Society*, 26 (1927), 249–259.

[5] Walter S. Monroe et al., *Ten Years of Educational Research*, University of Illinois Bulletin, Vol. 35, No. 51 (Urbana: University of Illinois, 1928), p. 87.

"centered very largely on marginal or secondary problems, important to be sure, but not the fundamental ones."[6] Although Henmon felt that the responsibility for this condition was not to be placed so much on the researchers as on the intransigent conservatism of college administrators, and while Monroe held out the hope that things were changing so that researchers would become more critical of each other's work to the end that the quality of research would soon be appreciably better, the problems they described seem very much with us to this day and the changes they hoped for seem to have been deferred.

The comparisons critics were making during the twenties and thirties were of educational research in the pioneer period—from the turn of the century to the first world war. Research recognizable by modern standards began with J. M. Rice's effort in 1894 to measure student achievement in spelling by giving a uniform spelling test to pupils in a number of cities. The effect of Rice's work was immediate. It was an inspiration to E. L. Thorndike, S. A. Courtis, L. P. Ayres and other researchers, but most educators reacted negatively. Ayres commented on the situation that developed after Rice had presented his research (1897) at a meeting of the Department of Superintendence:

> The educators who discussed his findings and those who reviewed them in the educational press united in denouncing as foolish, reprehensible, and from every point of view indefensible, the effort to discover anything about the value of the teaching of spelling by finding out whether or not the children could spell.[7]

It is clear that creativity and criticism in research, like the front and back of a bus, have always gone everywhere together, and indications are that the immediate future will not be different. Most of the criticisms of educational research were exemplified in the Inventory of Current Research on Higher Education, a project

[6] V. A. C. Henmon, "Contributions of Research to Higher Education," *National Society for the Study of Education*, 37th Yearbook, Part II (Chicago: University of Chicago Press, 1938), p. 239.

[7] L. P. Ayres, "History and Present Status of Education Measurements," *Seventeenth Yearbook of the National Society for the Study of Education*, Part II (Bloomington: Public School Publishing Company, 1918), p. 11.

sponsored jointly by the Carnegie Commission on the Future of Higher Education and the Center for Research and Development in Higher Education, University of California, Berkeley. Over nine hundred projects had been catalogued according to information provided by researchers on a questionnaire circulated by the Center, or as gathered from other sources, and abstracts were filed under eight main categories—students, faculty, administrators, structures, functions, governance, graduate/professional schools, and the demand for higher education. Probes on current research extended to sixty countries. While there were many well-designed, competently managed, entirely relevant research projects listed in the Inventory, and therefore the following comments are not meant to repudiate most current research on higher education, yet even a cursory glance at project abstracts shows that the bases for the persistent criticisms of the field remain. Researchers still have trouble defining a researchable problem, establishing control of experimental circumstances, designing testing instruments of sufficient sophistication to be serviceable, determining the authority of theoretical ideas, working through to the verification of hypotheses, and making findings known to educators willing to implement data in institutional situations.

Most educational research today, to turn to other matters, is a part-time operation. Between 10 and 20 per cent of the work seems to be the primary responsibility of graduate students, one of their several tasks, while the great majority of professors involved in research are equally committed to classroom assignments and other academic duties. Even in the major research centers, it is customary for senior personnel to have joint appointments in the sponsoring university and for them to give, officially, not more than half-time for research. No wonder the work proceeds so slowly and is disseminated so poorly.

"Knowledge," said Alfred North Whitehead, "does not keep any better than fish." The same must be said of research findings. A carefully organized, well-written research report can be very helpful if it is presented to an appropriate audience with all the freshness of fish drawn wiggling from the water. But few things are more useless and offensive, save perhaps fish left sunning on the dock, than research data unanalyzed or poorly disseminated. If research is to become a national resource, making research results known is as important as the research itself. At the present time there are few persons available for the task of development who have the skills necessary to work with both educational researchers and resourceful educators. Furthermore, it is not certain that the functions of research and development can be separated and delegated. The research and development process, Launor F. Carter has stated in his report of a study for the Defense Department on research and development associated with six successful weapons systems, was quite informal, often not well organized, and one in which personal interactions took on greater significance than formal lines of authority or communication. For Carter, the traditional assumption that there is a smooth sequence from research to development to utilization of results is false. These functions are often carried forward more or less simultaneously, with researchers involved all along the line.[8] It may be equally true for educational research and development. If so, the fact that research in this field is a part-time operation compounds the difficulty of relating research to practice and researchers to practitioners.

The paucity of sophisticated testing instruments in current educational research is another problem. Not only are the questionnaires and other data-gathering techniques sometimes crude mechanisms with which to get at complex issues—will Dame Research be killed by a blunt instrument?—they are also too often a hodgepodge of items collected here and there, items that may or may not have gained validation over time but that certainly represent varying and even contradictory theoretical conceptualizations. Surely the qualitative deficiencies of testing instruments are equally the cause, along with the quantitative deluge of questionnaires sent out, of the rising tide of resentment from administrators, faculty, students and various publics toward social science methodologies and the research they produce. Again, present complaints are variations on themes stated much earlier. In 1925, E. W. Butterfield, who professed to be at that time answering a questionnaire a day, mainly from graduate students, wrote:

For a time I was disturbed when I was obliged to give

[8] Launor F. Carter, "From Research to Development to Use" (mimeographed) (Santa Monica: System Development Corporation, 1966).

decisive answers to questions in fields where I had not the slightest interest or experience. At last I began to see the true principle of the questionnaire. The individual answer may be ill-considered or given in jest or even written on the wrong line. It may be the answer of a philosopher or a fool, a savant or a sophomore. It does not matter even if all the answers are wrong. All that is necessary is to gather them in sufficient numbers, count them, give them appropriate weights, apply the formula and in some mysterious way pure truth is the result.[9]

Thirty years later Kenneth Boulding would be addressing himself to the same phenomenon, and categorizing the chief problem as "data fixation":

Its principal symptom is a certain obsessiveness with arithmetic—the feeling that once a number has been arrived at by recognized statistical ritual something has been accomplished. . . . I must confess that I regard the invention of statistical pseudo-quantities like the coefficient of correlation as one of the minor intellectual disasters of our time; it has provided legions of students and investigators with opportunities to substitute arithmetic for thought on a grand scale.[10]

While there was a tendency in the early period of research, especially in the college surveys, to take on unmanageably large assignments and to come in with unrealistically sweeping recommendations—this was one of the criticisms of the much battered Allen study in Wisconsin[11]—the preference in recent times has been

[9] E. W. Butterfield, "The Plenary Inspiration of the Dotted Line," *Educational Review,* 68 (January 1925), 2.

[10] Kenneth E. Boulding, "Evidence for an Administrative Science," *Administrative Science Quarterly,* 3, No. 1 (June 1958), 16–17.

[11] The University of Wisconsin Survey (1913–1914), by William H. Allen. The words of Wisconsin's President E. A. Birge and Dean C. C. Sellery indicate the negative reception accorded this survey:

The outcome of the Allen survey is an accumulation of some 1200 to 1500 or more "suggestions" which are the "next steps" for the University. It is obvious that these suggestions cannot be considered in detail. Nor is it necessary to do so, for it is plain that these "suggestions" can be of little use in their present form. No organism (except perhaps a centipede) ever contemplates taking as many as 100 "next steps" at once, not to speak of 1000 or 2000. "Suggestions" in such number and variety, therefore, may serve to relieve the type of mind that makes them. . . . Dr. Allen is both in knowledge and in spirit wholly outside of every university. Dr. Allen's suggestions are, therefore, those of an alien. They are like those that an

for the discrete project that may substitute control for content and data for meanings. Much educational research is a small-bore operation.

Another limitation on current research is the circumscribed role given it. The "researcher" does that which could be done by a registrar or development officer, yet many administrators who give their institutional researcher circumscribed assignments of this sort are prominent among the critics who characterize research results as "junk." They do not see that the researcher has given them what they called for. It takes an artist of rare talents to produce interesting junk sculpture. Usually, sculpture done with materials drawn from the junk pile betrays its origins. So it is with educational research.

It would help to limit the use of the word "researcher" to those who are in fact free for research, even as units in the institution designated "research centers" or "research bureaus" must be understood to serve the college or university best only when they are free to do their work without compromise. The other jobs that need to be done—those that facilitate or implement existing policies and arrangements—should be carried out in offices other than those designated for research. Now it is impossible to separate the researcher from the technician or campus functionary and, consequently, almost all research efforts are either suspect or of limited value. The problem can only be solved at its source. Researchers must have freedom for research. If such freedom cannot be given, what is done should not be called research.

There is, therefore, the problem of knowing the end from the beginning. Allowed neither creativity nor criticism, the researcher gives back "findings" that conform to the values, goals, and assumptions of his sponsoring agency or administrator.[12] Daniel Griffiths, speaking about research on educational administration, develops this point and makes two recommendations:

---

educated Chinaman might write down, after six months in the country, as suggestions for improving the details of government in all of its grades from school district to nation.

[12] For more on this subject, see Paul F. Lazarsfeld and Sam D. Sieber, *Organizing Educational Research* (Englewood Cliffs, N.J.: Prentice-Hall, 1964), pp. 32–33.

One of the practices which is most damaging to the reputation of administrative research is engaged in by a large number
of professional organizations, state education departments, and
school systems. This is the practice of subordinating research to
policy development. What happens is this: an organization, say
a state education association, is confronted with a problem such
as the legislature considering a bill advocating compulsory merit
rating for teachers. The association, through its board of directors,
publicly goes on record as opposing the bill while indicating that
their research division will "study" the problem. What they
actually mean is that their research division will dig up the
evidence to support their stand.
It should be obvious that this sort of practice cannot be continued if research is to command a position of respectability in
the educational world. Two steps must be taken if respectability
is to be retained. The first step is that administrators must be
convinced that research should take place before policies are
formulated, not afterward, and the second step is that researchers
must be taught not to prostitute their labors to the whims of
their administrators. Neither of these steps can be attained easily,
but attained they must be or administrative research will continue to have little value in the actual administration of organizations.[13]

The recurrent charge against educational researchers that
their projects are lacking in theory, in purposeful theoretical frame-
works, requires qualification. Research projects are not lacking in
hypotheses or theories, though some show a pinched vision. There
may be a shortage of theory about specific facets of research—a
theory of student development, for example—but there are implicit
yet motivating themes about man and society underlying most
educational research. Two comments can be made in this connection: First, these theories of human development are largely unexamined by present-day researchers. Second, most of the fundamental values therein conform to straight-line western liberalism—
confidence in man, his abilities, worth, or essential goodness; confidence in democratic processes, tolerance, diversity, pluralism; confidence in the superiority of communicating ideas by cognitive

[13] Daniel E. Griffiths, "Research and Theory in Educational Admin-
istration," in *Perspectives on Educational Administration and the Behavioral
Sciences* (Eugene, Oregon: Center for the Advanced Study of Educational
Administration), p. 45.

rationality, coming to the emotions by the mind in preference to coming to the mind by the emotions. These and other ideas are intellectual assumptions of researchers as much as other academics. Martin Trow has said that research should "illuminate" realities.[14] Good research does that, but what is also evident is that research illuminates the researcher's values or the sponsoring agency's perception of the good, the true, and the beautiful. It has been often said that researchers find what they are looking for, and what they have found, given their values, on the evidence of their projects, makes them agents of socialization as much as the institutions within which they work. Data are, therefore, always purposeful—to a purpose.

Few research projects show promise of criticizing existing institutional values—as distinct from criticism of structural forms and organizational arrangements—or seem likely to turn up alternative models or point new directions. Few researchers regard their assignment to include the creation of tension within an institution. There is almost no confrontation research.

No claim is made that the Institutional Character study was free of the weaknesses that have characterized most educational research. The initial project design, the testing instruments employed, the interviewing methodology, the handling of data, these and other aspects of the study share many of the limitations alluded to earlier.

The most serious problems for this study were caused by the determination of the principal researcher to study educational issues in institutional settings that were too large to be neatly encapsulated. To make possible relevant data, given the subject of conformity and diversity in higher education, it was necessary to design research contexts—slightly structured interviews, open-ended questionnaire items—that could accommodate these big issues and welcome individualized responses. Consequently, findings were difficult to categorize, being as complex and multidimensional as life in the institution of higher education. And they were, of course, subject to a variety of interpretations. One alternative would have been to

[14] Martin Trow, "Social Research and Educational Policy," *Research in Higher Education* (New York: College Entrance Examination Board, 1964), p. 53.

tighten the subject to researchable proportions, given the state of the art, which means limiting the endeavor to concerns that can be quantified and proceeding no further in conclusions than empirical generalizations permitted by the data. Thus, thought about data is restrained to that which is the data. But, as a "natural area" of a campus may be destroyed by clearing away underbrush which, while an obstruction to hikers, is essential to the area's ecology, so too there is danger that controls introduced by the researcher on his subject may disrupt the delicate balance of factors essential to an understanding of that which he proposes to study. Another alternative, one less honorable but no less common, is to take findings resulting from a tight research design and rigorous methodology and force them into the mold of one's preconceptions or values, insisting all the while that the study was inductive or scientific.

If the first alternative is a variation of the dictum that "a bird in the hand is worth two in the bush," the second alternative encourages a delusion that the two in the bush are really in the hand. While the second course of action may be dismissed as deception, or self-deception, the first suggests a serious challenge to practices actually followed in this study. To say that a bird in the hand is worth two in the bush makes sense for falconers, but it is senseless for bird-watchers, and educational researchers are, or ought to be, more nearly the latter than the former. The bird-watchers' purpose is informed observation of activity in the natural setting. The control, therefore, must be in the observer, not the observed. The observer may have goals, and strategies to achieve them—the preservation of nature and the natural life there, the promotion of game refuges and natural areas—but as a bird-watcher he is not content to study a canary in a cage. He seeks to research his subject in its setting and accepts the risks attending his determination. Disciplined inquiry, therefore, whether the subject is birds or students, means disciplined inquirers more than controlled subject matter.

Once deciding to proceed with an open research design, it follows that data gathered under such arrangements may inform, or even persuade, but never demand. They are in the secondary, not primary, role. In this study, therefore, project findings have been brought to bear on theoretical conceptualizations, observations, experiences, insights of the researchers. The book is mainly about educational ideas and attendant problems, conditions, prospects; the project data have been used to illuminate—that is, to support, qualify, or contradict them. Thus the researchers, while affected by data, are not the agents of them. Nor are they neutral intermediaries or brokers operating between impersonal forces. The relationship of the researcher to his work is much more existential and heuristic; there is interaction, but in the end the data were made for man, not man for the data.

Crucial variables in the handling of the data, then, are the discipline and experience of the researcher, even as the factor crucial in reporting it is his honesty. Knowing how hard it is to control the context from which data came, he must work hard to control his use of what he gets. And most of all he must know and control himself—for the researcher assigns meanings to the findings, and, with the policy-maker, translates those data from a description or comparison of what "is" to advocacy of what "ought to be." That is an awesome responsibility, and the beginning of wisdom is to recognize that the human condition is the only independent variable.

Research of this sort cannot dictate, but it can advise. As an expression of disciplined inquiry, it may, as Fred J. Kelly said thirty years ago, modify the theoretical background in the minds of educators.[15] And as this orientation changes, changes in practice follow.

Acknowledgments

Every research project has a character of its own. The interaction between what the researchers bring to their work and what the subject studied brings to the researchers becomes the distinguishing feature of the project—its character.

That fact is no less evident when the research is on institutional character. The search for distinctiveness in colleges and universities reveals that which is distinguishable in researchers: where they look and what they see are affected by their attitudes and

[15] Fred J. Kelly, "Contributions of Research to Higher Education," *National Society for the Study of Education,* 37th Yearbook, Part II (Chicago: University of Chicago Press, 1938), p. 239.

values. Yet these qualities are not unaffected by external contacts. The institutions studied have assumptions and objectives, traits and distinctions that in turn influence the perspectives of the researcher. Character is the outcome of acting and being acted upon.

Research, therefore, must always be thought of as shared research, not only because its results are disseminated in some way with a greater or lesser degree of significance, not only because it builds on the findings of other projects, but also it is shared research in the sense that any project is dependent on the goodwill and cooperation of the institutions studied. Their formal contributions are the data collected in questionnaires and interviews. Their informal contributions, hardly less important, are the courtesies and services provided for visitors during the time of the project. Researchers involved in the Institutional Character study are greatly indebted to the participating schools for contributions of both types, and the character of the study has been, no doubt, affected by these relationships.

The nature of the project was also influenced by the methodological and professional diversity within the research staff. Edyth Short, Postgraduate Research Associate, Catherine D. Lyon, Research Assistant, and Judi Wilkinson, Research Assistant, came into the study from training in the social sciences, while David Kamen, Research Assistant, and Warren Martin, Project Director, were trained in the humanities. There was much cross-fertilization of ideas as the project progressed, but the perspectives of researchers remained in tension throughout and were reflected in the types of work done. Short, Lyon, and Wilkinson concentrated on "marginals," statistical "cross-cuts," and various methodological problems. Kamen and Martin dwelt on theoretical conceptualizations, syntheses, and field applications. Differences of opinion were frequent and substantive. There were times when the project itself seemed to be a test of the perturbational theory of learning.

Just as there was organizational diversity in the schools studied, so there were professional differences in the study's staff. Yet, as there were similarities in values across types of institutions in the sample, so there were shared interests among project personnel—for example, in cross-disciplinary research, in change and direction for higher education. Differences meant that similarities would be kept under scrutiny, even as that which was shared made differences tolerable.

James Curtis and Edwin Murray were project assistants who joined the aforementioned staff for short periods of time but, as with the others, made significant contributions to research design and evaluation.

The Center for Research and Development in Higher Education, University of California, Berkeley, provided a congenial setting for the project. Leland L. Medsker, Director, and other researchers created an atmosphere that was open yet critical, supportive without being sentimental.

Joseph Axelrod and Algo Henderson read the research report in preliminary draft, made useful criticisms and emendations, and then, in a demonstration of unforgettable magnanimity, read and commented on revised portions of the text. Paul Dressel, Roy Niblett, and Patricia Cross read portions of this manuscript and made useful criticisms. Editorial assistance was provided by Julie Pesonen and Julie Hurst. Moffett Hall was typist and occasional bibliographer. Other typists included Lilly Grenz, Ann Sherman, Rosemary Moyer, and Catherine Pernish. Typist for the final manuscript was Mildred Bowman.

All contributed to the ethos of the study as well as to its form and substance. The words of Martin Buber express the regard of the project director for his colleagues:

> The ones who count are those persons who . . . respond to and are responsible for the continuation of the living spirit, each in the active stillness of his sphere of work.

Berkeley, California   WARREN BRYAN MARTIN
September, 1969

CONTENTS

xxi

CONFORMITY

For two friends
who taught me to value ideas

I

Ideology, Organization, and Innovation

No theme has been more often mentioned by educators as a chief characteristic of American higher education than its diversity, the number and types of educational institutions, the various curricula, the range of opportunities afforded students—these and other features have been considered hallmarks of our system. The State of California has often been cited as providing an example of diversity among educational institutions, including as it does a nine-campus university, eighteen state colleges and nearly ninety junior colleges among its public institutions which, with its private colleges and universities, professional and special programs, brings the total of institutions to about three hundred. The University of California has been considered by many to be a model of program diversity—

1

10,000 courses provided in hundreds of different fields of study for 96,000 students.

Currently, however, there seems to be a slowly evolving shift in the American educator's understanding of this long-established theme, a shift by which diversity may come to take on a wider and richer meaning. Heretofore, although the concept was broadly defined, it actually stood for diversity in form and function. American colleges and universities have shown great variety in size, programs, sources of funding, and structural arrangements. However, there was comparatively little diversity at the level of educational assumptions, goals, and values. American schools have offered many routes to the goals of socialization and professionalism. The substance of socialization has been determined by what one may call an American value orthodoxy, usually associated with the Protestant ethic, a complex set of values revolving around a concept of work and competition that has been shared by most Catholics, Jews, agnostics, and atheists in this country as well as by Protestants. Both Protestant and non-Protestant traditions have made major contributions to the creation of such an orthodoxy, and institutions of higher education, as agents of socialization, were charged with maintenance and improvement of the tradition. Therefore, they taught a variety of means, including dissent, by which Americans were free to achieve orthodoxy's consensual end.

Meanwhile, the goal of professionalism has held sway on the campus. The same academics who were content for sociopolitical values to be set by forces outside the campus insisted on their right to give a professional cast to the curriculum. Professionalism developed first in response to the need of industrial democracy for well-trained personnel. It prospered under the belief that work dignifies, professional work most of all. Such competence could make it possible for members of the lower classes to obtain otherwise unobtainable social status. Professionalism came to the campus with the establishment of Johns Hopkins University in 1876, with its emphasis on rigorous graduate and professional education. From Hopkins, and later Clark University, professionalism spread rapidly to other universities, and even to liberal arts colleges. One of its ramifications was the standardization movement in education whereby qualitative and quantitative criteria were established to improve the widely dispersed and quite divergent institutions. Such developments, it was expected, would validate diversity, assuring the quality and integrity of American education's variety of ways to socialization and professionalism.

What was not widely recognized then, but has lately become better known, is that because means are ends in the process of becoming, an emphasis on diversity in means leads eventually to pressures for diversity in ends. This is now happening. The traditional emphasis on variety in structure, organization, methodology, and style in American higher education has culminated in contemporary movements toward more substantive diversity in goals, purposes, and values. This is not to say that these matters were entirely ignored until now—some diversity of assumptions and objectives is present in every epoch—but we may be seeing a shift of emphasis. Whereas until recently the assumption has been unchallenged that higher education should emphasize value similarities, the emergence of a concern for institutional as well as individual identity characterized by unique or distinctive values is upon us. In other words, excellence achieved through imitation seems now to be challenged by an interest in value differentiation. In addition to the likelihood that this shift is being affected by the interior logic of the American tradition—constant talk about diversity is finally convincing some people that it ought to be substantive—other factors are influencing the current trend, some external to higher education and some internal.

It is a commonplace that changes in education occur at a far slower rate than changes elsewhere in society. Innovations in medical science, for example, are said to proceed from research to development to general dissemination in three to five years, while innovations in education take thirty to fifty years. But such talk does not take into account one crucial, present development. In the past, changes in education came slowly because educators lived under what may be called the assurance of adequacy, under the confidence that what they were doing and, albeit to a lesser degree, the way they were doing it, was trustworthy or at least adequate to the need. Now, however, that confidence is badly shaken. Many educators are ready to admit that students under the existing system have too often been passive rather than active learners, that subject matter in the curriculum has usually been inert, not vital; static, not active; at best formal, at worst irrelevant. They also recognize now that higher education has been professionally functional but socially dysfunctional. Its technocratic orientation has belied its claims to value diversity, while the emphasis on quantitative criteria—with pressures for grades, credits, awards—has had negative qualitative consequences. Gone, therefore, is the old assurance of adequacy, indeed, the arrogance of adequacy.

While institutional anxieties stemming from a recognition of failures are internal prods to changes in higher education, there are also external developments that affect prospects for changes. Most alterations in education, viewed historically, have been initiated outside the institution and have literally forced their way into the structure. Today, the same thing is beginning to happen, although now external pressures for change are being heightened by internal uncertainties.

What are those pressures from the outside that are promoting educational changes? There is, for one thing, the technological-electronic transformation of the general society. It will affect education, and not only in terms of computer-assisted instruction or other adaptations of machine technology. The curriculum will be changed too. Colleges and universities will train the experts required, as John Kenneth Galbraith has emphasized, or risk having the corporations move into education and the information transferral business to take over the training of the personnel they want. Because universities do not want to lose their virtual monopoly in training the expert society, they may be expected to change to satisfy this demand. These new influences will affect not only institutions, but people. While some authorities fear that the consequence of computer technology will be the depersonalization of human beings, others see in the "technetronic age," with its new sources of power and new means of managing it, the prospect that man will at last be freed to be man—individual man; he will be free to do that which satisfies him personally rather than that which obligates him to others or to things.

Another external influence, the new youth movement, presses for change in an opposite direction. The radicals and revolutionaries of this force are indebted to the university for training and for issues, yet because they are being driven off campus, they may be viewed as an external influence. But what these youth do in the city affects students on campus.

That power is in the eyes of the beholder is an old insight given new emphasis among left-radicals. They see that the institution of learning, by its very nature as a humanistically oriented entity, has no authenticity apart from the student's acceptance of it. If the student refuses to agree to the tutelary relationship that has been the backbone of faculty-student contacts, the American university as traditionally conceived fails. And it is not only the learning process that requires student goodwill. Another fact of life is that the majority of educational institutions of this country are not financially strong enough to scorn student opinion—their financial survival depends on student support. They do not have the inexhaustible supply of applicants for admission presumed by the cry, "be done with the dissidents and make room for those who really want to go to college." Most colleges, as a matter of fiscal necessity, have to be reconciled to their student clientele even more than to their general constituency. The new youth movement is a force for change for yet another reason: This society worships youth. There are countless illustrations to show that what the elders denounce in the young today they seek to emulate tomorrow. Let there be no doubt about it, the youth have power. They have the strength of numbers, they have financial leverage, they have social appeal.

It is important to realize that the college students in the new youth movement are intellectually oriented, emotionally complex, aesthetically inclined, religiously liberal, unusually autonomous— possessors of those very intellectual and personality traits that have traditionally characterized the life of the academic.[1] Furthermore, all but a small fraction of these students are not bent on destroying the university's historic qualities, but are concerned to preserve them, especially those qualities that once were the hallmark of the professor. It is precisely because many faculty are abandoning these values for narrow professionalism that professors must be regarded as enemies of the reform movement.

Many of the protests, to be sure, have been aimed at ad-

[1] For more on this subject, see J. Axelrod et al., *Search for Relevance: Campus in Crisis* (San Francisco: Jossey-Bass, 1969), Chap. 7.

ministrators. This has been so because the explicit issues were often Vietnam and social injustice, and administrators, as the gatekeepers of academe, are the first to encounter all kinds of traffic. But whenever the issues are educational reform and the implicit values behind educational practice, student activists soon discover that the closer they come to the center of the intellectual city the more they are likely to find the barriers manned by faculty, not administrators. The more serious the academic challenge, the more faculty are threatened; what may appear at first to be student concerns disruptive only to the administrative organization are, in fact, concerns that threaten the present values of faculty. The point is not that the students are advocating the overthrow of those values that have traditionally marked the life of the academic but that they are insisting that those values are too important to be abandoned by faculty. The new youth education reform movement is an attack from within, and is, at least in part, a defense of old-line academic values and styles at a time when faculty are exposed as revisionists who are bringing heretical doctrines into institutions of higher learning.

Faculties a few decades ago were idealistic about men to the point of romanticism, individualistic to the point of anarchy—a curious mixture of the theoretical and the practical, in the world but not of it. The new students have taken up that style of life, while faculty are going over to the values of the business community. The image of the college professor as a contemplative, sensitive, available, vulnerable, poorly organized, politically naive but concerned scholar is fading fast. The modern professor is more often than not a "cosmopolitan," at home in the centers of power, capable of handling large contracts and public responsibilities, politically astute, selfish, well organized. He is professionally competent in his specialization, but he has little knowledge of and a declining interest in the broad traditions of the institution he represents. The students are moving into the House of Intellect as faculty move into the technostructure.

The causes for the shift in faculty values are varied and have been widely discussed. The rapid expansion of knowledge has made it impossible for a professor to encompass even one field of learning. Men have compensated by tightening their areas of specialization and by reshaping academic departments to conform to their interests. The positive consequence has been that research for a professor is reduced to manageable proportions. The negative consequence has been that schools are reduced to departments of specialists, where each person narrows his investigation until the subject is so esoteric that the individual can rightly claim to be the only living authority in the field, and only a few graduate students can understand him. And fewer still may care.[2]

There is no need to elaborate further on the characteristics of the prevailing specialistic guild orientation of faculties. But another dimension of the situation should be mentioned. While most faculty are isolating themselves in some specialization, burrowing into a pile of data and making that their home—except when they emerge to sell themselves to industry or government as technical consultants—and, while they are becoming the kind of specialist Alfred North Whitehead called "the most useless bore on God's earth," the new youth are moving in another direction. They have a wider range of intellectual interests. Very often they have double majors, or an area study major, or one that allows an inclusive approach to a discipline. They are, furthermore, pressing beyond established fields and, as is the case with the best professors, they are working at the borders between disciplines and mixing fields of study. Students are active in biochemistry, psycholinguistics, the sociology of education, and other blends.

Such experiences put students ahead of professors who work under narrow loyalties and only by circumscribed arrangements. Concerning learning outside their discipline, most faculty have to rely on whatever knowledge they picked up as an undergraduate. The English professor whose life goal is to say something about Jonathan Swift that nobody has said before may know a little philosophy, from Plato to Kant, as a legacy from his own sophomore course in philosophy, but almost nothing about contemporary existentialism or analytic philosophy. The problem can exist even

[2] My own Ph.D. dissertation was intended to make me an authority on the Clapham Sect, a group of eighteenth and nineteenth century evangelicals in the English Parliament. But the effect of this tidy bit of expertise has been disappointing. It does not even provide a conversational base at a party. Most people on hearing that my specialty is the Clapham Sect drop the subject immediately for fear of being drawn into discussion of a dread social disease.

within a discipline. If the professor was trained in economics before 1950, he probably will not have the math to do the new mathematical economics. And if he does, as Melvin Lasky has hinted, the mathematical economist can talk only with the statistical sociologist, and both can talk only to Ford. Students today are pressing beyond specializations, beyond established fields, and into parapsychology, occult literature, and nonverbal communication. They are ready to learn from all types of experiences, not just those accepted in the accredited classroom. They are exploring techniques for enhancing sensory awareness and for nonrational ways of knowing.

Academics have long espoused the maxim, "The unexamined life is not worth living," but the new youth movement is giving that maxim a comprehensive application that shows up too many modern faculty for what they are—one-dimensional men. Faculty have been committed to the rational examination of life, to rationality exclusively. This is, the new youth believe, a narrow treatment of the maxim. They also affirm that the unexamined life is not worth living, but they mean to examine it fully—by the use of all the senses, by reference to traditions East and West, by mixing the secular and the religious, the material and the spiritual.

In this, again, they are not revolutionary. Academic man has traditionally made a place for instruction through literature and the arts, through religion and the avenues of the spirit. Only in recent times, under the specialistic mentality, have the channels of communication and learning been narrowed to those reaching the head and carrying messages limited to rational forms. The new student is old-fashioned, then, in that he is responsive to truth in all its forms and is open to every approach. He is committed to the life of total intellectuality and approaches it with the spirit of celebration. He aspires to be a whole man in a world culture.

There are still other influences, largely external to education, that are factors in opening up the definition of diversity. This is the time of the "collapse" of the racial integration movement, in which so much activity was based on the denial of human differences at the level of basic values while acknowledging the presence of impediments to unity caused by socioeconomic differences. That collapse has exposed the fact that not only are the socioeconomic problems going to be more difficult to solve than the early burst of enthusiasm for the potentialities of advanced technology led Americans to believe, but it is evident now that there are deeply embedded value distinctions separating citizens. Men are not, apparently, "all alike anyway," and so the advocates of black power as well as reformed white liberals are gaining adherents in their campaign to get this country to recognize the extent of its social diversity and to accept the values of full individuation. The new radicals are actually calling for a reversal of an earlier condition. The old emphasis was on the eradication of social inequalities, while unconsciously promoting value conformity to standards set by the white middle class. The new emphasis is on diversity in values in the setting of uniform social opportunities.

When the potentialities of advanced technology are viewed against the needs of an expanding human population of infinite genetic variability, when the extended interests of modern youth are understood, when the ramifications of the demands of the awakened minorities are examined, one can begin to see how profoundly higher education is likely to be affected. No matter how extensive the concept of diversity was supposed to have been in the past, that concept must be immeasurably enlarged for the future; the range of opportunities for students must be extended, the judgment of their progress individualized, the meaning of educational experiences personalized. The radical challenge of the times is twofold: institutions of higher education are being asked to extend their traditional but often theoretical regard for diversity into complex social realities and political issues, and secondly, to enrich that concept of diversity by joining their established emphasis on structural or organizational variety with a heightened regard for diversity in fundamental values.

But where are the leaders who understand that the issues in the present situation are substantive and not merely procedural, qualitative more than quantitative? Are they present in our colleges and universities? And can they, if they are of this mind, prevail there? Or even survive there? Faculty seem to be increasingly involved in departmental and specialistic considerations at the very time that there is urgent need for them to be concerned for the relational nature of disciplines and programs. Students are still disenfranchised at the level of academic governance in most colleges and universities, though inchoate student protests are causing changes in the distribution of power at many educational institutions. Yet most students apparently have no sense of the whole and they lack philosophical sophistication or ideological clarity. Most administrators, meantime, seem so enmeshed in the minutiae of the day, in greasing squeaky wheels and getting out of the way, that they have no time to shape new objectives or even review existing ones. To be sure, some presidents, chancellors, and the like are usually ready to acknowledge responsibility for defining broad institutional objectives or for providing leadership in helping the educational community to achieve institutional distinctiveness; but when a concrete issue arises it is often difficult to distinguish the operational values of these administrators, or those of the institution they represent, from the values of society, or, less often, the values of faculty. Most administrators prefer to follow rather than lead.

But where are basic values, those assumptions and objectives of the society, to be reevaluated, revitalized, or even replaced? This task, educators generally say when pressed, is the work of the home, the church, and the individual conscience; yet the home and the church seem to be steadily losing authority at the level of norms for value judgments. Institutions of higher education may, therefore, be in a situation where their leadership in examining value options is urgently needed. The former loci of authority—home and church—have faltered precisely at the time when a desire for the affirmation of individuality, a concern for personal and institutional integrity, and a certain responsiveness to moral leadership are increasingly characteristics of the youth who are populating colleges and universities. Higher education is the home-church surrogate of those youth and, therefore, the institutions of higher education would seem to have no alternative but to become more, not less, involved in value judgments and value leadership.

There is no way for educators to avoid these issues, but there are many ways to approach them. Historical precedent may shed light. In traditional Christian cultures, the church and the Bible provided the authority whereby values were set, standards defined, and a sense of community achieved. In other cultures, concepts of natural and social law have served as buttresses for ethical positions. Recently, the individual person has, in the eyes of many, become his own authority. Heretofore, the conscience of the individual was joined with other referents, as in the Reformation when Luther gave to individual Christians the right to adjudicate differences of official opinion regarding the standards of both the Bible and the Christian community—although, admittedly, Luther seemed more impressed by the "conscience" of the German princes than that of the peasants, or the Pope. But perhaps never before in history has the solitary individual been regarded by so many as capable of judging matters affecting the basic social order.

In the context of this prevalent condition, is it possible to have standards for a community that are more than the sum of individual preferences or to have community values based on anything more than convenience? Is the chief threat to social organization that of randomness? The Heisenberg principle of indeterminacy brought out the fact that the efforts of an observer in the physical sciences may be expected to affect that which is observed—the point is also abundantly evident in social science research—but does it follow, then, that relativism must be absolutized? While acknowledging that absolute certainty is impossible, can one say that provisional shared beliefs for a community are still possible? What do men have in common—now? And what is their basis of authority—now? In education, for higher education, what are the answers to these questions? And do they provide a basis for intellectual community? For institutional character?

In organizing the research project that provided the findings for this book, it was assumed that administrators, faculty, and students in participating colleges and universities would equate institutional character with one or more of three aspects of educational life. The first and most obvious source of institutional distinctiveness or avowed character, project staff hypothesized, would be the stated educational philosophy and institutional objectives thought by members of a particular college or university community to give cohesiveness and direction to their work. To determine the philosophy and goals, the literature of the schools in the project, both formal and informal documents, was to be studied, and then administrative interviews were to be used as checks on and amplifications of printed themes. By these two avenues it was thought to be possible to arrive at an institution's philosophic and propositional stance or, to state it another way, the institution's formal ideology. Ideologies are, after all, still indispensable for social existence. It makes a great difference whether a college emphasizes the preservation of the cultural heritage and its inculcation in the young, or stresses the need to change or transform that heritage. Again, when a university speaks of being a "center of service," it is important to know whether the service is understood as essentially vocational training and the maintenance of prevailing notions of citizenship, or whether the institution thinks of service in broader and more inclusive terms, including the idea that the school may serve society as a center of countervailing power. An assumption in the study, then, was that such value commitments make a difference and that they can be components of institutional distinctiveness.

In investigating this first focus of concern, project personnel worked, of course, to go beyond statements of institutional ideology set forth by the president or public relations officer. It was important to determine whether faculty and student perceptions agreed with administrative pronouncements, and to find out whether the stated philosophy was actually applied as well as theoretically understood. Was the school's vision really contributing to the culture of the institution? And was it shared sufficiently to provide a basis for community?

Project personnel expected, as the second foci of concern, that institutional character would be thought by people in the samples to be related to what may be called the conventional criteria of institutional excellence—criteria that affect students, faculty, and administrators. At the student level, the conventional criteria of excellence include emphasis on, at entrance to college, Scholastic Aptitude Test scores, rank in high school class, and the distribution of college preparatory courses. During the college years the emphasis is on the student's identification with a subject-matter department and his success in specialization. The socioeconomic mix in the student body and student involvement in political and social issues, whether such involvement be from the perspective of prevailing societal values or from some politically deviant perspective, are important considerations for the institution as well as for the students.

Faculty characteristics that provide the basis for judging institutional excellence emphasize training at the right places in a precise discipline, location in a department with respected specializations, and advancement through the ranks by means of work characterized by research and publications. Guild standing and personal mobility are also features of what is called a professionally oriented faculty. How academic freedom is defined and protected on a particular campus and the role of the faculty in setting institutional policies and controlling curriculum change are additional dimensions of the norm.

Administrators, according to the criteria, have certain tasks to perform, professional qualifications to exhibit and, especially, a certain style to which they are expected to adhere. The prevailing administrative norms feature efficiency, order, and success in achieving the "supportive capabilities." Also, the college should show an ability to place its graduates in the best professional and graduate schools. It should turn out good citizens, happy and generous alumni and public leaders. A college is known by the company its graduates keep. Administrators are held accountable to these norms. The style dictated by present standards emphasizes that administrators should be modest, asknowledging, only half facetiously, that they are an evil and, as Sir Eric Ashby put it, hoping that they might be a necessary evil. They should know their place and stay in it. Administrators are to be fiscal and organizational facilitators of institutional programs, but they are not often thought of in the conventional wisdom as educational leaders—the curriculum is to be left to the faculty's care. Presidents, for example, are to be seen with wealthy benefactors but not heard, except when announcing a major bequest. Student personnel administrators, according to the standard's purists, are specialists but only quasi-professionals: orderly, predictable, well-mannered people who should be innocent as doves with faculty but wise as serpents with students. (Administrators are here caricatured in order to emphasize that present criteria have decreed their self-depreciation.)

The third aspect of educational life with which researchers assumed project respondents would associate institutional distinctiveness was the current national emphasis on educational innovation and experimentation. The theme of change is so much with us now that it seemed likely the image of an institution as seen by administrators, faculty, and students would be affected by it. Innovation and experimentation take many forms and mean different things. What may be involved at a given college is a shift in the assumptions, values, and goals of the institution. This can lead to significant change and be a major innovation. But how often does that happen? Again, an institution may define innovation in terms of the expansion of facilities, or perhaps by some creative effort involving environmental architecture. The institutional growth rate, numbers of students as well as facilities and funding are other developments often emphasized. Curriculum innovation is a better known form of change and, among most educators, a preferred way to institutional distinctiveness. Familiar expressions of it are changes in testing and grading procedures, the use of nonintellective variables in admission criteria, or opportunities for independent study. Course content changes by faculty and cross-disciplinary course arrangements for students are currently favored teaching-learning variations. Student-formed and student-led courses and student participation in institutional governance are less frequent innovations, although student responsibility for, or at least involvement in, social policy formulation on campus is common now. Colleges and universities that are going from private to public auspices, from small to large size, from a single professional emphasis (for example, teacher education) to a larger mission, must undergo changes representing differences in degree or even in kind. Institutional participation in consortia, whether state, regional, or national, may be regarded as innovative and as a distinguishing mark for a participating college or university. The process of innovation was regarded as a way to define and achieve institutional character. Troubling the waters even a little, we thought, could affect the contours of the shoreline.

This, then, was the situation as seen by the project staff: Diversity in structures and functions, a hallmark of modern higher education in this country, is now challenged by an element of the youth, by minority groups, by some educators, as well as by the resources of the new technology, to extend the concept of diversity in colleges and universities to hitherto unknown dimensions, including, indeed emphasizing, value diversity. But the institution of higher education may be ill equipped, even disinclined, to meet this challenge. Would the character of the institution accommodate such changes? How, in fact, was institutional character defined and measured? To help in answering these questions a research project —the Institutional Character study—was designed to reveal administrative, faculty, and student perceptions of the "integrative value system" of certain colleges and universities. Attention was focused on educational philosophy and institutional goals, the conventional criteria of excellence, and prospects for change, innovation, and experimentation, in the confidence that out of the commitment of administrators, faculty, and students to one or more of these areas of concern a sense of what is and ought to be would emerge.

II

Eight Diverse Schools

Each of the institutions participating in the Institutional Character study has certain characteristic features in organization and administration, in structures and functions, that serve to set it apart from other schools. Indeed, such differences in form and activity at these places and elsewhere provide the basis for claiming diversity as the mark of American higher education. Some of these special qualities, or, more often, characteristic quantitative distinctions, of participating colleges and universities are presented here so as to begin to know the institutions of the study and to start examining how different or alike they actually are. Also, the preconceptions or assumptions of the principal researcher concerning these colleges and universities will be shown as well as the realities of the schools' past and present existence that became known to researchers during the course of the study.

16

MultiEastern

Founded as a private institution in 1766, MultiEastern was one of nine colonial colleges. In its long history, however, the institution would experience several changes in basic affiliation. After 1864, MultiEastern was the state's land-grant college. The main effect of this change was to give the university schools of agriculture and engineering and, eventually, a large ROTC program. Multi-Eastern was designated as the state university in 1917 although still a private institution but, in 1945, it was incorporated as a public school along with various academic divisions and special programs it had been gathering. MultiEastern's growth has been due in part to its willingness to draw together isolated units—a college of pharmacy, schools of law and business administration, as well as another campus specializing in professional schools.

It had been announced, prior to the Institutional Character study, that the future expansion of MultiEastern, particularly in undergraduate programs, would follow the federated college model. By using this structural concept, older established units could move ahead in their own way and at their own pace, while the university grew and was revitalized by the introduction of new colleges. Innovation and experimentation could be tried in the new units without upsetting the traditional order within older programs; conventional wisdom would not be uprooted but new insights might be planted.

The federated college idea seemed especially appropriate in a state that had been slow to develop a master plan for higher education or to provide a clear delineation of the role of the state university vis-à-vis other educational institutions. There have been only a few community colleges in the state, although many are projected, and the state college system remains weak. Many of the state's students, particularly those of high intellectual aptitude, have in the past gone to schools out of the state. Some observers believe that this state's failure to provide for the educational needs of its youth has been scandalous. Developments during recent years show an awareness among state political leaders of past deficiencies and present urgencies; yet at the time of this study, authorities at Multi-Eastern did not know how far statewide planning would go and, therefore, the federated plan seemed best as a mechanism for internal growth and change as well as a way of providing a flexible way to meet external challenges.

Another view of the establishment of the federated college plan at MultiEastern is less favorable to the vision, courage, and creativity of the institution's central administration. This view has it that not until the federal government made known its intention to dispose of a nearby military installation did university people act —and then for the wrong reason. Realizing that MultiEastern should move with dispatch to acquire the adjacent military property, administrators began to think of an educational justification for their acquisitive intentions. From this critical perspective, the federated plan looks like academic opportunism—a way to extend the property and power of the university without engendering much internal division.

The truth, project personnel thought at the time of the project's beginning, was that the university was sensitive to the need for a radical expansion of higher education in the state and fully cognizant that if MultiEastern did not move to meet that need the political and social climate was such that other ways would be found to do so. MultiEastern would thus have found its supremacy and its control of higher education in the state threatened. There was, also, an element of educational idealism in the decision to double the size of the university by establishing several new colleges on the old military installation. The interest in innovation that had been developing nationally in response to student unrest, social conflict, and the economic complexities of modern higher education, as well as the desire to meet the challenges of the postindustrial age, had reached and motivated certain leaders on campus. They knew MultiEastern was going to grow. They were also interested in providing ways for it to change.

Theorists of the dynamics of change in complex organizations state that the following factors are at work whenever considerable institutional alterations are achieved: an ideology that motivates and unifies; a social matrix that has certain features conducive to change and others that challenge through contrast; strong leadership; an effective carrying mechanism to move specific changes forward; and, finally, provision for self-renewal and criticism, because all efforts at change are subject to attrition and compromise and must be constantly reaffirmed and updated. While the federated college plan provided a carrying mechanism for change, there was much to be learned about the unifying, motivating ideology for change at MultiEastern as well as about the prospects for leadership, regeneration, and support in this institution's own matrix.

The addition of MultiEastern to the Institutional Character project in the spring of 1967 was occasioned, therefore, by a desire to include a public, fairly large institution that was definitely in transition, a case study of the processes of change. MultiEastern had gone from private to public auspices, from small to intermediate size, from few and comparatively simple programs to diverse and complex ones, from an imitative stance to one supposedly innovative. Furthermore, it was thought to provide an approximate parallel for the other public university in the institutional sample, and, in some ways, for the two private universities as well, due to the declared intention of MultiEastern to expand and develop undergraduate programs by the creation of semiautonomous colleges as the other three universities were doing. So here as elsewhere project personnel were interested in the process by which priorities were determined for the new colleges, how these means and ends were communicated to various interest groups, how they were received and implemented by administrators and faculty and, finally, what the consequences were when avowedly innovative ideas were introduced into a long-established and essentially traditional university.

Because of the focus of the research on undergraduate education, two of MultiEastern's colleges were studied but none of the professional or graduate programs. The colleges are designated Alpha and Theta. Both are on the Riverview campus, the former a college for men, the latter a college for women.

Eastversity

Located near the center of the most populous area on the eastern seaboard and close to four other institutions of higher education—three universities and one new liberal arts college—East had been a commuter school for thirty years at the time of the study, with a student body vocationally oriented and motivated by middle-class values. The university's dependence upon student fees for its operating budget had in the past caused the curriculum to be skewed toward those offerings to which students could be expected to subscribe. The faculty contained a core of dedicated teachers who felt that the university's mission was to take youth who would come to them and to help these students toward their educational goals. But another segment of the faculty was oriented to the metropolitan area near which the school was located; their pattern was to come out to the campus, fulfill their lecture schedule, and return to the city. Many of these were able specialists with a strong disciplinary and professional bent. A third segment of the undergraduate faculty consisted of young instructors and assistant professors who were working on advanced degrees at the major universities of the area, and were teaching at Eastversity for bread and experience.

What were the prospects for a sense of community and the unity of shared purposes in a situation such as this one? What was being done to meet challenges raised by the newer and older universities nearby? East's experimental program, here designated Zeta College to distinguish it from the more conventional undergraduate program coded Beta College, was obviously one answer. It was a way for East to provide a "living core" or academic focal point for certain otherwise widely dispersed students. And if, as the research from Jacob to Feldman and Newcomb indicates, the greatest impact on college students comes through informal, outside of class, residential encounters, the approach behind East's experiment in Zeta could be exceedingly important. But would students from lower-middle-class homes be interested in such an innovative curriculum? And if some were, what ideological divisions would emerge between the university's conventional programs and this new one? How did students, faculty, and administrators take to the new plan and what did they think it meant for the future of the university?

The administration's second response to the competition's challenges to East's future was its announced plan to give the university a 50 per cent residential student body. What effect would this development have, project staff asked, on the character of the institution after it had been from its inception almost entirely a commuter school? Having never been burdened by cumbersome parietal rules and the plethora of social regulations that accrue to most residential colleges, how would the student life committees go about setting up a "code of behavior"? Would they be innovative or imitative?

The prognostic literature on the future of American higher education, of which there has been an increasing volume in recent years, has uniformly emphasized the trend toward the democratization of colleges and universities. While approximately 40 per cent of college age youth are now enrolled in post-secondary institutions, the percentage will increase to nearly 70 per cent within the next two decades. This development is expected to have profound qualitative as well as quantitative ramifications.

Most important will be changes away from the single-model, middle-class, elitist value orientation of present institutions of higher education to a diversity of programs and values hardly imaginable in the past but now deemed essential for the realization of the equality of opportunity our democratic ideology requires. While there will be growth and change at the upper and elitist end of the educational continuum, most of the action will be in junior colleges created to serve the bottom third of this population influx as well as in mass institutions that are or will be in urban centers. Therefore, what is happening in such places now may provide models, good or bad, for the next several decades of unpredecented expansion and alteration.

The Institutional Character project personnel wished, therefore, to learn how a university with the experiences and location of East was likely to relate to all these developments. East is comparatively young, has increasingly diversified programs, is strategically located in a populous, influential metropolitan area. This combination of opportunities and constraints seemed to constitute a microcosm of the situation likely to be facing private universities like East, and those of less privileged and secure status, public or private, in the next decade or two. How was institutional distinctiveness being achieved at East when potential and peril seemed so inextricably intermingled?

MultiWestern

In May and June 1966, four campuses of this multicampus university were enlisted in the Institutional Character project—Valley, Hilltop, Seaside, Bay. The selections were deliberate. Project personnel wanted two of the older campuses of the university and, for comparison, two of its new campuses. In addition, all four of those selected satisfied criteria set down for inclusion in the project: they were all in the process of substantial change, and all were thought to be distinctive. The two older campuses had traditions—Valley, with its expansion out of the agricultural tradition, its bicycles and smiles; Seaside, all sun, surf, and energy—while the new locations, Hilltop and Bay, were claiming distinctiveness through innovation and experimentation.

In the last fifteen years, Valley had changed dramatically in size and scope of function. From a small campus known mainly for excellence in agriculture and home economics, Valley had become a large, diverse university complete with medical school. Although administrators during this period did not hesitate to expand the institution's numbers and programs, they had understandably shown a great reluctance to give up the informal and friendly tradition that for years had been epitomized by the chancellor waving from his cottage office at bicycle and pedestrian traffic through a large, deliberately conspicuous plate glass window. One interest of project staff, therefore, was to analyze the way institutional objectives were being transmitted and accepted by a growing, increasingly disparate community.

The monumental physical proportions of the development of the new Hilltop campus of MultiWestern—involving the creation of one college per year over the span of more than a decade—has been matched by the audacity of the organizational arrangement conceived for that campus whereby individual colleges were to be sufficiently free to establish their own character and ethos without loss of MultiWestern's established regard for high academic standards. At Hilltop, the colleges were expected to have an academic focus or emphasis, in the humanities or social sciences, for example, but they were to also show that they were a part of MultiWestern.

The other new campus of MultiWestern, Bay, was to be

similar in general organization, yet providing for larger colleges. Because of the greater size, it was hoped these colleges could be essentially self-contained units covering the main divisions of undergraduate education. Bay's plan called for clustering colleges into groups of three or four, thereby providing the essential features of a university in each cluster, and having four such groups.

Both of these new campuses had, therefore, innovative master plans. Project staff were concerned to determine just how the various campus constituents understood their opportunities, how they defined institutional distinctiveness, and what values and educational objectives they brought to their situation. This was as important for the success of the new programs as the ability of the first planners to convey to their colleagues the vision of the future they had. It seemed important also to try to ascertain how procedures, traditions, and restraints existent on the older campuses of the university, particularly those emanating from the powerful academic senate, would impinge on the faculties and curriculum innovations of the new campuses. Hilltop was entirely new, while Bay was beginning with a strong graduate tradition and had many faculty members whose experiences in graduate programs had been gained in approximately the same geographical location. What difference would it make to establish undergraduate programs from the top down, that is from the graduate level, as would be tried at Bay, while moving at Hilltop from undergraduate colleges to graduate offerings?

No campus of the university has had a more varied history than Seaside—from female academy to teachers college, from an education emphasis to liberal arts mini-university, and then in recent times to general campus of a complex university system. As a consequence, Seaside was thought to provide a situation in which at least three blocs were present in the faculty—the remnant of the old teachers college, the faculty that envisioned Seaside as a small liberal arts university concerned for academic quality, and the new "cosmopolitans" in the faculty with their professionalism and national mobility. How was institutional character to be achieved, given this mix?

About one third of the student body at this campus lives in apartments not owned or operated by the university. Thus, many students are unaffected by the social restraints experienced by dormitory occupants. What were the consequences of these conditions for the academic life and, especially, for the assumptions, objectives, and values that various elements in the university community brought to their work? Seaside has had the reputation of a "fun and games" campus or, more accurately, the "surf and sand" school. What were university officials doing to change this image? Or should they change it? Perhaps having campuses compatible with the needs and interests of various student subcultures is also a part of the university's commitment to diversity. But would the sort of faculty that this university draws want to work in the relaxed, sensate atmosphere suggested by the image this campus has had?

Westversity

Current publications of West often carry one of two banners —"[The State's] first chartered institution of higher learning" or "First with today's cluster college concept." The first word and the last word—that is the image West seeks.

Chartered in the mid-nineteenth century and intended by the founders to be "an institution of the grade of a university," West has been, in fact, a little of almost everything on its way to becoming a university. There have been four name changes and three primary locations in two different cities with recent expansion into two additional cities. West was chartered as a university, offering separate programs for men and women, but it soon moved toward becoming a college, divesting itself of an early medical program. At another period the college added several graduate and professional programs; still later the curriculum was limited to upper division work and certain graduate courses, leaving lower division responsibilities to a publicly funded community college. In recent years, again a university, West has added professional schools and graduate programs (including two Ph.D. programs) plus new undergraduate colleges. In the present era of great change, West ought to prosper, for it has always been characterized by change. Certainly this state's first chartered institution of higher learning has experienced most of the changes that have happened singly or in small doses to other colleges and universities in the state.

The cluster college concept at Westversity provides a good

example of the style of operation that has typified the school's history. By 1960, West had three urgent problems. It needed, first, to broaden its base of financial support. The university's operating budget had to be raised mainly from tuition income supplemented by the efforts of the president and development office staff, because of its very limited endowment, marginal financial assistance from a Protestant denomination, a middle-class alumni that had not developed a tradition of support for the university, and a board of trustees whose financial contributions, with some exceptions, had been token. The cluster college idea, it was thought, would attract wealthy benefactors (whose names could be assigned, not to a building or an academic chair, but to a whole college) as well as from foundations with an eye for innovation and from an extended clientele as new college alumni came into being.

There was need, second, to establish the university's identity. Friendly, easygoing [West] College, well known throughout the region for its football teams and conservatory of music, had again become a university. In a state with extensive public educational services (the university, state colleges, and junior colleges) there was reason for anxiety about the future of private higher education, and especially about West's place in the sun. Graduate and professional programs would, of course, be added as soon as possible. But they were expensive. Library and laboratory resources were very limited. The institution's geographical setting was not especially attractive for scholars and their research—better than some places, worse than others. The cluster college concept seemed a viable means to the achievement of institutional identity: Funds for programs of the new colleges should become available from benefactors; most facilities could be built with government money; programs in the humanities and social sciences would not be too expensive; students and parents might be attracted to an innovative approach to liberal education. (The last assumption was not borne out in reality. It was assumed that getting students would be no problem, whereas, in fact, all three of the cluster colleges now established have been undersubscribed.)

Above all, in establishing the institution's identity, the concept of the "West family" with its emphasis on the advantages of small size and the spirit of community would be enhanced by the presence of these colleges at the same time the university was expanding. West would, as the president was wont to say, grow larger by getting smaller. The university would be first with today's cluster college concept, thereby achieving identity for the university even while the new colleges were establishing their identity within West's community.

The idea of federated colleges was not new in 1960 when West's administration began planning for, as was then said, "fifteen colleges in fifteen years." The Atlanta complex of colleges and the Claremont colleges had been established long before. Of course, these other places were essentially autonomous institutions with only loose and limited working relationships between them. But neither was the idea of experimental subunits within a university new at that time. In the East, Wesleyan University had already launched its subject area specialization colleges. In the West, in 1957, Nevitt Sanford proposed a one-year experimental liberal arts program for the University of California and, in the next year, he urged that the University of California establish "within its own body" a two-year experimental liberal arts college. In 1958–59, then president Clark Kerr of the University of California began planning for a new campus to be based on semiautonomous undergraduate colleges. What Westversity did, to the credit of its president, was to take ideas then in the air and move quickly to apply and implement them. West was first to get the cluster college concept under way.[1] Plans were made in 1960–61, and the university's first college, here coded Omega College to distinguish it from the university's long-established liberal arts college, Delta College, was opened in 1962. A private, comparatively small university put into motion within two years what it took five years to launch in a large, complex state university.

The first college, West's president and academic vice president decided, would be an innovative, liberal arts college with an enrollment of 250. The president decreed this size for all cluster colleges. The figure was determined not on the basis of a feasibility-

[1] Defined as provision for semiautonomous, holistic academic programs to function under the aegis of a central administration which keeps certain rewards and sanctions, particularly financial ones, under its control (as contrasted with plans that give to each college both academic and fiscal autonomy).

statistical study, or on the basis of faculty thinking at West about the ideal size for the best learning environment, but as a result of several trips by chief administrators to Oxford and Cambridge where they were told that the glories of the British Oxbridge system were achieved when the college enrollments were about 250.

Particular innovations that might be incorporated in the first cluster college, according to the academic vice president's planning, included a prescribed four-year curriculum featuring a balanced distribution of work for all students in the three classical divisions of the liberal arts—humanities, social sciences, natural sciences. A special feature of the curriculum was to be a science program as an integrated sequence, moving from physics to chemistry and finally biology. The total program was to be of high academic quality, more intensive and inclusive than customary liberal arts arrangements.

Living facilities for the college would be new, separate (although on the same campus), and complete. The Oxbridge influence was again manifest in the emphasis on served meals as an expression of gracious living and with various physical stylistic touches to suggest the school's assumed lineage.

Academic innovations proposed by the first planners (the president, the academic vice president, and the new school's provost, working occasionally with other university administrators as special considerations arose) emphasized the liberal arts ideal and exuded confidence in the adequacy of that ideal. Subject-matter specialization was played down and broad course distribution featured. The concept of community was seen as crucial to all else—students and faculty would learn together. Administration was to be kept to a minimum. One of the virtues of the cluster college idea, everyone thought, was the chance it gave innovators to leave many duties, such as fund raising and admissions, to central administration.

The leader upon whom all else depended in the formative period was the university's president. His predecessor, West's president from 1919 to 1946, had controlled every facet of the institution's life while claiming to be uninterested in educational philosophy. He had allowed faculty to develop departmental identity but preferred not to involve them in institutional policy formulation.

He had kept the faculty dispersed but individually related to himself. The leadership of the current president at West since his appointment in 1947 had been no less dominant, but it had been more discreet. He kept certain important decisions to himself, mostly financial ones, but freely delegated others. West in recent years has been run by an oligarchy with a democratic front. Yet it may well have been precisely because of this limited distribution of power that the cluster college concept could be established there. The president had long and openly insisted that faculties are both conservative and slow. He believed, therefore, that the planning for the university's expansion and improvement must be kept in the hands of a knowledgeable coterie. This he arranged, and it may have been the feature enabling the first three colleges to get under way quickly. As stated, Omega opened in 1962; the second cluster college, a program for training Latin American specialists, with most of the student body from South American countries and with most lectures and discussions in Spanish, opened in 1963; the third cluster college came into being in 1967 with a liberal arts program featuring a sophomore year in India and a non-Western emphasis in the curriculum.

Center researchers were interested in Westversity's quantitative and qualitative transition, with tight administrative leadership and cluster colleges as the chief mechanism to effect change. An ancillary interest was in the effect of the cluster college concept on the administrative structure of the university. No major administrative shift or innovation had been devised for the management of the new institutional configuration. Rather the centralized governance umbrella characteristic of West's past was simply extended to cover new colleges. Even the old academic departments had considerable autonomy to set their curriculum schedule, so long as available financial resources were not overextended. The new colleges would have academic autonomy but not fiscal freedom. Central administration would determine general growth patterns and the formulas to attain them. Cluster colleges would follow line-item budgeting, not program budgeting. Budgets would be adjudicated by central administration in consultation with college provosts.

The obvious advantages in this plan are that duplication of efforts within a university can be avoided and emphases favored by university administrators can be advanced. The disadvantages are that college or program provosts or deans are dealt with separately and hence have no more than a very general knowledge of what is going on financially in programs other than their own. This is a situation in which the head knows what the hands are doing, but the right hand is ignorant of the left. Tension and suspicion can build up among the body's members. Also, because everyone is dependent on central administration, one effect can be a reduction of criticism and an increase of adulation. When resources are very limited, as is certainly true at West, it is understandable that the administration would see centralization as an aid to efficiency. However, studies in administration show that centralized government fosters efficiency at the price of creativity.

Omega, the first of the cluster colleges, was chosen for the study along with the core liberal arts unit of the university—Delta. These two colleges were thought to be representative of developments at the undergraduate level in this university.

Plans for the growth of the university initially called for holding Delta fairly stable in size, while the expansion of the university's undergraduate population was to be carried out in the cluster colleges. Although not decreed, it was expected that the weight of tradition and the force of habit would make Delta the conventionally oriented liberal arts program while the new colleges sought their identity through various innovations. Each new college, the president had said, would feature its own unique characteristic or program to justify its separate existence in the university and to give the colleges separate personalities and the university diversity in programs.

Delta, however, has had considerable difficulty in establishing its identity since 1962 when the university's new subunits began to open because, as a legacy from the former president, loyalties there developed along departmental lines or according to special programs. Furthermore, Delta seemed to have no more right to the traditions of the university than other units and, indeed, some people in the college were not sure that they wanted to be saddled with those traditions. Certain younger faculty wanted Delta to establish its identity as an innovative, aggressive member of the university community, not as guardian of conventionality. But many, perhaps most, Delta faculty were content to continue life in their departments pretty much as before. They had never been encouraged to think about broad institutional objectives and educational philosophy; the administration had kept these matters under its control, and faculty meetings were almost entirely perfunctory and ceremonial. Faculty had, therefore, developed various forms of privatism and were quite content to leave business and general policy to the president.

The Delta faculty did have an understandable interest in its own professional welfare, and consequently there were unrest and disquiet when the cluster college plan was announced. It was not a turbulence caused by administrators taking over prerogatives that many faculties would regard as their own so much as it was a concern for how limited financial resources could be stretched to cover new ventures. Although assurances were given that supplementary sources of income would carry the burden, Delta faculty were anxious—prophetically, as it worked out. Yet, even issues such as this one were insufficient in the early years to unite the Delta faculty. When plans for the first two cluster colleges were announced, the typical faculty member shrugged and said that since he had not been consulted he would leave the new programs to their own devices while he got on with his teaching and research. Various proposals for innovative programs had been announced at the institution before; these new ones, like those, it was predicted, would soon be forgotten.

However, as the new colleges became visible entities, leaning heavily on Delta and the university and, of course, striving to establish their presence by reacting vociferously to the habits and attitudes of the sponsoring body, their innovative programs got considerable attention. The infant colleges romped like tiger cubs in the presence of a tired, sagging mother. It soon became clear that the success of Omega could not be taken for granted. It was time for the mother to cuff the cubs and reestablish her authority.

This process was under way at the time of the Institutional Character research project (1966–67). A reaction against the "excessive claims" of the Omega administration and faculty had set in. Assurances were heard that Delta students and faculty were as good academically as those at Omega and, furthermore, that Delta with its larger size and diversity of programs in the arts and sciences was the more attractive setting within which to teach and learn. The president of the university had stated that one of the benefits of the cluster college notion was the competition that could be expected to develop among units. It was evident by the time of the study that he had accurately predicted what would happen, but it was not certain that what was happening was a benefit to the university.

South College

South College was a logical choice for the Institutional Character study because it was comparatively new at the time of the project, and, from its beginning, had declared a determination to achieve institutional character by giving rigorous attention as a community to its philosophy of education and to innovation and experimentation in undergraduate instruction. South was also committed to making a fresh examination of other important developments in higher education—the liberal arts program and the Christian college in the contemporary world. At a time of renewed interest in the place of religion in higher learning, and with student anxiety and disquietude about values and "the meaning of it all" evident on every hand, project staff had special interest in a new educational establishment where, it was said, matters of this sort were of fundamental concern to the academic community.

No less interesting for research were south's specific curriculum innovations. This institution had put into practice an "interim term" program, making thereby a significant change in the conventional calendar. There was also an innovative curriculum "core" that provided a cross-disciplinary integrative learning experience for all students in the social sciences and humanities throughout the four-year academic program. (A sophomore-junior science core was also in use but, during the period of the study, had not been integrated with the other, more ambitious program.) Overseas study, travel opportunities, independent study, advanced standing and other better known, more widely used innovations were also available options.

At the time of the study, South College had been in the planning and operational stages for about a decade—four years in planning and six years in actual operation. The state synod of a Protestant church had decided in 1956 to conduct a feasibility study for the establishment of a new church-related college in their state. A group of educators and public leaders had been brought together, and they issued a report emphasizing two points: There was a place in the state for a new private institution of higher education, and such a college ought to offer a program of high academic quality. No mention was made at this time, apparently, that the proposed college should be avowedly innovative. By 1958, the feasibility study had been circulated, evaluated, and approved by the synod, and a successful Protestant minister was named president. He soon invited a professor at another church-related college to join him on an extensive trip financed by a grant from the Ford Foundation for the purpose of studying current developments in higher education. The professor accepted and later became the first dean of the college. As a result of the trip, the attention of the men focused on the formation of a college that would not only be Christian but would emphasize the liberal arts—the dean insisted that faculty candidates be willing and able to respond to the "liberal arts questions"—and would be different. South would be innovative, characterized, as it later worked out, by (1) the core curriculum, (2) an emphasis on independent study, (3) the winter interim term calendar arrangement—probably influenced by the planners of New College (Amherst) in 1957–58, although South would be the first institution actually to implement the plan, and (4) special emphasis on values and the search for a Christian philosophy of education.

It was a matter of interest to the project research team that the catalog of South College has been and remains open and explicit about the centrality of innovations in the program of the college. Besides the usual emphasis on personal education found in the publications of most colleges, the catalog presents South as "pursuing a policy of experimentation." The college "adopts experimental attitudes in attempting to reach its goals through unique but carefully considered means." This emphasis on "living research" should be carried, according to the catalog, into the realm of ethics and morality. South would learn by such "research" how students can best make moral evaluations informed by the Christian tradition: "We do not presume that [South] College is the first college to assume the necessity of a moral end of education, but we are experimental in trying to find out how best such an end can be realized."

The college has been unapologetic about being a "Christian community," a vision calling for the merger of intellectual rigor and social concern. "[South] College acknowledges as primary in the search for truth a knowledge of God and of ourselves as revealed in Jesus Christ." Yet the college also asserts that its doors are open to qualified students of all faiths.

This college, then, did two things that went against contemporary institutional styles. South emphasized innovation at a time when most colleges regarded avowed commitment to change efforts to be risky for an institution's reputation. Also, it proclaimed itself to be Christian in a day of increasing secularization. And all of this within the framework of a new, independent liberal arts college founded in a period of educational history when most discussions center on merging such schools or closing them.

Southeast College

Southeast College seemed when the study was launched to be a prime example of a Negro college in the border situation between acceptance by the educational Establishment and obscurity. It had the advantage of location in a major city and had a working relationship with certain other colleges in the area, including two that are nationally known, with the consequent prospects for financial assistance from national foundations and other funding agencies. But Southeast had a legacy of paternalism, social conformity, and academic mediocrity by conventional standards of excellence. Nevertheless, at a time of increasing attention to higher education for Negroes, Southeast seemed to be interested in change. If so, by what style and standard? How self-conscious was the college about its future prospects? Were leaders there—faculty, students, administrators—thinking in radical or conservative terms? Were they seeking excellence in traditional ways or by new tracks?

This liberal arts college was established shortly after the Civil War (1869) and has had a long affiliation with a Protestant church. It draws perhaps one fifth of its entering students from elementary and secondary schools that do not prepare their graduates adequately for college level work. The faculty seemed increasingly divided between an older, academically tolerant but socially stringent faction and a newer, younger group who wanted to reverse the school's tradition and tighten up academically while relaxing social regulations.

In Southeast project personnel saw a college that, given its associations with other colleges in the area, might gain strength by setting aside its traditional concern for autonomy and participating more actively with its fellow institutions. Could the cluster college concept be activated in a very contemporary form within a group of colleges that were among the first to join in a loose confederation of institutions? Perhaps confederation should proceed to federation.

Midwest College

The justification for the existence of Midwest College is difficult to find if one limits himself to a consideration of generally accepted criteria for academic success. The location of the college makes faculty recruitment difficult—graduate libraries and cultural centers are located some distance away. The college is not favored with a large endowment or generous, wealthy benefactors. This church-related college is within 200 miles of several other Christian colleges, and certain of these competitors have national reputations. Midwest's conservative theological tradition has militated against achieving the socioreligious mix in student body and faculty that is generally regarded as essential to a vital learning environment. The facilities of the college are adequate but unimpressive.

However, developments at Midwest during the last decade made the college important for this research project. There appeared to have been a shift in the theological perspectives of the institution. Department of religion personnel had changed completely. Although that department apparently still exercised great influence on the total institution, a new and more liberal theological stance—one more open and rather more malleable—was now in effect. The college's president and dean, both comparatively new to their posts, were advocates of academic freedom, intellectual rigor, academic innovations, growth, and change. There was no interest in making the college secular, but there seemed to be a determination to make the college socially relevant. Despite the location, though occasionally because of it, a new group of professionally oriented young faculty had been brought in. While they did not slight teaching, they were more guild-conscious than the faculty of former years. They worked for the college, but they were also giving attention to their own professional advancement.

The faculty work load at Midwest had been reduced in the years around the study from fifteen hours to twelve and even to nine for a few persons. The cover letter on the 1966 student application listed 55 per cent of the faculty as having Ph.D.'s. In 1962, Cass and Birnbaum had listed 22 per cent at Midwest. A large proportion of the current faculty was educated in the midwest, getting their graduate degrees at "Big Ten" schools. About 60 per cent took undergraduate work either at Midwest or another of two colleges related to the same denomination. Many colleges with lower faculty salaries (although Midwest's are not high) and fewer advanced degrees among the faculty can claim a much wider range of geographical and ideological diversity. Administrators said that they had reduced the baccalaureate degree inbreeding problem by 10 per cent in five years, but admitted that there were still too many faculty members from the same background.

The contract letter for faculty stated:

> [Midwest] is a college of the [denomination] and proud of its contribution to the Church. As far as humanly possible, we strive to fulfill in word and deed the precepts of our Lord and Savior Jesus Christ. It is important that each of us maintain these precepts with our colleagues and students. We respect the confessions of the Church and urge all who are a part of our community of faith to study them in relation to their faith.

Despite this theological commitment, the college was concerned to maintain academic freedom and to bring more ideological diversity into the faculty—including in 1967–68 a Catholic, and perhaps a few discreet agnostics. Also, recently the college arranged to grant tenure to faculty who were not affiliated with the denomination.

The faculty has been weighted toward the lower ranks. In 1966–67 there were eighteen full professors, sixteen associate professors, forty-four assistant professors, thirty-one instructors, and two teaching associates. Improvements in recent years in salaries

and benefits, and in professional and scholarly arrangements, made
Midwest attractive to certain faculty. The college offered a comfortable environment—an academically respectable school that still
had freedom from much pressure to publish, a geographical area
where the cost of living was low, a chance to work with obedient
students who respected authority—all of this in an environment
that provided religious men with religious ambience. Therefore,
Midwest probably had a relatively large number of people who
had some mobility but who would not leave it.

Still there was considerable turnover in the faculty. Given
Midwest's financial condition and forty-four assistant professors,
personnel shifts seemed inevitable. This fact, along with the school's
growth in the student population, explains the presence of twenty
new faculty in 1966–67 and twenty-two in 1967–68. None of these
were "name" faculty; most were young (the increase in instructors
was pronounced). The strategy seemed to be to get two or three
outstanding leaders—teachers and, hopefully, scholars—per division,
if not in each department, and put young faculty around them.
An example of the effectiveness of this plan is seen in the department of biology. Five years before our study all members of that
department had resigned. A chairman who was capable but without national standing was brought into the vacuum, and through
the intervening years built one of the strongest departments in the
college. There was no evident division in the faculty between "cosmopolitans" and "locals."

The financial condition of Midwest has been and remains
an obstacle to Midwest's ambitions. About 80 per cent of the
regular operating budget came from student fees. The endowment
was less than $2 million. The development staff had been raising
about $1 million per year from external sources. Included in this
figure was approximately $200,000 given annually by the church.
The church, thus, was not a major source of financial support, but
most students came from church-related homes.

The student body continued to be drawn from a four-state
area, with a large percentage from rural areas or small towns, but
the college had succeeded in adding minority group students—
more than thirty Negroes in 1967–68—and, by the use of the winter or interim term idea, students were undertaking national and

international study and travel. Money from various sources, largely
government loans, made possible new facilities, and morale in the
college seemed to improve apace with the anxiety level of some
conservative elements in the constituency.

Midwest had been in the process of changing its institutional image, and what was happening there, it seemed, might lead
to a change in institutional character. Project staff wanted a better
understanding of the formal and informal dynamics of that process.
How self-conscious were they—students, faculty, administrators—
about what was going on? What were the new assumptions, values,
and goals that undergirded and gave direction to their efforts? Was
the college interested in alternative institutional models, if these
be available, or did this school prefer to strive for excellence as defined by the standards of the educational status quo? Given the
college's limited resources, what changes were viable? Were there
clues in this situation for solving the puzzle of the future of small,
private colleges?

North College

The fourth liberal arts college in the study was North—a
proud, old, well-established, church-related school that has undergone a physical and qualitative transformation in the past ten years.
What happens in a college of approximately 1500 students and
fewer than 100 faculty when, rather suddenly, the old ploy about
"We have no problems that a few million dollars wouldn't solve"
can no longer be used because that college has the few million
dollars and, indeed, more than a few millions more? North has the
sort of benefactor all college presidents dream about. He has given
millions to the college in the last decade, thereby making possible
many of the changes that now distinguish the institution. Not only
has he been generous, he has also been content to leave policy formulation in the hands of the college leadership.

What happens to a faculty when their salaries rise dramatically and security is assured? What is their vision of the college
then? And how is academic excellence defined and achieved? By
following the path laid out by elite colleges? By using new-found
resources to devise new means to new ends, or new means to traditional ends? Is the spirit of community encouraged or diminished

by affluence? What sort of students are drawn to such a college? Do they come only when scholarships are available to them? What does such a college have to offer them that these students could not find elsewhere? Or is the whole point in the fact that North can now supply what students can obtain in the "better" schools of the country?

Concern had been expressed by college leaders that North should become better known for its international programs, for its innovations and individualized or personalized instruction, for its cultural and aesthetic opportunities, for a strong academic program increasingly applied to current social realities. Can such distinctions be achieved quickly? Which of them could be bought outright? And through it all, what would be the assumptions, values, and goals that would be used to determine priorities and measure success? North had been given a unique opportunity to become a leader in innovations. What was the college doing about it?

North was also important for the Institutional Character study because of the prospects for studying the effects on innovation in a situation where administrative leaders were confronted, on the one hand, by an increasingly professional and liberal faculty and, on the other, by a rather more locally oriented constituency and a conservative funding agent. Innovations are always explicit or implied criticisms of the status quo, and the research staff wanted to follow developments in a college where it seemed that money was available from sources that might be opposed to significant changes, particularly changes that might alter traditional institutional values. Had North seized the opportunity for radical innovation, or were the new resources to be lavished on established programs and traditional objectives? Had the level of expectation changed, and, if so, in what direction? When a school's administrators suddenly have considerable financial resources, do they act as they said they would if the money were available—or do something else? What? Why? It has been said that the issue for most church-related liberal arts colleges is not survival but significance. That statement seemed especially relevant for this college. Project personnel were concerned to find out how administrators, faculty, and students at North defined significance, or institutional character, and what they were doing to achieve it.

III

Institutional Character Study

The Institutional Character research project was an effort at relational research, an attempt to understand and evaluate the interaction between theory and practice as perceived by the three main interest groups on college and university campuses—faculty, administrators, and students. By an integrative research methodology, by showing interest in the multiple perceptions of complex learning environments, as well as by the previously stated concern for specific theoretical conceptualizations, the Institutional Character study tried to go beyond most present educational research efforts. Rather than erring on the side of a pinched vision and a constricting project design, researchers of this project preferred to err on the side of broad theory and methodological openness.

Certain ideas about complex organizations, learning environments, human characteristics, and the purposes of higher education figured in the design, the implementation, and the evaluations of this study. Several of these were indicated in Chapter One, those dealing with the emphases and values of modern higher education. Ideas and preconceptions concerning the institutions participating in the study were given in Chapter Two, while others having to do with the organization of the research project itself will be stated here.

As already mentioned, project personnel reflected in the organization of the study their concern for ideational as well as environmental factors in the achievement of institutional character, especially the interaction of the two—the ideational at work in the environment, the influence of social forces on ideas and ideology. The institution of higher education was understood as complex and multidimensional, a place where learning is affective or noncognitive as well as cognitive, where all dimensions of life are political and moral, in process, capable of change but inclined to inertia.

Two questionnaires were designed, one for faculty and one for students. The belief that an intellectual environment as well as other social settings can be internalized by an individual to the extent that he can in turn influence the external world and effect changes there led researchers to design a faculty questionnaire that represented an "open stance." It was intended to provide the respondent with opportunities to be formational as well as informational, to work with themes or problems that are infinitely complex, and to do so in a personal and open-ended way. The student questionnaire, in contrast, was entirely a structured instrument— a condition determined by the need to satisfy the interests of several research projects within budgetary limitations imposed upon all. At the administrative level no questionnaire was supplied; the information received was gained entirely through interviews. There were methodological risks in this procedure, but these risks were seen as no greater, although different, than those in more structured techniques.

In selecting colleges and universities for participation in the Institutional Character study, no attempt was made to secure schools that would collectively represent the full spectrum of American higher education. Nor was the sample random. Schools in the study were selected because they have been recently characterized by one or both of two developments: they were in the process of substantive change, or were involved in some variation of the cluster college plan. The changes might have to do with size and facilities, constituencies and programs, particular innovations or efforts at experimentation. However, regardless of the form of change or how it was defined, participating colleges and universities were places where it seemed likely, in the opinion of campus participants as well as the research staff, that changes under way there would affect the character of the institution.

The cluster college concept, whereby a university authorizes establishment of a comparatively small and in some measure autonomous unit within the general structure of the university, has drawn considerable attention in recent years as one way to solve the problems of large size and impersonality. In addition to being curious about the way this idea was being expressed and received, project staff saw in the cluster college plan a situation that could be used for program comparisons, either on the same campus or with other segments of a multicampus university.

Many more institutions than those actually selected for the study meet the two general criteria specified above. There were, obviously, other factors influencing the selection of schools, including a desire for some measure of national geographical representation in the sample and an interest in having the sample include both colleges and universities as well as both public and private institutions. Representation of large and small schools was another consideration, as was evidence of strong individual leadership as a factor in institutional change.

In the initial organization of the research project, during the summer of 1966, three private liberal arts colleges, two private universities of medium to small size, and one large state university were included in the institutional sample. Four campuses of that public, multicampus university were specified. In the spring of 1967, after the student and faculty questionnaires had been distributed at the campuses mentioned above, it was decided that the interests of the research effort would be served by adding another independent liberal arts college, one openly committed to major innovations, and a state university in another section of the country that was pledged to expansion via the organization of new and innovative undergraduate colleges. This was done. The time of addition precluded student contacts, but the study was conducted in the established manner in two such institutions at the faculty and administrative levels. Within each of the universities enlisted for the study, therefore, were subunits or colleges that were treated separately because of the interests of both the project and the institution in the cluster college concept or the idea of federated colleges.

Because of the desire to share project data with the leadership of participating institutions at the earliest opportunity, and also because of the need to have the impressions and conclusions of project personnel checked by institutional representatives, a preliminary report was written for each school and these individual campus reports, along with an introduction and some comments on findings, were distributed to members of the project dissemination committee on each campus in the spring of 1968. One of the principal researchers visited all campuses in May or June 1968 to discuss this report and to elicit comments and criticisms from local personnel. Finally, in June, copies of the complete preliminary report, containing all of the individual institutional case studies, were mailed to participating schools. It was understood that the contents of this report were not for publication or quotation due to their provisional nature as well as to the fact that the actual names of project schools were used throughout the preliminary documents.

For the final report, the case study approach to individual institutions was retained because of the opportunity this arrangement provided for the most relevant sections to be lifted out and circulated locally, but the names of participating colleges and universities were not used. Instead, a coding procedure was employed that designated schools by their general geographical region.[1] In

---

[1] In the final technical report of the project, as submitted to the U.S. Office of Education, the coding ran as follows: four liberal arts colleges, North College, Midwest College, Southeast College, South College; four universities, UniEastern (College A and College B), East University (College C and College D), UniWestern (Campus G, Campus H, including Colleges H_1 and H_2, Campus I, and Campus J, including Colleges J_1 and J_2), and West University (College E and College F). In this volume, as will be explained presently, the coding of the institutions has been retained, albeit modified. (The report as submitted to the Office of Education was entitled *Institutional Character in Colleges and Universities: Interaction of Ideology, Organization, and Innovation.*)

this volume, institutional case studies will not be featured, but findings by schools will be given on the main areas of concern—educational philosophy and institutional goals; the conventional standard of excellence; and change, innovation, and experimentation. The code names are used less to conceal the identity of project schools than to promote the generalization of findings. With actual colleges and university names removed, the reader may be able to apply the findings more generically, or, perhaps even better, to his own situation.

Chapter Seven, "Faculty," provides cross-cuts of faculty data. There the liberal arts colleges are designated the "Libarts" group; institutions that adhere mainly to the conventional criteria of excellence are termed "Standard Bearers"; innovative colleges showing some prospect for experimentation are called "Radicals"; recently established cluster colleges are "Newcomers"; and the parent institutions out of which these new programs have come are listed as "Elder Siblings." In several cases an institution will operate in more than one category.

Administrative interviews for the study averaged eight per campus, over 100 in all. Each campus was visited three times for administrative interviews, with four persons at the Center responsible for these sessions. Conversations with administrators were thematically structured and lasted from thirty minutes to two hours. Interviewers recorded their summaries on tape immediately after the interviews or, in some cases, made their reports in writing.

The total of the entering freshmen constituting the student sample for the study was about 12,000. Most of these data will be reported separately, but some are used in the following chapters. The faculty data ($N=577$) constitute the principal research resource of the Institutional Character study.

The distribution and collection of faculty and student questionnaires by colleges and universities went as follows:

South College. At the time the faculty questionnaire was distributed (spring 1967), South College had sixty-five full-time faculty members. The sample polled numbered twenty-eight, or 43 per cent of the total. Twenty-two questionnaires were returned, giving representation from 34 per cent of the total faculty. This comparatively high rate of response provided researchers with a

sample notably larger than the 20 per cent of full-time undergraduate teaching faculty that had been set as the project norm.
No student questionnaires went out here, but a number of students
were interviewed.

Southeast College. The faculty testing instrument was
mailed to a sample of twenty-four full-time faculty at this college.
Fifteen questionnaires were returned, a 20 per cent sample of the
total faculty. No student questionnaires were sent out, but students
were interviewed.

Midwest College. At the faculty level, the Institutional
Character questionnaire went to forty-seven persons from a roster
of 111, thus, to 42 per cent of the full-time faculty, including all
ranks. Faculty at Midwest returned thirty-three questionnaires, a
72 per cent response from the sample and a 30 per cent representation of the total faculty.

The student questionnaire went to the entering freshman
class of 1966–67. Completed questionnaires totaled 498.

North College. Thirty-five questionnaires were returned
from the faculty sample at North, giving a representation of 29
per cent of the faculty.

The freshman class filled out 485 questionnaires. Project personnel also had access to data on North students from the Omnibus
Personality Inventory and the College and University Environmental Scales.

Eastversity. Student questionnaires from Beta College gave
a sample of 546, and from Zeta College a sample of eighty. The
Omnibus Personality Inventory had also been administered to the
freshman class, and these data were available to the project staff.

There were 167 faculty at Beta College and six in Zeta
College at the time of the study. Content with comparatively small
N's, seventy-two Beta faculty were contacted (a sample of 43 per
cent), as were all six faculty in Zeta. Emphasis was on undergraduate teaching faculty in the selection of the sample. Forty-two
questionnaires were returned from the Beta faculty polled—58 per
cent of the sample and 25 per cent of the total. Five instruments
were returned from Zeta, giving representation from 83 per cent
of the total.

The third dimension of the study consisted in the interviewing of key administrators. Seven administrators were interviewed, four of them in several different settings.

Additional contacts at Eastversity included a luncheon with five student leaders and two informal meetings with small groups of faculty (six individuals). Attention was also given, here as elsewhere, to catalogs, press releases, informal documents, the student newspaper, and several campus reports.

MultiEastern. The population sample at MultiEastern was limited to administrators and faculty in two colleges on the Riverview campus. One college was the long-established college of arts and sciences, the other the university's college for women. The former had been a loose coalition of schools and departments that were at the time of the study drawing together into a more cohesive unit; the latter had been and remains a small community cohering around a commitment to the liberal arts. Administrators were interviewed, while faculty perspectives were gathered through a questionnaire. The faculty questionnaire was distributed in the spring of 1967 to 174 persons at the college here designated as Alpha, and to ninety-eight persons at Theta College, all of whom at both places were involved part time or full time in teaching undergraduates. At Alpha the sample polled was 42 per cent of the total staff of 415, and the Theta sample was 43 per cent of 228. Questionnaires were also given to a few persons then planning the first of several new colleges; their responses have been included in the returns for Alpha. The faculty of this college returned fifty-one questionnaires, 29 per cent of those polled and 12 per cent of the total faculty there. Twenty-seven questionnaires (two too late for inclusion) were returned from faculty at Theta; this was 26 per cent of those polled or 11 per cent of the total faculty in that college.

The rate of return was lower at MultiEastern than at all but one of the project's participating institutions. One reason may have been that the questionnaire was circulated late in the academic year and faculty by this time were probably suffering from physical and psychic fatigue. Another possible reason for the comparatively low rate of return was that the MultiEastern faculty had passed through a period of considerable controversy over the federated college plan in the late winter and early spring of 1967 and they may have been uneasy about the intent of our inquiry in the context of institutional uncertainty. No attempt was made to collect student data due to the unfavorable circumstances engendered by the time of year when it was necessary to carry out project assignments. A number of students, however, were interviewed.

Westversity. After a working relationship had been established for the study with administrators in Delta and Omega, as well as with general university administrators,[2] project samples were established from these two colleges.

The faculty questionnaire was distributed in fall 1966 to forty-nine faculty members in Delta College and nineteen at Omega College. The forty-nine persons at Delta were a 56 per cent sample of those faculty involved at least in some measure in undergraduate teaching (total faculty being then eighty-seven). Researchers chose a 100 per cent sample of the Omega teaching faculty because of the small number on the staff there. Both faculty samples were stratified to get distribution through the ranks and, as a presumed ancillary benefit, a rough age distribution. In the Delta sample, thirty-eight questionnaires were returned. This was 78 per cent of the number invited to take part and a 44 per cent sample of the teaching faculty in that college. Omega faculty returned eighteen questionnaires, a 95 per cent return on the sample and the same percentage of the total faculty.

Student questionnaires designated for the project were given to all 416 entering Delta freshmen in September 1966. Omega freshmen received the same instrument, eighty-eight persons being involved. Students in both entering classes had also been given the Omnibus Personality Inventory, and data from the scales of this instrument were made available to project personnel.

MultiWestern. In the fall of 1966, 234 faculty questionnaires were mailed to faculty on that campus of MultiWestern which is here designated as Valley. This was a 33 per cent sample of those persons involved, as best the researchers could determine, in undergraduate teaching. One hundred and fifty-one questionnaires were returned, 65 per cent of the sample and about 22 per cent of the total faculty there.

[2] Administrative interviews on this campus were conducted by Ernest Palola, research sociologist from the Center; Edyth Short, project research associate; David Kamen, research assistant; and Moffett Hall, bibliographer.

In 1966–67, the faculty at Hilltop campus was small. Thirty out of the forty-two persons then associated with the first cluster college on that campus, here designated Gamma, and thirty out of the thirty-nine then at Kappa, the second college, were polled. Thus 71 and 77 per cent of the faculties in these colleges were contacted. Returns were adequate to the needs of the study. Fourteen questionnaires came back from Gamma faculty and sixteen from Kappa —a 47 per cent response from one college and 53 per cent from the other. This meant representation from 33 per cent of the full-time teaching faculty at Gamma and 41 per cent of faculty at Kappa.

The response at MultiWestern's Seaside campus was considerably better. From a faculty numbering some 420, project personnel selected a sample of 169 that was stratified to include, here as elsewhere, distribution through the ranks as well as by disciplines. This was a 40 per cent sample of the total. Seaside faculty returned ninety-five questionnaires, 56 per cent of the total number distributed, providing a working sample of 23 per cent of the full-time faculty.

At Bay campus, sixty-nine faculty questionnaires were circulated to a faculty estimated at the time to number 186. Thus, 37 per cent of that faculty were contacted. Returns from Bay campus were proportionately smaller than for any school in the study. Eighteen faculty questionnaires were returned, 26 per cent of our sample but only 10 per cent of the full-time faculty (fourteen questionnaires from Sigma College and four from Lambda College).

Entering freshman classes at all four campuses of Multi-Western, excepting only Gamma College of Hilltop campus, received in September 1966 the student questionnaire designed for the project, as well as the Omnibus Personality Inventory. Student questionnaires returned by schools numbered: Valley, 1523; Hilltop, 213; Seaside, 2676; and Bay, 480. This questionnaire contained seventy-four items, thirty-two of which were used for the Institutional Character study.

While certain assumptions and interests influenced the organization and implementation of this research project, no attempt was made to define words, phrases, or concepts for respondents. Project staff believed that it would be best for individuals in participating colleges and universities to tell the researchers what they meant by the use of such words as "distinctiveness" and "innovation," or phrases like "educational philosophy" and "institutional character." The desire of the researchers was to learn what these words and phrases meant to administrators, faculty, and students.

Although key terms were not defined in the project testing instruments, as a way of giving respondents freedom to use them in their own way, certain words and phrases appear frequently throughout this volume that should be understood to be used in the following ways:

Change—the act or process of alteration, usually conveying in the context of this study the idea of hope of institutional improvement.

Distinctiveness—the quality of being different or unique; the special character of a college or university, having to do with structures and functions or fundamental values.

Experimentation—new means to new or "open" ends, implying "process" and a situation where conventional assumptions and goals are challenged.

Innovation—new means to established ends, implying that conventional or traditional goals and values are essentially sound but capable of improvement.

Institution—refers for the purposes of this study to colleges and universities providing postsecondary, undergraduate educational programs.

Institutional character—the consequence and manifestation of an institution's "integrative value system"; also that which, in turn, gives the institution its essence, sense of community, and basic ethos.

Value—"a standard held with conviction" (Leonard T. Hobhouse). Values act as fundamental motive forces for human action, be they from known or unknown sources, but are not to be confused with things valued.

There is one further delimitation. The Institutional Character study was an activity in time, and its findings represent conditions or perspectives on conditions at a certain period in the history of the institutions involved. At most of the schools of the study there have been developments since the period of data-gathering that qualify or perhaps radically alter certain findings of the research. Because the project had to have its perimeters, it was impossible either to retest in the light of subsequent changes or to keep the report open to later accretions of data or conclusions. What could be done, and what is hereby done, is to acknowledge that life in the institutions of the study is organic; that schools like people can be heuristic; that the results of the study as revealed in the preliminary report helped in some cases to effect substantive change; and that, as a consequence of all these factors and developments, the Institutional Character study findings are more a description of aspects of life in the participating institutions at a recent period in their history than a definitive representation of current conditions there.

It should also be said that few of the schools have changed greatly while many have changed little. Furthermore, the assumptions and goals, problems and conditions described on these campuses prevail at many other colleges and universities. For those who have eyes to see and ears to hear, the findings may have significance.

IV

Educational Philosophy and Institutional Goals

What are the basic values present in academe today, and what difference do they make? Is every college and university, to paraphrase Pitirim Sorokin's question about cultures, "an integrated whole, where no essential part is incidental but each is organically connected with the rest"? Or are they, again as Sorokin put it, "mere spatial congeries of cultural objects, values, traits, which have drifted fortuitously together and are united only by their spatial adjacency, just by the fact that they are thrown together, and by nothing more?"[1] If the first condition exists, what is the

[1] Pitirim Sorokin, *Social and Cultural Dynamics* (Boston: Porter Sargent Publisher, 1957), p. 2.

principle of integration? If the second, what holds the disparate conglomeration together?

The attempt to answer these questions led researchers to an examination of three areas of concern in the colleges and universities of the Institutional Character study. It was hypothesized that the principle of integration—or, alternatively, that which holds the disparate conglomeration together—could be found in one or more of the following dimensions: the formal ideology, that is, the educational philosophy and the institutional goals of the college; the institution's commitment to the conventional standard of excellence; or an institutional identification with change, innovation, or experimentation. There could be, patently, some overlapping of these concentrations, but within them the integrative value system of most institutions of higher education could be found.

In this and the next two chapters, data drawn from the Institutional Character study will be evaluated within the context of these areas of concern. First, information relating to educational philosophy and institutional goals, as found in the literature of colleges and universities participating in the study, will be given and analyzed; then, in an interwoven fashion, the perspectives of administrators at these campuses as they relate to the same subject area. Finally, faculty views as drawn from questionnaire items, and some student data, will be introduced. The universities of the study will be examined first, then the liberal arts colleges.

Statements and Perspectives

The Institutional Character study included two public and two private universities, two of which were medium to large in size (the public ones), with the others comparatively small. The strongest impression gained from our examination of the literature and through conversations with administrators of the large public universities was the notable absence of attention by the leaders to institutional assumptions, values, and goals compared with their almost frenetic regard for quantitative, financial, procedural, implementive considerations. The imbalance between these areas of concentration was somewhat reduced in the smaller, private universities, but was, even there, more noticeable than in the liberal arts colleges. Still, all of these differences, across institutional lines and among types of institutions, were matters of degree only and were insufficient to spare administrators from the charge of delinquency in attending to first principles. It has taken the student activist movement to bring to the fore those general norms, positive and negative, by which the modern institution of higher education organizes itself and measures its style of life. Perhaps it would not be so hard for administrators now to command respect for their pronouncements about the nature of the university had they shown themselves over time to have been good stewards of their institutions' integrative value system. Having neglected to lead, or to even show until lately much more than lip service to educational philosophy and institutional goals, they are having trouble asserting leadership and persuading the public as well as students of their expertise in these matters.

MultiEastern. At this state university within which two undergraduate colleges were studied, Alpha and Theta, the 1967–68 catalog for Alpha carried several paragraphs that explained the shield of the Alpha coat of arms, and several publications associated with the college (for example, the freshman handbook), gave space to a history of the university; but neither the catalog nor the literature available to researchers stated Alpha's present educational philosophy or its broad institutional objectives. Elsewhere in university publications one can read that "[Alpha] continues to uphold the intent of the . . . College trustees as stated in 1771, namely, to pay 'strictest regard . . . to everything that may tend to render students a pleasure to their friends and an ornament to their species. . . .' " Or a statement from the inaugural address of the current President would be quoted: "It must therefore always be the ultimate aim of the University to provide the atmosphere and the intellectual conditions in which alone the free spirit can survive." However, beyond such occasional generalizations researchers were unable to find in the literature any expression of concern for the role of the college in the contemporary world that would match the attention given to Alpha's history and social traditions.

Are visitors to assume that because the catalog says, "diversity of function is the hallmark of a university," Alpha gives no thought to general ideological considerations because, in a university, these are no longer appropriate concerns? Are there no fundamental normative standards operating in the university? Clearly there are. The university makes value judgments about its history and about what it means to be a "Alpha man." The freshman Handbook (1967) stated: "At [Alpha] no one will tell you how to dress or conform to the '[Alpha] image' because there is no such thing as a 'typical' [Alpha] man." Yet in the same publication a picture showed all frosh wearing dress shirts, ties, and other conventional clothes. So, too, judgments are made about the meaning of liberal education in an institutional setting—for example, the superiority of intellectual analysis over noncognitive learning, the character and importance of academic freedom, the role of the university in modern society. If these are aspects of operational values in the university, but are not stated in the literature, how are they conveyed? Are they more caught than taught? Should they be spelled out? They were not found in the Alpha catalog. In the catalog of the other college of this study, Theta, there was a short and general statement:

> The purpose of the College is to discover and to develop the possibilities for growth in its students, so that they may find the fullest satisfaction in rich and responsible personal lives and serve usefully as citizens of a democracy. The College believes that a sound liberal education, in which both practical and ultimate values should be sought, offers to most young women the best means for attaining these objectives. However, since a liberal education does not completely meet the varied needs of all its students, the College offers also courses in important professional fields. By this two-fold offering it aims to serve adequately both the individual and the State.

Whereas in one college, then, nothing is made explicit about educational philosophy, in the other we find a statement that is almost qualified away. The conclusion of the project researchers was that the publications of MultiEastern did not at the time of the study help one to understand the propositional stance of the university. MultiEastern, while very concerned for its historic image, meant apparently to convey the substance of that image by function, act, and attitude rather than pronouncements.

What impressions came from interviews with administrators that might indicate the educational philosophy and broad institutional purposes of this university? First, these conversations gave the impression that general policies were formulated mainly by the university president and a few of his administrative colleagues, and that such policies were usually conveyed by various informal means to other administrators and lesser functionaries. Chief administrators knew that matters of the curriculum were in the control of faculties, but they also knew that they had leverage with those faculties through control of or influence over certain rewards and sanctions. Therefore, leadership by administrators at the level of general institutional planning was possible.

The administrative style at MultiEastern had been patterned after English antecedents and this meant that informal contacts were preferred to formal statements, personal leadership was favored over programmatic, systematized arrangements. University leaders, it was said, were not ideological but pragmatic, more likely to operate with short-term plans and improvised schedules than on fixed, long-range ones. There seemed to be general agreement that this style had been effective in the past at MultiEastern, but concern was expressed by some as to its adequacy for a greatly expanded institution with a complicated future.

Project researchers concluded that the literature of the university faithfully reflected the position of key administrators regarding major philosophical questions even though their views were not explicated. These leaders assumed the adequacy of the liberal tradition; they were confident that the values of the society were basically sound, that the university served those values, and that this relationship could be assumed without being constantly asserted or constantly reaffirmed. They were aware of the social malaise in this country, but they did not believe it to be the place of the university to take a particular position on controversial issues. Rather, the university was meant to provide a setting in which contending points of view could be heard and where representatives of differing philosophies and causes might safely study and teach. MultiEastern was proud of its defense of academic freedom, but the university itself was not thought of by the chief administrators as an agent of social change. Whether they were aware of the extent to which the university has been and is an agent of the social status quo was not clear. That it was to serve the society was certain; just what elements of that society it was serving, and why, did not seem to be regarded as matters for continual review. Therefore, an educational philosophy was operating but was not announced and, perhaps, not even understood.

On the question of the university's role in the state, administrators gave the visitor the impression that MultiEastern for many years had been sensitive to the charge that the best students of the state were going elsewhere for their higher education and that this problem was especially serious at the graduate and professional levels because students trained outside the state were unlikely to return to the state and establish themselves there professionally. Thus the state had suffered a brain drain, a concern to industry as well as to education. It was expected that expanding MultiEastern into a first-rate, complex university with a wide variety of advanced programs would help solve this problem.

No compromise with academic quality was anticipated during the university's expansion period. If MultiEastern was concerned for charges of elitism, administrators gave no sign of it. They were, in fact, concerned for qualitative improvement even during the time of quantitative expansion. This was the university's chance to move up into the first line of universities in the nation, and all energies were to be directed to that goal.

Administrators appreciated MultiEastern's obligation, on the other hand, as the state university, to extend and improve undergraduate educational opportunities. This, indeed, was the principal rationale given for the proposed organization of three new, large (3500 students) undergraduate colleges on the newly acquired 500-acre site. This also influenced consideration at the time of the study to establish one of those new units as an "upper division college," featuring programs of special value to graduates of the state's budding community college program. The state legislature had authorized a community college in each of the state's thirteen counties; thus, in the near future 10,000 to 15,000 students could be graduating from county-run junior colleges and inquiring about transfer into the state university. Considering that the university's present yearly rate of student attrition was 6 per cent, an attrition that made possible the introduction of only about 250 transfer students per year, the pressure of this situation could be great.

MultiEastern needed to expand if the state was serious about keeping students in the state for their higher education and if Multi-Eastern was to continue its monopoly as the state university. The political ramifications of this situation were also apparent. The counties would be supporting community colleges, but would a state legislature with close political ties to these counties be willing to support MultiEastern financially if the university embarrassed the community colleges by refusing to accept their graduates? The tension between MultiEastern's two goals—improving the university qualitatively while also serving a greatly expanding constituency—was evident in the speculations and reflections of administrators during project interviews.

There were problems no less difficult within the university, especially regarding the purposes, objectives, and relationships of MultiEastern undergraduate colleges. There was no apparent concentration among administrators interviewed on the task of securing agreement or understanding at the level of educational philosophy as an essential prerequisite to programmatic planning and the delegation of responsibilities by schools. Philosophical presupposition may have, again, been assumed, and assumed acceptable to all parties, but the parties interviewed did not show any such shared understanding.

For example, it was mentioned that the central administration apparently had decided that Theta College would be a full participant in the federated college plan and that, additionally, if the Theta faculty were to keep abreast of the professionally oriented faculties presently available or those being secured for expanding programs elsewhere in the university, they would need to show accomplishments in research and writing, association with faculty guilds, and other professional activities. Some administrators and faculty within Theta were in full agreement with this shift away from the college's historic autonomy and toward professional integration with the university, but insufficient attention was being given to the question of the meaning and place of Theta, qua Theta, in the new university configuration. When the question was raised in administrative interviews as to which criteria would be used to determine the advancement of Theta's faculty—given the school's long-standing emphasis on teaching vis-à-vis the university's developing emphasis on research—it was admitted that here lay a source of confusion and an issue that, in fact, could not be decided without a consensus on institutional priorities. Another consideration hotly debated by faculty and students within Theta was its future as a college for women. But, it was pointed out, this issue also had to be seen in the context of larger university developments, and there was insufficient dialogue at this level. Also, there were questions about the prospects within the university under the federated plan for faculty innovators. Would "change agents" be supported and rewarded by central administration? What was the prospect for Theta as an innovative college, competing, perhaps, with the newly developing federated colleges for recognition in this connection?

Decisions were being made, or would soon have to be made, in all of these areas of MultiEastern's operations. Yet at the time of the research project, there was little evidence that any sense of shared purpose existed among administrators or that they were even aware of the institutional goals being set for them by somebody else's educational philosophy.

MultiWestern. The other major university of the study was MultiWestern. Four campuses—Valley, Hilltop, Seaside, and Bay—were visited and evaluated. At that time the catalogs of the various campuses did not carry statements on the university's philosophy of education or the general educational objectives of the institution. No attempt was made to define liberal education or to state the responsibilities and privileges of the modern university. The culture of the institution was not described, the academic community not defined. These matters were mentioned in various special publications, as in *Unity and Diversity, the Academic Plan of [MultiWestern],* 1965–1975, issued by the president's office. There, in a section titled "The Role of the University," the reader is told that the university is "responsive to the needs of its state and of society and to the traditional free inquiry that has governed great Western universities since their medieval origins." Furthermore:

> Universities today play a vital role in the preservation of free societies. They are the principal center for the discovery and publication of new ideas; they preserve the heritage of the past for future generations; they maintain precious freedom to ex-

plore all points of view; they instruct the young and the mature alike in the most fundamental conceptions and advanced skills known to our civilization. Increasingly, their contributions are being recognized as basic to the vitality of our culture, the prosperity of free economics, and the very survival of freedom.

This document emphasizes that the achievement of distinction in the years ahead will be conditioned by five overriding imperatives, then six are named: Growth, "The State . . . .is faced with a burgeoning population . . ."; Diversity, "The University will strive deliberately to foster diversity among its campuses, so as to present the broadest range of high-quality educational opportunities to the people of [the State]"; Balance, ". . . an appropriate balance must be achieved and sustained among the basic academic disciplines . . ."; Perspective, "A great University has a duty to the future as great as its duty to the present. . . . Intellectually it must be both more conservative of established values and more bold in trying innovations than may be fashionable at any given moment"; Freedom, "Originality and creativity cannot long breathe any other air"; Responsibility, "Self-restraint, mutual tolerance, and shared concern for the good of the whole community are the obligations of freedom."

Nowhere in this document, or in others known to the research staff, were answers given, or discussion generated, on those questions of what men have in common now, or the basis for authority among the educated. At a time when doubts are being raised not only about the efficiency and flexibility of institutional arrangements but also about their very rationale and necessity, when the institutions of higher education are required to show the validity of their structures and functions, researchers found it disturbing that the university's major publications gave no indication that the institution was consciously, actively probing its assumptions, goals, and values. The attendant fear was that, in this case, the literature faithfully reflected the general condition in the university.

Yet two qualifications on these judgments must be given: First, this university is in this respect no better or worse than other large educational institutions, public or private. All such places have, generally speaking, no sense of the whole. Secondly, the new campuses of the university, especially the two in this study—Hilltop and Bay—have put into their printed materials various statements calculated to show their determination to establish an educational philosophy and follow a set of general objectives. They would be different; and the authorization for substantive diversity had come from the president's office:

> Major differences of emphasis are being planned among new campuses. . . . As each campus also develops its own individual character, vision of excellence, and sense of history, its students, faculty, and staff are better able to engage imaginatively in the enterprise of discovering knowledge.

But the implementation of the president's mandate was left to the individual campuses. One purpose of this study was to see how that task was defined on certain of these campuses, how and if it was being carried out, and what the consequences were.

MultiWestern's Valley Campus. At this older, established campus, conversations with administrators tended to focus on the relationship of the campus to the central administration of the university. The consensus among those interviewed was that statewide administration had tried to give individual campuses sufficient freedom for innovation as well as growth, but that, despite theoretical autonomy, statewide budgetary allocations were handled so as to encourage conformity and discourage innovation. One administrator illustrated the problem by referring to the difficulty in getting money for computer runs necessary for the servicing of innovative admissions procedures. In order to test out this particular registration change, computers at the county office and a local dairy were used.

A further complication was created by university regulations specifying a strict division of labor for administrators, faculty, and students on the several campuses. The consequences have been, first, the creation of a separate administrative caste, working, thinking, talking with their own kind, while the same thing was happening for faculty and students, with the result that it was difficult for any one of these interest groups to understand the needs and feelings of the others. Second, these rigid divisions destroyed the prospects for a community attack on problems and any sort of broad, integrative planning. Thus it became exceedingly difficult to form a philosophy of education or general institutional objectives except, as is now the case, for statements carrying the most superficial, general meanings.

While certain Valley administrators complained about the leveling effect of statewide regulations and guidelines, most administrative leaders professed to be committed to keeping certain Valley traditions intact. One was the tradition of friendliness. The chancellor and others emphasized various structural arrangements whereby students and faculty were encouraged to meet (for example, beautiful lounges at strategic locations, with money provided for student-faculty coffee times, or the "lodges" along the creek that traverses the campus, two of which were near the main buildings and where students and faculty could meet for classes and conversation). Administrators seemed to put great stock in their ability to facilitate friendly encounters.

The chancellor's door has always been open to students, visiting researchers were repeatedly told, but the chancellor's office had been removed during the year of this study to the top floor of a new administrative building some distance from the main flow of student and faculty traffic, and researchers got the impression that the university was growing too large to permit the same measure of informality and immediacy that had characterized relationships in the years prior to the expansion program. However, the dean of students remained (1966–67) in one of the old, centrally located cottages and was eating in different student dining halls at least three days a week. The academic vice chancellor invited more than one hundred students to lunch or dinner at his home in the year prior to the research project. Valley still appeared to be, despite new buildings and numerical growth, friendly and comparatively relaxed. There was some substance to one administrator's claim that the essential distinction of Valley could be reduced to the word "friendliness" or, perhaps, "courtesy."

Administrative leaders acknowledged that changes were coming—a school of medicine, a school of law, a more professionally oriented faculty in arts and sciences. It was evident that the distinctiveness of Valley in the future would be different from the past. Already there was some awareness of the radical changes confronting the culture of the campus—as symbolized by the stress and strain in the student body during the year of the study over the continuation of the "Wild West Days" funfest (canceled by the student body president, but with petitions circulated to have it revived) and a dispute over the appearance of the controversial San Francisco Mime Troupe (canceled by the chancellor, in conjunction with the student body president, but with this decision later reversed and the performance arranged for a later time). However, there was, so far as project staff could determine, no group at Valley thinking about the tacit assumptions that should provide the basis for community on a campus where community was deemed important but where neither the "ag tradition," nor the bicycles, nor the coffee lounges were likely to provide it any longer.

The faculty were drawing more and more into the security of their various specializations—this despite the best efforts of the academic vice chancellor, who had the task of helping to assimilate 145 new faculty in 1965 and over ninety in 1966, and who had arranged at fall orientation time to divide the newcomers into subgroups with deans distributed among them, all in the interest of encouraging community. Administrators were more and more sacrificing faculty fellowship for administrative efficiency. They were so busy with buildings, budgets, and state politics that they could do nothing more than provide structural supports for community. They had less and less time to be a part of it. Students, meantime, were becoming diversfied in values though, as both the student questionnaire and the Omnibus Personality Inventory data showed, they remained pretty much straight-line, middle-class youth. They were, however, beginning to ask the very questions about the nature of the university that faculty and administrators found harder and harder to answer.

MultiWestern's Hilltop Campus.   It was surprising to the project staff that the philosophy or educational objectives of Hilltop, one of the new MultiWestern campuses, were nowhere stated directly. The integrative values, the tacit assumptions, the ultimate basis for authority and for community—these matters were not discussed in the literature. The viability of the university in its institutional forms, with its subject matter disciplines, hierarchical organization, and middle-class value orientation, appeared to be assumed. In various ways, however, the shared aims of the colleges were indicated to be:

—to ignite curiosity,

—to increase knowledge, and with it understanding of the significance, methods, interrelations, and inadequacies of our various ways of looking at the universe,

—to cultivate the skills involved in inquiry, expression, and the handling of ideas,

—to teach habits of honesty, accuracy, sensitivity, and independence,

—to enlarge the student's understanding of his own and other cultures; to develop the student's ability to stand outside himself, to understand as a consequence his location and opportunities, and

—to foster a sense of competence in the academic area by encouraging some expertness.

These aims were more seriously pondered at Hilltop, in the judgment of the researchers, than at most colleges and universities. Nevertheless, was enough attention being given, in the formative years, to the meanings that would be assigned, in a time of great change when traditional definitions can no longer be assumed to be accepted, to time-honored expressions like "liberal education," to words such as "honesty" and "independence"? The pressures to get on with the quantitative task, the immense job of launching a college a year, seemed so great that already one of the core administrators lamented the fact that he felt shy of time for the theoretical conceptualizations of long-range planning. Another administrator, when asked how the assumptions, values, and goals of Hilltop had been communicated to him, replied that he had no memory of explicit conversations or the presentation of printed statements on these matters. He had read the general literature, watched, listened, tried to somehow "catch" what was not specifically taught. He wondered about the absence of a statement of objectives and tended to believe that there should be one. Perhaps a formal statement of ideological commitments would be no more influential at Hilltop than it is at most other places. Perhaps the ideological commitments can become part of the campus ethos without being explicitly stated. But, one way or another, they must be present if Hilltop is to have colleges of consequence.

MultiWestern's Seaside Campus.   At Hilltop, beginning as

was done with the college plan and with the intention of creating graduate units later, the campus is being built from "the bottom up." However, it may be Seaside, not Hilltop, that is building from the bottom up. Given the value priorities of the university, Seaside began much farther down the ladder than Hilltop. It was once a teachers college, and from that "bottom" is now moving toward full parity in the university system.

Interviews with administrators made it clear that an institutional course had been set to give Seaside full standing—in size and in the variety of programs, undergraduate and graduate, in colleges, centers, and institutes—and that the residue of faculty from the old teachers college days, as well as those from the era in which Seaside was intended to be the elite undergraduate liberal arts campus of the university, would be expected to adjust to the new challenge. It was apparent to campus visitors from the project that most administrators at Seaside felt that they had been given such a mandate from "statewide," the president and regents, and it was their intention to carry it out.

It was acknowledged in interviews that some faculty had been hesitant to accept the long-range plan, in part out of academic idealism—they feared that the liberal arts would be deemphasized—and in part for pragmatic reasons—they doubted that the present campus could handle the large numbers of students assigned to it. But the administration argued that in order to achieve what the faculty wanted, it would be necessary to pay the price of large size.

Most administrators whom project personnel encountered seemed to have adjusted their thinking to the accoutrements of the large complex university, even though some of these trappings have come under attack in recent years. One administrator, for example, stated that Seaside would make increasing use of teaching assistants and large classes, and he presented a spirited defense of both. In defending the use of teaching assistants he spoke of their closeness to students and their freshness in the subject matter. Then, defending large lectures, he spoke of the advantage in having one capable lecturer work before several hundred people rather than having several less skilled and less well-trained teachers work with small groups of students. This same administrator also argued that large classes were necessary to pay for small ones.

At no point did interviewers sense uncertainty concerning the university's basic educational objectives and structure. No inclinations to holistic innovation were manifest—such as revising the role of the university vis-à-vis the contemporary society, or radically changing the authority structure of the institution of higher education. There seemed to be no anxiety about having centralized administration or about the likelihood that it may encourage operational efficiency but discourage personal creativity. In fact, certain administrators made a point of claiming that relationships between this campus and statewide offices had been good, first, because of a number of personal friendships and, second, because of the willingness of administrators at Seaside to "play ball" with statewide officials. One administrator illustrated the latter point by citing an incident that had occurred two years before the study when an appeal was made from statewide officers for university campuses to accept more student applicants than had been initially projected on their growth charts. The Seaside administrators decided to cooperate, despite the crowding of facilities that such a change would necessitate. The administrator's comment was that he was sure statewide officers were grateful for this sort of flexibility and accommodation and that, in return, Seaside could expect cooperation from "statewide" in the rapid development of its graduate programs. The effect of this decision on the undergraduate student's educational experience was not discussed, although, surely, administrators must have been confident that no essential sacrifice of quality would result.

However, some adverse qualitative effects must have accompanied this and other quantitative decisions. At the time of the study, Seaside was running over 30 per cent behind its building schedule while it was 20 to 30 per cent ahead of student enrollment projections. (After experiencing a comparatively modest student population growth rate for several years, this campus was increasing its student enrollment 20 to 30 per cent per year.) The decision of the administrators at Seaside to be good "company men," as two of them put it, suggests their concept of organizational leadership, even as their repeated use in the interviews of expressions such as "the people of the state must be served" and "those students who qualify must be accepted" suggest their philosophy of education.

Encounters such as these are, in fact, very revealing. They show that institutions, like individuals, do not operate in a value vacuum. Institutional representatives may not declare the tacit assumptions by which their programs are directed. They may even play down the need for thematic conceptualizations; they may claim to be action-oriented. Nevertheless, the institution is defining itself by some sort of norms, and in these it also finds its validation.

The priorities at Seaside, as listed by one of the chief administrators, were: First, to balance the undergraduate program with strong, varied graduate offerings. The campus had suffered, he said, by having its direction and image changed several times, but now plans for the future were definite. A second priority was the establishment of institutes, centers, and special programs. The Seaside campus provided the headquarters for the university's statewide overseas study programs, and several other special programs had been begun; but, by and large, this campus had not developed a variety of centers and institutes. Such a development was seen as part of Seaside's expansion into the status and complexity of a general university campus. The third priority of the administration was the establishment of new and innovative programs.

MultiWestern's Bay Campus.   Given the emphases of this research project on educational philosophy, the conventional standard of institutional excellence, and innovation and experimentation, Bay seemed to be an especially appropriate candidate for the study. With a distinguished institute of oceanography as a nucleus, this campus of MultiWestern had started at the graduate level, widening its program in 1959 to a school of science and engineering, five years before admission of the first undergraduates. Indeed, until 1966, graduate students outnumbered undergraduates and more research dollars per faculty member had flowed to this campus than to any other in the world. As a brochure quotation put it: "[Bay] has started at a higher level of distinction than any university since Johns Hopkins in 1876, and Chicago and Stanford in the early 1890's." It seemed certain, therefore, that the conventional standard of institutional excellence would be well represented at Bay.

Nevertheless, in 1966 there was considerable impetus toward innovation and experimentation. The long-range academic plan for Bay was unique, proposing to divide 27,500 students into twelve colleges of about 2300 students each. Each college was to have not only a distinctive architecture but also a distinctive academic character. Each was to have its own characteristic approach to each of the divisions of the liberal arts—natural sciences, social sciences, and humanities. The student would have at least two thirds of his curriculum in the college in which he was enrolled and not more than a third in adjacent colleges. Four colleges would be grouped together, colleges varying in style and emphasis but, taken together, offering nearly the full curriculum of a university.

There seemed to be, therefore, every reason to think that the concern of the project for innovation and experimentation in undergraduate education would be well met at Bay. The publications of the new campus claimed that it was unique and, if the colleges could combine on that campus a commitment to the conventional criteria of institutional excellence and a commitment to innovation and experimentation, they would indeed be unique. And were this to be accomplished, the third of the project's areas of interest would certainly be prominently featured. If the Bay campus were to succeed in its ambitious intentions to achieve distinction by both the standard of the status quo and the mandate of change, it would certainly give attention, researchers thought, to the creation of an integrative value system appropriate to its vision.

Interviews with key administrators made clear the point that they were basically satisfied with the conventional criteria of academic excellence. There was general support among them for the idea of having the university organized by departments and specializations, with standard criteria emphasized in the selection of faculty, with a division of responsibility whereby the academic senate controlled curriculum and corresponding programs and the administration handled public, political, fiscal, and structural matters. There seemed to be no uneasiness about the fact that the faculty's relationship with students should be essentially tutelary and was in fact asymmetrical, or with the tradition that the university should be characterized by rational discourse and intellectual analysis. Administration seemed satisfied that the meaning of liberal education or humane learning was known and generally accepted and that the conventional standard was the way by which this meaning was to be measured.

The embodiment of the standard for Bay administrators was, it seemed, the oldest and most prestigious of the university's campus—originally the state university. Administrators at Bay were consciously or unconsciously tied to the structures and functions, to the values and norms, of that older campus. Researchers got the impression, reinforced by several explicit statements from administrators, that they regarded their own campus as the emerging standard for their part of the state and that they were out to emulate their precursor, and, if possible, surpass it. Their attitude and intent seemed to be "more of the same, done better."

The interest of Bay administrators in change, therefore, took the form of innovations. In the later chapter on change, innovation, and experimentation, details will be given on the form and substance of innovations undertaken at this campus. Here it is enough to state that knowledge gained through administrative interviews confirmed the claims of the institution's literature that Bay was committed to reforming undergraduate education. However, most administrators interviewed seemed either oblivious of or indifferent to the troubles likely to result from advocating change in a university whose dignities have been achieved through fidelity to the conventional standard of excellence and conservatism toward change.

Contrary to expectations, then, few administrators at Bay, especially among those in the central administration, were actively probing the preconceptions of the university's programs or were trying to shape new philosophical perspectives for a campus avowedly interested in change. It was assumed that a new House of Intellect could be built on the old foundations.

Turning to the private universities, East and West, more explicit statements in the literature on philosophy and purposes were found; but conversations with administrators gave visitors the impression that the rhetoric of their own public pronouncements as well as the printed ideals in the literature were determined mainly by a superinstitutional value orientation to which they readily adhered. They might talk of unique goals and values, but they were in practice committed to those of the conventional standard of excellence.

Eastversity. Publications at East presented several ideas about the purposes of higher education for the individual in society and the place of the institutions of higher education in society. The university, according to the literature, is private, nonsectarian, co-educational; it is responsive to "a society becoming increasingly complex and demanding an enormous breadth of spirit and knowledge of all who live meaningfully within it"; it is committed to the liberal arts and thereby it "hopes to implant in its students a respect for reason, spiritual values, creativity, speculation, the abstract, eagerness to evaluate new ideas, and a sense of history and of the excitement of participating in the future."

East officially encouraged research and publications among faculty, but it was also stated that the primary function of the faculty is teaching. The students of the university deserved a broad range of programs; these are provided, and students were expected to make use of them. All of these emphases were included in the official literature. The "dreams and hopes" of East were summarized by the President: "To teach, to educate, to lead, to illuminate, to provoke, to stimulate, to urge and guide toward far horizons, toward wisdom and understanding, never in the process forgetting to cherish and to care." These words, presumably, were intended to apply to students rather than to society, or perhaps to students directly and through them to society. The impression that the university was considered an agent of social change was not conveyed by the literature or through conversation with administrators. Rather, East apparently was considered a service-centered institution, reflecting societal values and responding to society's needs. So far as the university's philosophy of education and its institutional objectives were concerned, researchers concluded that there was nothing in the publications or interviews to suggest that East was trying to be innovative or experimental at this level. University officials wanted a complex university with diverse programs, yet they were shepherding students in the manner of conventional residential colleges. They wanted to foster faculty research and publications, but also to emphasize teaching; to have strong departments and professional specializations, yet to build this house of many rooms on a liberal arts foundation; to lead, to provoke, to stimulate, but without alienating constituents by variant behavior patterns. It is all familiar, honorable, and well-nigh impossible.

The board objectives of the institution were shaped in the president's office, with the help of the board of trustees, then brought to administrators for discussion and the preparation of implementational strategies at the meetings of the deans' council (heads of colleges and programs, plus central administrators). There were also numerous informal personal contacts. Project personnel sensed that there was a strong feeling of institutional loyalty among administrators.

It soon became apparent, however, through a review of the literature available to the public, and even more from conversations with East's administrators, that the university officials were keenly aware of the institution's limitations as well as its several bright prospects. They were trying to decide how to create a functional operational base, especially with regard to finances, and how to build an institutional character on that base that would sustain and project East into creative growth. Accommodation and character were pivotal considerations in East's planning. The implicit tension between the concept of accommodation, implying compromise, and the concept of character, suggesting the lonely splendor of principle, had already become explicit.

Interviews with East's administrators, as well as the literature, made clear just how this university proposed in 1966–67 to achieve character through accommodation. First, East intended to move as quickly as possible to gain general university status, offering a wide range of programs that would thereby broaden its base of support by appealing to the needs and interests of a very heterogeneous constituency. The traditional graduate and professional divisions of a first-class university were to be promoted, with first priority to law. Some faculty and administrators preferred to see East do a few things well, and they resisted the inclination of the university to jump into new programs two or three years before needed resources were available. Nevertheless, it had been decided a few years before this study to abandon the brief tradition East had established as a liberal arts college and to meet the future as "one of the nation's youngest universities," a university with three distinguishing qualities: "a youthful willingness to experiment; a dedication to the pursuit of scholarly excellence; and an abiding concern for those who—whatever their need—turn to the University."

Student needs about which the university was to be concerned included, apparently, the need for East to offer three undergraduate degrees and a variety of Master of Arts programs, a Master of Science in Education, a Master of Business Administration, and advanced study beyond the master's level in several fields. Restraint had been shown, however, in initiating Ph.D. programs, and it was not until the year after the project commenced that modest beginnings were made at the doctoral level.

East is located within a few miles of a competing private university, about ten miles or so from an innovative college being established by the state university, an hour's drive from another private university, and about the same distance from yet another campus of the state university. These facts must have contributed to the urgency of East's expansion. A matter of special concern to some of East's administrators, it seemed, was to stake out claims to key programs before new campuses or expanding and opportunistic ones could get ahead of them.

Administrators did speak of plans for cooperation between at least some of these institutions. Monthly meetings had been set up involving administrators of East and the private university close by. They agreed not to duplicate expensive library acquisitions (single purchases over $300), to offer reciprocal use of library facilities, and to share a Spanish language program, another in classics, and one in inter-American studies. East, researchers were told, would not try to duplicate the other school's fine program in dance and, meanwhile, East had been assured that the neighboring university would not compete for the school of law that, at the time of the study, was designated for the area and which since has been awarded by the state to East. Cooperation with the other private university in the area was less likely, it was said, because of the greater distance involved and because of certain personality clashes. (The institutions had become extensions of their leaders' personalities.) The same problem was perhaps the main reason the neighboring institutions had been slow in making a start toward greater efficiency and economy through purposive cooperation.

The main competition for East was expected to come, not from either of the private universities in the area, but from the new campus of the state university, where $110,000,000 was to be spent to establish what the university's president had predicted would be "the most experimental college in the state system and one of the most experimental in the country." There, in the shade of the last great stand of trees for miles around, for the campus site had been a huge estate, students would pay about one-fourth of East's tuition charge.

How would East meet such a formidable challenge? The East way was not only to expand into university programs that would draw students by meeting their individual needs but also to assume an innovative stance for the institution by showing "a youthful willingness to experiment." Zeta College was one manifestation of this determination. The year the study began was the year Zeta completed its evolution into a three-year degree-granting college of the university. This was an innovative college, striving for distinction by close student-faculty relations, opportunity for independent study, a sense of community, and a unique curriculum.

East had other distinctions. A commuter university from its inception, East began arranging in 1966–67 for about 50 per cent of its student body to live on campus while 50 per cent remained commuters. In terms of national practice this was not innovative, but it was a radical change for East. The university's decision to build four high-rise dorms with appropriate service facilities, using $10,000,000 or more in federal money, came at a time when students in some universities were rejecting residential collegiate life, particularly the regulations and ethos associated with conventional dorm life. Would students from local communities leave home to "live in"? Could the university broaden and enrich the socioeconomic composition of its community by bringing students from the northeast and the eastern seaboard? Certain administrators had high hopes that this would happen. They wanted to break up the provincialism of East's students and saw the residential plan as a way to do it. Furthermore, they said, so long as the university had only about $1,000,000 in endowment, and 90 per cent of its operating budget came from student fees, the program of the university was hostage to students. Any class or activity they wanted must be set up, tailored not only to their needs but to their taste. The university had to cater to its clientele. Having 50 per cent of the students in residence could bring new order and stability—students would not directly allocate their tuition dollars to particular courses —and might bring a different type of student.

Did East really want the type of student likely to occupy their new dorms? Or, indeed, the types likely to respond to the innovations at Zeta? East students had been aspirants to the middle class—practical, no-nonsense young people. There had been, to be sure, some sorority-fraternity makebelieve, but that had been peripheral to East's central mission, which had been to educate lower middle-class masses of the metropolitan area. But the students likely to occupy the new dorms would be those who could afford them—students from middle to upper middle-class homes. Moreover, students attracted to Zeta would be "intellectuals" with an idea orientation, not East's job-study types. What would be the consequences? Would East innovate toward the style of the elite just when the national challenge was to educate the masses of students in the so-called "bottom third"?

The administrative answers reflected the character-through-accommodation theme characteristic of Eastversity. They seemed to be saying that the residential plan could reduce the instability of the commuter tradition, using government loans and grants, mainly on self-amortizing buildings, to establish a new financial and academic base for the future. The administration's direction was set by pragmatic considerations, but they considered their act idealistic pragmatism. They were using the resources they could muster to create what they wanted, and what they wanted was a university with the stability and programs to compete with the other private universities in the area, as well as a school with the flexibility to compete in innovations with the state university's innovative programs.

Critics of the residential plan and Zeta College argued that the heavy indebtedness associated with the creation of a major university, and the expensiveness of innovations, would cause the university, despite the fact that the dorms are self-liquidating, to try to satisfy the high rate of occupancy required for the buildings by giving priority to students able to pay for space there or able to pay for a place in Zeta. These emphases might some day jeopardize the institution's long-standing commitment to commuters and divert scholarship money that has gone to them. There was also the threat that the university might become overextended financially and academically. Some administrative contacts wondered aloud whether there were sufficient resources to sustain graduate programs, particularly at the Ph.D. level; others saw quantitative expansion competing for limited resources needed for the qualitative improvement of existing programs. East was already in such a bind that "unprofitable courses," that is, those with an insufficient enrollment, were cut off despite their importance for those enrolled. The free-market approach was being carried to dangerous extremes, however understandable it was for university administrators to cast about for new sources of revenue.

The university has shown its innovative capacity by installing wheel-chair lifts and by modifying curbs and other facilities to allow physically handicapped students to study with a minimum of difficulty. Also, East has allowed faculty freedom to organize their classes according to their own best judgment and has provided numerous institutes and special programs. It may be, indeed, that the programmed innovativeness that is supposed to be a feature of the new East will result in programs less daring than those of the past. One member of the university argued that faculty members in Beta College have been freer to innovate in their teaching methodology and in course content than faculty in Zeta, where certain innovations have been required of all faculty participants. The research staff were especially interested in these currents and cross-currents of thought and practice bearing on East's philosophy of education and institutional objectives. Related concerns had to do with whether those themes and goals would best be achieved by fidelity to conventional standards of excellence, or by experimentation, or by innovations which might, on the one hand, reconcile differences, or, on the other, bring differing methodologies into the community.

Westversity. The catalog and other Westversity publications emphasize two objectives in the school's undergraduate programs. No matter which college, "it is the concern of the university that every graduate be a liberally educated person"; providing a "comprehensive liberal arts education" is the first objective. The means to this end, according to the catalog, is

> . . . a core of subjects leading to the discovery of the fundamental nature of man and the universe, and a general acquaintance with, and appreciation of, man's history and creative achievements, presented in such a way as to develop alert critical thinking, self-expression, and skill in discovering truth.

The second objective emphasized in this university is community or fraternity, that ineffable but unmistakably important factor that gives life to what is frequently referred to around campus as "the West family." West has long had the reputation as a friendly, close-knit community, and one of the most attractive features in the cluster college concept was its promise to personalize and unify the learning experiences of participants, providing a basis for community in the subunits even as the university grew larger and human relationships at that level became more dispersed, formal, and impersonal. Yet the emphasis on community was a university concern in 1966–67. The catalog referred to privileges and responsibilities:

> The University believes in a friendly mutuality between students and faculty, and in a program of student activities to give opportunity for creative expression and the development of leadership. At the same time, the University holds that privileges are inseparable from responsibilities, and a student who accepts the one is expected to share fully in the other. Thus the student earns the right to continued instruction, residence, work and fellowship.

Of course other emphases figured in the objectives of the institution—preparation for a vocation through academic specialization, graduate programs, and professional schools, and the university's dedication "to Christian principles." Above all, however, West seemed committed, as shown in the literature, to undergraduate programs featuring the liberal arts worked out in the setting of an academic community.

These same themes were even more explicit in Westversity's Omega College publications. The cornerstone of cluster college planning was the confidence that out-of-class supports for the student's learning experiences were more important than in-class activities and that, therefore, facilities, schedules, and everything else must contribute to the creation of a close-knit community serving the needs of the whole person even as the whole person was to become involved in the life of the community. The curriculum of Omega was deliberately structured to provide a balanced program in the liberal arts. Whereas most colleges and universities limited general education to the first year or two of the student's baccalaureate career, moving him quickly into some specialization, the Omega curriculum provided almost three years of liberal arts learning. The college would not be all things to all men but, rather, would strive to do a few things well. The Omega graduate would move on at the fourth year into graduate or professional specialization after a three-year experience in the liberal arts that had its own integrity yet offered at least an introduction to a discipline.

These emphases of West's publications were confirmed in administrative interviews. The primacy of the liberal arts and the necessity for the spirit of community were persistent themes. Neither Delta nor Omega officials indicated that they had doubts about the essential validity of either emphasis. They, as did the university's central administration, seemed to assume that the values of the Western liberal tradition, of which, after all, the liberal arts are an intellectual and now an institutionalized expression, were the values needed by contemporary students. The central administration at the time of the study expressed these values through a business ethic and bureaucratic mode of operation. Administrators in the two colleges expressed these values in a more academic mode and with emphasis on a consensual operation, yet they all seemed to be sociopolitical liberals of the sort who are coming under increasingly heavy attack from the new youth movement.

The concern for community also carries value assumptions that, judging by the interviews, went unchallenged by West's administrators. The essential prerequisite for community is goodwill. If goodwill between interest groups is ever lost, the spirit of community is lost. But the basis for goodwill is a body of shared assumptions about man and history and man in the world. Without that, what one man calls benevolence another may call a strategy for enslavement. Shared values of a fundamental sort seem, therefore,

to be essential to the achievement of community. It is precisely at
this point that trouble may emerge at West. A consequence of the
cluster colleges has been to introduce into the university a growing
number of youth who do not share the values of the liberal tradition. Hence, the concept of community is threatened, at least as
conceived by the first planners of the cluster colleges. There will
surely be more confrontation within the community—that could
be hoped for—but such differences among interest groups may
eventually destroy the very objective the concept of innovative colleges was meant to foster. Community could give way to anarchy,
or, fearing anarchy, community could give way to tyranny.

    North College.   Publications at North—catalog (1966–67),
brochures, and various reports—state the institutional purposes:

> [North] College is a Christian liberal arts college that endeavors
> to unite excellence in academic achievement with dedication in
> service.

> Believing that worthwhile life and a free society hinge upon en-
> lightened intelligence, the College takes its primary task to be
> the sharing of great ideas among growing minds.

> Taking good will rooted in faith to be basic, the College seeks
> to constitute a community exemplifying the spirit of brother-
> hood. Christian in spirit, and . . . background, but not sectarian
> in outlook . . . [North] seeks to cultivate in all its students con-
> structive citizenship and aspires to bring out in many fearless
> zeal for justice, freedom and human well-being.

> The business of [North] is that of changing students . . . to help
> the student develop his greatest potential so that he may become
> an effective agent in helping to guide and mold forces at work
> in the world, rather than being merely affected and 'driven' by
> them.

    The views expressed on these and related themes in the
college catalog seemed more explicitly stated than were similar expressions in the literature of any other school in the study. But, as
is so often the case, these broad generalizations were not being discussed, refined, and applied as a community endeavor. They were
goals assumed by the administration, interpreted by faculty in terms
set by their own increasing professionalism, and largely ignored by

students. There was an articulation and transmission problem. It was not clear from admissions staff interviews, for example, just what sort of directives, if any, had come to that group from top college administrators on general institutional objectives. There was a major change in personnel in the admissions office during 1960–61, at about the time the "new North" drive began with its consequent vigorous recruiting program, but the goals of the college were presumed to remain the same in a time of rapid change, and presumed to be known and accepted by all concerned.

The type of student sought by North was the well-motivated, bright, self-disciplined youth who embodied the values that have come to be associated with the American middle class. From administrative interviews we received the impression that the interest of some admission counselors in more dissident students was not supported by the committee on admissions and, therefore, nonconformists, trouble-makers and boat-rockers tended to be rejected. Observation and interviews gave the impression that students were orderly, well scrubbed, and essentially conservative, with theoretical interest in controversial issues—black power, civil rights, political radicalism, and the views of the developing "adversary subculture" —but that very few of them were personally active in effecting social change. Several faculty complained about the docility of students. They wanted a different mix in the student body. No discussions could be uncovered on such subjects as the correlation between student characteristics and institutional values.

South College. The contrast between North College and South College on the articulation of goals was marked. In the formative years of South there was spirited and continuing discussion between administrators, faculty, and students on subjects in the area of educational philosophy and institutional objectives. Three factors seemed to contribute to this unusual situation. One was simply the fact of newness. The college had been in operation about seven years, and throughout that period had been forced to think about what and why and so what. The second factor was the leadership of the academic dean, a gentleman who took it as his mission to see that everyone from the president through faculty and student body to nonacademic personnel understood what the college was all about. This responsibility proved to be too much for one man, and of course he was never entirely alone in carrying it, but for years he was crucial—and made a difference. The third factor was that from the beginning South had made use of faculty for their ideas on institutional goals and design as well as for their disciplinary expertise. Faculty members from other institutions were active in the initial planning activities for the college, and of a total of twenty-two involved in one or the other of two planning committees, fourteen actually joined South's faculty. Thus, from the first, a large proportion of faculty knew about and became identified with the educational aims and academic program that characterize the college. Administrators emphasized in the interviews that this sort of substantive involvement in the most basic considerations by the faculty had been essential to the success of the college thus far.

Midwest College. If North College seemed to emphasize an educational philosophy featuring the conventional criteria of institutional success, and South College was a self-conscious community disposed to innovations, Midwest College, at least in the opinion of its president, was distinctive in its "religious climate." The president saw the college as the "cutting edge for the church," and he was prepared to live with the friction this working relationship created with some church people. The president's occasional sermons were distributed to the constituency, and thus constituents were "educated" to accept the fact that the educational experience at Midwest was a combination of security and risk.

Midwest College is frequently called, in conversations and in printed materials, "a community of learning and a community of faith." The concept of community is very important, and is another point of distinction in the college's self-perception. The academic community is called "a vital link between the Church and the world" and "a Christian community engaged in higher education." The role of the community of faith is emphasized in daily quasi-voluntary chapel programs. Students are told:

> Students who come to [Midwest] for their education join a community that gathers once each day Monday through Friday, for the expression and communication of common concerns and faith. . . . The daily worship service . . . is not designed primarily for individuals who want to worship God, but for a community existence under God in which the individuals assume respon-

sibility to and for the community by their presence . . . concern
. . . participation and contribution.

An examination of school publications and interviews with administrators indicate that Midwest plans no change in its stated educational philosophy; nevertheless, its traditions appear to be yielding to evolutionary change. This change was initiated, first, by the college's decision to improve the academic quality of its faculty, and secondly, to broaden its social and religious representation. The incentives for these changes were inherent in the situation but the initiative for them seemed to come from the chief administrators, the president and academic dean.

If these changes continue, Midwest may well experience increased questioning in the student body of the relevance of Christian faith and the Judeo-Christian tradition for contemporary social and political problems, as well as pressure from faculty for the further professionalization of the academic program at the college. Both developments are likely to produce strains for the college's cherished concept of a religiously based community.

Southeast College. At Southeast, leadership in the area of institutional objectives had come, administrators said, from the Board of Trustees and the President. The trustees had been loyal to Southeast's church affiliation and, therefore, it was claimed, through them the church has influenced the ethos of the college but not the academic program. Church affiliation contributed significantly to student recruitment, but the church was only moderately influential through direct financial support. Many churchmen, one researcher was told, felt that Southeast had been and should remain an arm of the church, whereas the leadership within the college had become increasingly vigorous in asserting the independence of the school.

The preceding statement is not intended to suggest that Southeast's administrators proposed to use their independence to promote radical sociopolitical ideas or radical educational experimentation. The impression gained in 1966–67 was that the administrators of the college, with the exception of the new president, who was then just beginning to be known on campus but who was already showing signs of discomfort with the status quo, were moderates on most controversial issues. They appeared to be moderate on questions of race, economics, and politics, moderate regarding personal and community styles, moderate in educational expectations and program planning. They were interested in being distinctive if that meant being better by conventional standards of academic excellence than were most Negro colleges of the southeast. They were not interested in being distinctive if that meant being different from the good white or black liberal arts colleges with which they wanted to be identified and who were responsible for the standards by which Southeast people judged themselves. They did want the distinction of highly regarded Negro colleges and the satisfaction of success judged by conventional academic criteria. They had too long had the "distinction" of being regarded as inferior. Thus, we feared, Southeast's administrators were interested in innovations that showed promise of moving the college toward what other administrators, in institutions where the dominant model had long been sanctioned, were now trying to innovate away from. At the time of the southeast study, a new spirit of independence was just beginning to emerge, but it was clearly a harbinger of things to come and not a distinguishing characteristic of existing realities.

Interviews with Southeast administrators revealed that they had decided to work toward greater cooperation with the other colleges of the complex. They gave the impression that Southeast personnel were for many years concerned primarily to establish the identity of their college and the integrity of its program, and that only recently had they gained the confidence in themselves prerequisite to creative, successful efforts at cooperation with schools previously thought of as competitors.

Southeast draws most of its students from the state it is in and a bordering state, from small towns or rural locales, from church-related homes of limited social and educational opportunities. The city in which Southeast is located is a mecca for such students, and they readily identify with the middle-class values of the area and the college. Indeed, their vocational and social status aspirations, combined with the educational limitations in their background and earlier experiences, limit the innovations open to the college and sustain the middle-class character of the institution. Fraternities and sororities, for example, figure prominently in the life of Southeast. Some of the administrators interviewed felt that the

"Greeks" were too influential and that their leadership was essentially anti-intellectual. Others thought that the "Greeks" tended to lift the academic life of the community and that they fitted in rather well with prevailing institutional values—neither elitest nor sharecropper, not intellectually esoteric, but oriented to materialism and competitive capitalism, democracy, social conformity, and liberal Christianity.

Faculty Attitudes

Several items in the faculty questionnaire used for the Institutional Character study illuminate the extent to which faculty at the participating schools had been drawn into a consideration of general institutional objectives and educational philosophy, their views on how such matters were regarded by colleagues, and faculty understanding of the responsibility for leadership in shaping and protecting the integrative value system of the institution of higher education.

The first item in the faculty questionnaire read:

> When you were negotiating for your present job, was attention given through the correspondence, during the interviews, or in casual conversation, to the educational philosophy and objectives of the institution, particularly as compared to the details of the particular task for which you were being considered?

An assumption behind the question was that if the institution regarded general ideological considerations to be of prime importance to the educational experiences offered students, as well as to faculty satisfaction and the future vitality of the school itself, administrators and department chairmen would emphasize these considerations at the time the faculty member was employed. Four response options were provided, which yielded the data given in Table 1.

Attention is drawn to the differences between newer and older institutions, especially the differences between the newer, innovative colleges and the older, conventional ones. At both Multi-Western and Westversity these points were evident. The new Hilltop and Bay campuses of MultiWestern, at least during their first formative years, were giving much more attention to institutional ideology than was true at the older campuses of Valley and Seaside.

Table 1

UNIVERSITY FACULTY REPORT ON EMPHASIS DURING INTERVIEWING FOR THEIR CURRENT POST

(IN PERCENTAGES)

	MultiEastern		East-versity	Westversity			MultiWestern				CIT*
	Alpha College (N=51)	Theta College (N=25)	Beta College (N=42)	Delta College (N=38)	Omega College (N=18)	Valley Campus (N=151)	Hilltop Campus, Gamma College (N=14)	Hilltop Campus, Kappa College (N=16)	Seaside Campus (N=94)	Bay Campus, Sigma College (N=14)	(N=577)
Institutional objectives were treated at length, indeed, at greater length than the particulars of the job	6	4	5	13	78	4	79	69	4	36	16
About equal attention was given to institutional objectives and job description	14	20	17	26	17	13	21	19	19	36	22
The institutional philosophy and educational purposes were mentioned, but in a tangential or ancillary way	16	32	17	29	0	15	0	6	17	0	15
The emphasis was clearly on the work of the department and the way my own training and interests would relate thereto	59	40	48	26	0	60	0	6	51	7	40
No response	6	4	14	5	0	8	0	0	7	21	7

* CIT (Composite Institutional Totals) include the four liberal arts colleges. (Cf. Table 3.)

NOTE—Totals in this and subsequent tables do not always equal 100 per cent, or equal to N, because of rounding percentages and the few variant responses not accommodated by code categories.

82

The older places showed the same trend toward departmental concentration as found in the composite institutional totals. The interest in institutional objectives at Sigma College, Bay campus, may be the most remarkable accomplishment of all the colleges, given the graduate orientation of faculty there and the national tendency for graduate faculty to be highly specialized.

Data for the cluster college at Westversity, Omega, suggest again that faculty members coming into a new and innovative program are required by the nature of the situation to give more attention to the broad, inclusive objectives of the college than is true in an older, conventional college. In the older college, institutional assumptions, values, and goals are apparently assumed to be known and accepted, or subsumed under departmental emphases, or simply ignored. But, if it is correct that Westversity has always emphasized both the liberal arts and the spirit of community, can these emphases, in a time of expansion and change, be assumed or ignored without risk to the enterprise? Is it not likely that other values will emerge and become dominant—for example, the superinstitutional norms of conventional excellence? Such a development may be viewed favorably, of course, but if so, it should be pointed out that educators usually consider such norms to be in conflict with values emphasizing community. They also represent a threat to a conception of the liberal arts which emphasizes the unitary nature of liberal learning.

At MultiEastern, with its two long-established colleges, the emphasis at recruitment time was on departmental and professional consideration, although this was less so at Theta College than at Alpha. Only one campus in the total institutional sample ran higher than Alpha on the response rate favoring departmental concentration. Only three institutions in the study, all major state university campuses, gave a higher percentage response to the priority of departments than did Eastversity faculty. The "No response" rate at East on this item was also high. These data match the emphasis some administrators put on departmental autonomy at East and indicate the presence of a professionally oriented faculty. These data, taken together, indicate that most faculty, with the exceptions noted, did not remember that their initial professional contacts with the universities where they were employed emphasized attention to educational philosophy and institutional goals.

At another point in the faculty questionnaire, respondents were asked:

> What proportion of the present faculty do you consider to be seriously concerned, pro or con, with the formal institutional purposes that are intended to give direction and character to your college?

Research personnel held the position that a high percentage of faculty sharing at least a surface manifestation of concern for the ideological or propositional stance of their college would suggest the possibility of openness on their part to substantive involvement in setting and achieving institutional goals. Data from the university faculty samples to the six response options are given in Table 2.

The central tendency on this questionnaire was for faculty respondents to regard about half of their colleagues as seriously concerned for the formal institutional purposes of their university. However, when the newer, innovative colleges are set over against the older, conventional ones, marked differences again become apparent. For example, these data show that faculty at Valley campus and Seaside campus of MultiWestern, the older units, differed significantly from faculty at the new campuses, Hilltop and Bay. The same distinctions were evident at Westversity. MultiEastern's long-established colleges gave roughly comparable response patterns, very much like those at MultiWestern's older campuses.

Because there were only six faculty in Eastversity's innovative Zeta college, responses from this small sample were not included in Tables 1 and 2. However, it may be noted that all five of the respondents from Zeta regarded their colleagues there to be seriously concerned about general institutional objectives.

Readers will attach varying importance to having faculty seriously concerned about the formal institutional purposes that are supposed to give a college direction and character, but there can be little doubt that faculty samples on these campuses viewed their colleagues quite differently. Some auditors will argue that the excitement of new beginning alone, not greater seriousness of purpose or philosophical sophistication, explains the greater attention to in-

Table 2

Proportion of University Faculty Concerned for Institutional Purposes (in percentages)

| | MultiEastern | | Eastversity | Westversity | | | MultiWestern | | | | CIT* |
	Alpha College (N=51)	Theta College (N=25)	Beta College (N=42)	Delta College (N=38)	Omega College (N=18)	Valley Campus (N=151)	Hilltop Campus, Gamma College (N=14)	Hilltop Campus, Kappa College (N=16)	Seaside Campus (N=94)	Bay Campus, Sigma College (N=14)	(N=577)
Almost all	8	12	14	10	72	13	57	50	7	43	19
Well over half	22	20	31	21	28	24	43	38	24	21	26
About half	28	24	36	42	0	26	0	6	27	14	26
One fourth or so	26	24	19	13	0	15	0	6	22	0	14
Very few	12	8	0	10	0	9	0	0	10	14	7
Such things are not the concern of the faculty	0	0	0	3	0	0	0	0	0	0	0
No response	2	8	0	0	0	11	0	0	10	7	6

* CIT (Composite Institutional Totals) include also the four liberal arts colleges.

85

stitutional objectives on the new campuses. But, if so, is this not an argument for new beginnings, for new campuses or the reshaping of old ones, if that development brings participants to think about the nature and worth of shared values?

When faculty attitudes at the four private liberal arts colleges were compared with responses from university faculty on the same questionnaire items (see Table 3), the strongest impression received by project staff was a more even distribution across categories for the faculties of the private colleges than had been the case with university faculty. There was still an alarmingly small percentage declaring that institutional objectives had been treated at length when respondents were hired, as was also true when they were trying to determine the percentage of colleagues seriously concerned for institutional purposes; but there was a definite shift of percentages toward a more balanced presentation in the recruiting process between institutional priorities and those of the department, and toward a higher proportion of colleagues concerned for that which is regarded as giving direction and character to the institution.

Faculty responses at South indicated that the college's emphasis on its philosophy and objectives, as shown in the literature and through administrative interviews, had been conveyed to candidates for positions on the faculty. Furthermore, a high level of salience for incoming faculty of the school's philosophy and objectives had been reasonably well sustained. This conclusion is based on comparative data; of course, South's record may be viewed quite differently from the perspective of the institution itself. It may be a matter of concern to the college that seven years after its founding, even 13 per cent of the faculty sample thought that half or less than one half of its faculty were seriously concerned for broad institutional objectives.

The data in Table 3 show that the Southeast faculty sample remembered a departmental and subject-matter emphasis in their negotiations for employment in percentages that equate with the university faculties. More evidence for departmental "autonomy" or, at least, the department as focal point of faculty attention—both points made by several Southeast administrators—appeared in the lack of response for the first category. It might be assumed that a

Table 3

RESPONSES OF FACULTY AT LIBERAL ARTS COLLEGES
(IN PERCENTAGES)

	North College (N=35)	Mid-west College (N=33)	South-east College (N=15)	South College (N=22)	CIT* (N=577)
When you were negotiating for your present job, was attention given through the correspondence, during the interviews, or in casual conversation, to the educational philosophy and objectives of the institution, particularly as compared to the details of the particular task for which you were being considered?					
Institutional objectives were treated at length, indeed, at greater length than the particulars of the job .	14	12	0	64	16
About equal attention was given to institutional objectives and job description	29	67	27	32	22
The institutional philosophy and educational purposes were mentioned, but in a tangential or ancillary way	23	3	13	0	15
The emphasis was clearly on the work of the department the way my own training and interests would relate thereto	20	15	47	0	40
No response	9	3	13	0	7
What proportion of the present faculty do you consider to be seriously concerned, pro or con, with the formal institutional purposes that are intended to give direction and character to your college?					
Almost all	11	30	7	46	19
Well over half	37	42	0	41	26
Almost half	43	27	47	9	26
One fourth or so	6	0	13	4	14
Very few	0	0	27	0	7
Such things are not the concern of the faculty .	0	0	0	0	0
No response	3	0	7	0	6

* CIT (Composite Institutional Total) includes also the four universities.

school with only about sixty full-time faculty and a long tradition as a church-related college would effectively communicate its general institutional objectives to faculty and that they would be actively, noticeably committed to them. But such was not the case at Southeast.

One cautionary note in the item dealing with the emphases during job negotiations was raised by several respondents at Midwest College. They made it known that at the time of job negotiations they were already well acquainted with the general objectives of the college. When this fact is joined with data provided through the question's structured response options, it is evident that the stated purposes of that college were well known to faculty. But this factor did not apply to other schools.

Robert Hutchins, former president of the University of Chicago and now president of the Center for the Study of Democratic Institutions, Santa Barbara, California, has been for twenty-five years one of the most provocative figures in American higher education. He has been forthright and controversial, as was a quotation from him used to elicit faculty attitudes on a question related to faculty concern for general institutional purposes. The question was, "Is it the responsibility of the faculty to be active participants in the formulation of educational policies and programs?" Hutchins put the matter positively: "The duty of the faculty is to formulate the purposes and programs of the university. The duty of the regents [trustees] is to interpret and defend them." Faculty were invited to agree or disagree with that statement, and space was provided for written qualifications. The staff anticipated that respondents would approach the statement as a view of what ought to be and not as a description of existing conditions or even immediate possibilities. Nevertheless, the item would provide an indication of the extent to which faculty thought they should lead in charting the course of institutions of higher education. When the responses from all colleges and universities were combined (CIT, composite institutional total), the percentage of faculty agreeing with Hutchins ran to 80 per cent. Only 16 per cent disagreed.

At MultiEastern, 82 per cent of the Alpha College respondents and 88 per cent of those at Theta College agreed with the notion of faculty leadership. It may have been, of course, that both

MultiEastern samples were answering in the context of anxiety about what the university's increasing dependence on the state for funding would mean for academic autonomy. But the attitude expressed by the faculty on this subject, at least when considering it theoretically, may also indicate a willingness to become more actively involved with the university's administration in the formulation of general policies and new programs. Thus, the decision of the central administration to involve Alpha faculty in planning subsequent colleges on the new site may be especially propitious.

Responses to the quotation at South College showed 59 per cent of the sample agreeing to a leadership role for faculty, while 41 per cent disagreed. Of those choosing to enlarge their answer, 23 per cent expressed qualified agreement and 32 per cent qualified disagreement. About 9 per cent suggested various ways the responsibilities could be shared. In an institution where much has been made of the faculty's actual participation in the formulation of policies and programs, and where broad institutional purposes are emphasized, the response to this question falls considerably below the results of the CIT (composite institutional total). Does this suggest that the principle of collegiality is the one favored by the South College faculty, that they prefer a plan of shared responsibility due to positive experiences thus far, or does the result suggest that the college's interest in innovation does not extend this far and that the school's commitment to experimentation is confined, in the thinking of the faculty, to curriculum developments? It would be innovative to have fundamental purposes as well as programs set by faculty, with trustees put in a supportive role. But is this notion too radical, or perhaps aristocratic, to gain really strong support at South? This may have been an area of the school's program where, at the time of the study, there was little interest in innovation of this sort or perhaps little thought on the subject.

A point of interest to project personnel was that the same faculty who said they had, in the majority of cases, been hired into the institution because of their professional competence and potential for departmental service, and who indicated that many or even most of their colleagues were not seriously concerned for integrative institutional objectives, nevertheless believed that faculty should formulate university purposes as well as programs. It was a case of,

"That which I would, I do not; and that which I would not, that I do."

If the Hutchins quotation is to be regarded as providing data only on theoretical possibilities, another item in the faculty questionnaire explicitly dealt with reality factors: "Who would you say has the most powerful voice in determining educational policies, i.e., the general objectives rather than the particulars of a given program, in your college?" Respondents were invited to select from a list of nine options, plus open ended or free response sections. Table 4 shows the treatment of the question by the faculty samples at MultiWestern campuses and colleges. The centrality of faculty leadership in general educational policy formulation is asserted by these faculty samples, although on the two older campuses, where there has been a tradition of strong administrative participation, that fact is acknowledged. At Valley campus, where the administration had seen itself as existing to implement faculty decisions, the faculty responded by making the strongest comparative claim for faculty leadership. The report from Hilltop is confused by the fact that Hilltop's Kappa College faculty were at the time of contact just getting established and could only respond to the question by acknowledging the leadership of administrators in planning the college, whereas Hilltop's Gamma College faculty reported shared leadership during the one year they had been working together. The spirit of collegiality seemed stronger there than in the other samples.

In the other colleges and universities of the study the leadership of certain strong administrators was evident in faculty data from this question. At North College, 49 per cent called the dean or provost of the program the most powerful voice in determining educational policies, a tribute to the authority of their executive vice-president and provost. At South College, 68 per cent pinpointed the academic dean, with only 14 per cent crediting the general faculty. Eastversity faculty considered that the greatest influence had been exerted by the president (38 per cent), with the dean and the general faculty tied for second place (17 per cent). In only one other institution, namely, Westversity (55 per cent), did a larger percentage of faculty name the president as having the most powerful voice in policy formulation.

Table 4

EDUCATIONAL POLICY DETERMINATION AT MULTIWESTERN—FACULTY VIEWS (IN PERCENTAGES)

	Valley Campus	Hilltop Campus, Gamma College	Hilltop Campus, Kappa College	Seaside Campus	Bay Campus, Sigma College	CIT
Trustees or regents	4	14	6	5	0	5
Chief administrative officer of your *campus* (president, chancellor)	12	21	31	21	0	20
Chief administrative officer of your *program* (dean, provost)	15	14	19	6	7	18
Division head	0	0	6	2	0	1
An executive committee	6	0	0	1	21	6
The general faculty	46	36	0	42	57	33
Students	0	0	0	1	0	0
Constituency	1	0	0	0	7	1
Statewide coordinating agency	2	0	0	3	0	1
Others	3	7	6	1	0	2
No response	11	7	31	17	7	12

91

At MultiEastern, opinion on the leadership variable was rather evenly distributed. About 20 per cent of the Alpha College sample said "Chief administrative officer (president, chancellor)," 24 per cent gave the most powerful role to a dean or provost (the "Chief administrative officer of your program"), and 26 per cent marked "The general faculty." These positions were shifted somewhat by the Theta College sample, which judged that for this college the president was more powerful than the dean (20 per cent for the former and 8 per cent for the latter). However, the faculty at Theta, as at Alpha, was regarded as most powerful of all (Theta, 36 per cent and Alpha, 26 per cent).

If the position is taken that faculties are inherently conservative, and hence unlikely to advocate change at a time when change is essential if higher education is to meet the needs of a new age, then there is reason to promote the creation of new colleges, especially innovative ones. It is in those places, these data show, that innovative faculty leadership has the best chance for success.

Student Views

The student questionnaire distributed to the entering freshman class at most project schools in the fall of 1966 contained an item asking students how much they thought they knew about the "general philosophy of the college" they had just entered. Response percentages by schools varied considerably, with a higher percentage of students at the new campuses claiming an understanding of the purposes of their schools. Table 5 presents the differences in professed knowledge at the four campuses of MultiWestern.

Eastversity entering freshmen differed, as did MultiWestern's, according to whether they were attending the established larger college or the innovative, smaller one. Nineteen per cent of the freshmen at Eastversity's older college, Beta, thought they knew a lot about their school's philosophy, while the students entering the new college, Zeta, who were this confident totaled 36 per cent. Those who said they "know a little about it" came to 69 per cent at Beta College and 55 per cent at Zeta. Ten per cent at Beta said they "don't know anything about it," while this view was taken by 9 per cent of entering students at Zeta. These data, when compared with the CIT, show that Beta is rather low on the "Know a lot"

Table 5

ENTERING STUDENTS' KNOWLEDGE OF INSTITUTIONAL PHILOSOPHY
(IN PERCENTAGES)

	Valley Campus ($N=1523$)	Hilltop Campus, Kappa College ($N=213$)	Seaside Campus ($N=2676$)	Bay Campus, Sigma College ($N=480$)
Know a lot about it ..	20	61	12	40
Know a little about it .	69	36	70	52
Don't know anything about it	10	1	15	4
No response	1	2	3	3

NOTE—No student questionnaires distributed at Gamma College, Hilltop campus.

end of the scale and high on the "Don't know anything" end. The 10 per cent of students claiming "Don't know anything about it" was second highest among project schools. However, considering the preponderance of commuting students and the lack of tradition in this university, we conclude that Eastversity had made its philosophy fairly well known to entering freshmen.

Forty per cent at Midwest College answered, "Know a lot about it," and only 2 per cent checked "Don't know anything about it." Apart from the three colleges founded less than five years before the time of the study, Midwest students claimed to have more knowledge of the school's general philosophy than did students at any of the other institutions.

Only 18 per cent of the freshman class at Southeast College thought that they had considerable knowledge about institutional purposes, while 68 per cent claimed to know a little on the subject and 6 per cent professed ignorance. Of ten different college units participating in the study, these data put Southeast eighth in the "Know a lot about it" category. The advantage that an observer might assign to an older college in conveying to counselors, student applicants, parents and others the philosophy or general objectives

94 Conformity

of the college is, therefore, not sustained. As a matter of fact, comparative data show that the new college has the advantage.

About 61 per cent of the freshman class at Westversity's Omega College, the cluster college, professed to know a lot about their school's philosophy, whereas 17 per cent of the student respondents at this university's core college, Delta, felt that they could say as much. Only one entering class in the study showed a lower frequency than did Delta on this item. Similarly, 9 per cent of the Delta students said they knew nothing about the general philosophy of the college at entrance whereas only 1 per cent of the entering frosh at Omega gave this response.

Just as the history of man shows that to know the right is not necessarily to do it, so, surely, to profess to know a school's philosophy is not necessarily to know it or to follow it. Nevertheless, it is fair to surmise that the vitality and character of an institution are more likely to be enhanced by a knowledgeable entering class of students than by those who know little or nothing of these matters.

Further insight into how well educational philosophy and broad institutional purposes were being conveyed to students in project schools was gained by a questionnaire item reading: "Do you see this college as having some special quality that distinguishes it from other colleges and universities?"

At Southeast College, entering students divided their answers as follows: 74 per cent thought that their school was "Not greatly different from other colleges," while 21 per cent felt that it "Has a special distinguishing quality." This result is instructive in that the percentage of freshmen thinking that their college is "Not greatly different" was the highest of any participating institution.

Eastversity freshmen enrolled at Beta College responded with 39 per cent saying that "It has a special distinguishing quality," but 59 per cent saying it is "Not greatly different from other colleges." A dramatic difference in student perception was evidenced at Zeta College, Eastversity, where 82 per cent thought their college had a special quality while only 18 per cent answered negatively. The innovative nature of Zeta's curriculum had, it seems, been communicated to most entering freshmen.

More entering freshmen at North, in 1966, saw their college as having a special distinguishing quality than did such students on other of the older campuses, but fewer than students on new campuses. Some 31 per cent saw the college as "Not greatly different from other colleges," while 67 per cent saw it as having "a special distinguishing quality." Not surprisingly, but perhaps significantly, in two innovative new colleges the student confidence in the existence of a special distinguishing quality at their college ran as high as 90 to 100 per cent.

These data are representative of the total sample, and they show that some institutions are much more successful than others in getting before students the distinguishing characteristics of their philosophy and programs.

Having examined student, faculty, and administrative perspectives at a variety of colleges and universities on the stated educational philosophy and institutional goals of the place where they were personally involved, and having commented on the extent to which a significant percentage of each of these interest groups seemed to be uninformed and little affected by the propositional stance of their institution, attention will be given next to an analysis of the way these same persons and groups responded to the superinstitutional value standard provided by the conventional criteria of excellence.

V

Conventional Standard of Excellence

A student's Scholastic Aptitude scores and related verbal or mathematical skills, his success in college preparatory courses, student-body offices held, and other indices of social and emotional as well as intellectual abilities—all these characteristics and accomplishments are features of the conventional criteria by which high school youth are judged as they try to advance into college.

Once at the institution of higher education, the student is accountable to the grading system; needs to secure acceptance in a respected department as an apprentice to a renowned professor; must prove himself capable of the intellectual discipline and social restraint of the educated man, by success in rote memorization, the massing of factual information, and the utilization of theoretical conceptualizations and modes of inquiry within the established disciplines. At graduation, the student should be able to bridge over by the recommendation of his major professor and a strong Graduate Record Examination into a recognized graduate or professional program, taking up, certainly, the professor's methodology and possibly, someday, his mantle.

But the conventional standard of excellence applies to faculty and administrators every bit as much as to students. It decrees for faculty that they have the right degrees from certain universities. (There are, in fact, about ten graduate schools offering diplomas that are international currency in academe.) The professional life of faculty must be characterized by a good teaching reputation (but not too good), a style and sociopolitical preferences that are in the academic mainstream, and research culminating in publications honored by professional journals but with a permanent home between the book covers of a distinguished university press. Meanwhile, occasional stints on committees of the academic senate must be coupled with duties for the national guild and various engagements that encourage visibility and assure professional mobility. Now, more than in the past when community service was honored in the breach, the criteria include an expectation that the professor will by words and occasional deed show himself to be a concerned citizen—a law and order with justice citizen.

Administrators, too, have norms to which the standard holds them accountable. They are seen as facilitators, implementers, interpreters of the institution's life. Their success is measured by their ability to provide the money, facilities, conveniences, and services the system has decreed to be essential components of a professional environment. As they prove their competency by assuring these "supportive capabilities," administrators have some prospect, especially if they can also show earned degrees in academic subjects, of being accepted by faculty as "professional."

In the preceding chapter, while discussing administrative, faculty, and student responses to the avowed purposes of the colleges and universities in the Institutional Character study, there were repeated instances when it became clear that various schools were committed less to unique or even particular institutional goals than to professionalism's superinstitutional norms, called here the

conventional standard of excellence. The institutions, and the individuals within them, might not be measuring up to the particulars
of the criteria—indeed, most of them were not—but the point is
that at the level of aspiration, or with regard to desire and intent,
they were beholden to these norms. At the center of the picture
dominating their imagination was the standard. Additional evidence
of the authority of the conventional criteria with institutions of
various sizes and types follows. It will become evident that it is by
these measures that, for almost all colleges and universities, institutional character is determined, achieved, and protected.

South College. Despite professed interest in experimentation at South College, there were numerous signs that innovation,
not experimentation, was under way. Established educational values
were not repudiated. Conventional norms guided operations and
determined successes. Innovations were not regarded as means
of breaking with conventional criteria so much as they were seen
as means to the achievement thereof.

The Freshman Class Profile 1966–67, published by the college, showed 860 applications for admission with 499 accepted. The
CEEB Scholastic Aptitude Test scores profile revealed that in the
year of the study, of 116 applying with 600 or higher SAT verbal
scores only three were not accepted, and of 106 applying with SAT
scores of 600 or higher in math, six were not accepted. A comparison of SAT mean scores for four years showed a modest but steady
increase each year, with the figures for 1966 standing at 600 verbal
and 588 math. The rank in class section of the Profile also supports
the conclusion that South has not been unmindful of standard
criteria in its student selection program.

South's involvement in another of the emphases normally
associated with the standard of conventional institutional excellence
is suggested by the attention given at the college to the success (50
per cent) of South's graduates in entering graduate or professional
schools and in receiving major fellowships—six Fulbrights, ten
Woodrow Wilsons, one Marshall, and twenty other assorted awards
in the first three graduating classes (from a total of only 234 persons).

Faculty excellence, again measured by conventional standards, was assured at South by securing a staff 76 per cent of whom held Ph.D.'s and 78 per cent of whom had published in professional journals in the year prior to the research project. On the other hand, and in fairness, South's faculty were also committed to teaching, according to the literature and administrative opinion. The faculty is called the "heartbeat of a college" and every member selected "combines scholarship and teaching to an extraordinary degree." The catalogs studied by project staff contained the full range of rhetoric found in publications of all liberal arts colleges and most universities concerning the importance of teaching, but research indicated that in this case practices confirmed rhetoric.

Southeast College. The difficulties engendered by adherence to the conventional standard were shown at Southeast College. Southeast administrators wanted better students—as defined by standard criteria such as College Board scores and rank in class— and they felt that there had been a slight improvement in these areas over the past decade. However, there were two serious problems in this connection: first, limitations in the elementary and secondary schools as well as in the homes from which most Southeast students came were such as to make a considerable number of entering freshmen, perhaps 20 per cent of them, incapable of doing collegiate work. Also, the 70 per cent who successfully enrolled at Southeast but who failed to graduate seldom transferred to other schools. Yet the college had not revised its program sufficiently to meet the students where they were, nor was it able to lift these youth to a level adequate for them to remain in college. The basis for continuing with a dysfunctional arrangement was that the college did not want to compromise its academic aspirations. It was bound to the standard.

A related problem for Southeast and schools of its type has been that wealthy northern white colleges compete so aggressively for the best southern Negro high school graduates that these academically oriented students are often lost to northern institutions. The complex of colleges of which Southeast was a part had held a luncheon for high school counselors of the cosmopolitan area for the first time, in 1967, in an effort to enlist their help in getting first-rate Negro students into local institutions. (The letter of invitation to counselors, project personnel were told, may have been the first public document in the history of the complex to be signed by the presidents of all the colleges.)

The faculty handbook of any institution of higher education is a good place from which to elicit the personal and professional values that the institution proposes to promote by its rewards and sanctions. The handbook at Southeast emphasized the criteria for faculty selection and advancement that are used in the great majority of prestigious or upwardly mobile schools. Project staff noticed only one major exception: there was no mention of academic freedom. Presidential reports to trustees are also indices of institutional emphases and, here again, the conventional value structure of Southeast College was documented. One presidential report stated that 20 per cent of the instructional faculty had earned the doctorate, and that the college was concerned for teaching excellence, research and publications, professional affiliations, and various forms of public service. From interviews with administrators and an examination of the college's literature, project personnel concluded that Southeast, if it had any self-image, defined itself by a Christian and liberal arts educational philosophy, with curriculum and social objectives that were standard American.

Southeast wants faculty trained in the better graduate and professional schools—a professionally oriented faculty. This emphasis, which of late has become quite marked at the college, created uneasiness among older faculty and, furthermore, has probably contributed to a high turnover of personnel and the low faculty retention rate. Younger, aggressive, intellectually inclined faculty saw the school's Council for Academic Affairs dominated by older department heads and academic traditionalists. Yet to visiting researchers, these junior faculty, who are committed to strengthening departmental autonomy and to the success of their students at graduate schools, seemed more concerned for general institutional policy matters and more faculty responsibility for academic policy formulation than were older faculty.

Midwest College. The rise of conventional criteria for excellence in the faculty is one of the developments that has come to characterize Midwest College during the tenure of the present administration. However, in the opinion of administrative leadership, this development has meant an expansion in institutional emphases more than substitutions for earlier emphases. The commitment to historic Protestant Christianity remains, for example, but has been opened and extended considerably. The academic dean, who has been pressing for a more scholarly and liberal emphasis at Midwest, joins the president in contending that the most distinctive quality of the college is the religious nature of the community. Religion provides unity and continuity in the curriculum—students are involved with courses in religion in the freshman, sophomore, and junior years—and the religion faculty is academically strong and politically influential. The theological commitments of the college have been changed but not dropped and, additionally, they have been extended to include contemporary issues such as civil rights and the ecumenical movement.

Students at Midwest come mainly from the small towns and rural parts of Minnesota, Iowa, Wisconsin, and Illinois. Most are affiliated with the sponsoring denomination. Although entering freshmen are told in college literature that success depends largely upon "the student's self-management and his campus citizenship," the programs of the college to which the student is expected to give himself are arranged to take up almost all of his time, and the rules of the college see to his citizenship. The life of the student is heavily structured with social, athletic, and religious activities. In these areas the youth participate actively in governance—there are five major committees on which students sit. To the time of the project, they had not been involved in academic policy formation or in academic governance. Administrators stated that, in their opinion, students were concerned about food, dorm hours for women, and the honor code, but had no desire to be on faculty committees where academic policies were made. Furthermore, they said, the atmosphere of the college was very open, access to the leadership of the college easily arranged, communication between all levels free and frequent. The president, for example, had a weekly luncheon with the four vice presidents and certain other administrators, as well as a few faculty and some student body officers. There was seldom an agenda, meetings were relaxed, and "any issue" could be raised.

Midwest administrators declared their willingness to see

students become more formally and actively involved in educational policy matters but the students, it was said, must first see the need and demand participation—and they were not yet ready. Nor, apparently, were the faculty. One administrator suggested that the issue of student participation in academic policy formulation was more threatening to faculty than to administration. Another said that the student course evaluation form then in use on a voluntary basis could help to create student interest in academic matters and impress faculty with student concerns, but, he said, many faculty did not share his enthusiasm.

The faculty at Midwest appeared at the time of the study to be increasingly interested, not in student participation, but in their own involvement in matters of general institutional governance. Some of the younger element were pressing for more specific policies regarding faculty ranks, salaries, tenure, professional leave privileges, and so on. One specific issue concerned the place of assistant professors in the academic senate. They had not been voting members of the senate, and this meant, with instructors added in, that well over half of the full-time teaching staff could not vote on academic policy matters. Young faculty were impatient with this arrangement. The college administration encouraged faculty discussion on this and other issues, but seemed committed to a slow, deliberate change of policy. Several administrators said that the traditions and procedures of the college might easily be disrupted by introducing a large number of comparatively new and inexperienced assistant professors into the academic senate. Furthermore, given Midwest's location, there would be considerable flux and movement among younger faculty, so they might have little to contribute. Perhaps a better policy, said one administrator, would be to give early advancement to promising young professors into the associate rank and hence into the senate.

Problems of this sort may be expected to increase as the college grows. It is a development assured by financial pressure on the school and the need to utilize available resources. As more assistant professors and instructors are brought in, as necessitated by the ascendancy of faculty in the job market nationally and the unfavorable bargaining position of a small liberal arts college, pressure will build. And the problems will be accentuated by the achievement of the conventional goals Midwest has set for itself. New faculty for whom the college traditions have little meaning, and who are themselves capable and strong-willed, will press for changes that make professional sense to a professionally oriented faculty. But will their proposals really make sense for Midwest?

North College. Of the freshmen enrolled in 1966 at North College, 82 per cent were in the top fifth of their high school graduating class. The college ranked high in the number of National Merit Scholars in its student body. The school's literature emphasized the success of North by these measures. Administrators confirmed that at the time of the study student applications were judged mainly by SAT verbal and math scores (with special emphasis on the former), student rank in class, high school student body offices held, extracurricular interests, athletic accomplishments, and, in some cases, nonintellective variables.

A local newspaper reported that the administration at North had released figures showing that 67 per cent of the faculty held Ph.D. degrees in the year of our study, compared to 30 per cent five years earlier. And this faculty, particularly the newer contingent, had impressive credentials—Fulbrights, Woodrow Wilsons, Danforths, and other awards—with advanced degrees coming from prestigious schools. Origin of academic degree, number of publications, previous teaching positions, success in teaching, and evaluation of peers were the main criteria for faculty appointments. At North, however, unlike many places where standard professional criteria are employed but teaching is treated lightly, there were indications that teaching was important. In the previously mentioned newspaper article describing the number of Ph.D.'s, a chief administrator was quoted as saying that the college was not going to forsake its traditional commitment to teaching in a preference for faculty research and writing, but a "balanced emphasis" had helped to lift North into the circle of top church-related colleges, and administrators were confident that the balance between teaching and research could be maintained.

No division between "young Turks" and "old guard" in faculty was acknowledged in administrative interviews, and an emphasis on the creation of a united academic community was evident throughout these conversations. One person cited the prac-

tice of the provost in making himself available for discussion with
the faculty about once a month on any matters of concern to the
community. About a third of the faculty members, it was said, took
this opportunity to exchange ideas, criticisms, and evaluations.

The faculty had become more insistent in recent years on
participation in policy decisions directly affecting faculty welfare.
Its personnel committee reviewed faculty salaries with the administration but did not yet share in the allocation of the annual budget.
Decisions in these areas remained with the budget committee of the
board of trustees. But the budget was published each year, and the
faculty was becoming more interested in the intricacies of budget
preparation. There had been changes in the extent to which faculty
members were involved in these considerations, and certain administrators allowed that there probably would be others in the
future. At North, the board of trustees had for some time included
in its organization an education committee, a student life committee, an investment committee, and others. The faculty had become increasingly active in these same areas. It was not evident,
however, whether the faculty wanted power in order to change the
shape and direction of the college or to control the status quo and
secure its place in it.

MultiEastern. MultiEastern provided an opportunity for
researchers to examine the role of the conventional standard of excellence among administrators and faculty who were in the process
of redistributing power within the university while also planning
for new, innovative colleges. While administrators at MultiEastern
showed a readiness to work with faculty in planning for the future
of the university, they also favored a division of responsibility in
formulating the institution's basic commitments. Researchers got
the impression that administrators expected that the faculty would
advance the interest of the university in research while administrators would have the responsibility of advancing the university's
concern for teaching. One administrator emphasized that faculty determination to move MultiEastern into the first echelon of institutions would be the motivation for research, while the administrators'
control of rewards and sanctions and their concern for the classroom
would be the safeguard of effective teaching.

Faculty salary decisions at the time of the study were handled by department chairmen and deans. However, while each dean respected the authority of the departments and of the faculty's academic senate (appointments, for example, were approved by senate sections organized along disciplinary lines, and administrators did not intrude on their deliberations), administrators had leverage through their control of the budget. Nevertheless, there was congruence between administrators and faculty on the centrality of the conventional standard of excellence as the means for achieving institutional distinctiveness at MultiEastern. And their respective roles within this theoretical framework were clearly understood; faculty controlled the curriculum, and administrators by and large worked through faculty to achieve change in this area. Administrators were the "gatekeepers" between the university's many programs and the paths leading to the world beyond the campus. Administrators were responsible for these broad relationships, and faculty were expected to cooperate.

But, of course, developments at one end of the spectrum of responsibility impinge on those at the other. The state legislature had been conservative in budgeting allocations for the university at the time of the research personnel's association with Multi-Eastern. The effect had been to heighten the budgetary competition at a time of expanded plans among the several schools and colleges within the university. MultiEastern had practiced program budgeting to the colleges, with the provost's office and an administrative triumvirate making the final decision on the amount to be allocated to each. This office also controlled the "lines" (job allocations per academic program). The provost had stated to his associates that he was willing for these decisions to be made under some other administrative plan, but no one had come up with a viable alternative. The deans acknowledged that they were not prepared to accept responsibility for dividing available money among themselves, nor were they "mature enough," as one put it, to negotiate with each other on the "lines" since it would eventually involve revealing salaries for individual faculty members within colleges. The university had a published salary schedule, but the position of an individual within an academic rank on the scale was information not generally shared by deans across college lines. It would be a source of endless controversy, leaders felt, to have to justify the standing of individual faculty on the salary schedule.

Theta College of MultiEastern had over the years enjoyed greater autonomy in handling its budget than other programs in this university for reasons acknowledged by all to be historical but believed by some to be irrational. Some Theta people held that the separate budget offered a measure of protection for innovation and program flexibility in the college. Recently, however, in changing times at the university, if the amount available through its separate budget proved inadequate to the college's needs—as was increasingly the case—there was no recourse for the college, no general university resources to which they could turn.

Theta College had suffered a pinch at the time of the study in the allocation of "lines." In the year prior to the project Alpha College, MultiEastern, had received nine new lines and in the year of the study twenty more, while Theta had received none in either year. Officials at Theta emphasized that this condition, while very unsatisfactory, was due to state economics rather than to prejudice against Theta in central administration. However, concern was expressed for what would happen to Theta, which had emphasized teaching and the liberal arts, when the emphasis in the university was shifting to research, tight specializations, graduate and professional programs.

The creation of new colleges seemed likely to require faculties and administrators to think much more and much harder than had been their practice about the fundamental values of the university's educational experience. MultiEastern leaders had been slow to reflect on their integrative value system—how they would legitimate the learning configurations in their institution for new times. But new colleges must think about these things and, because they do, the older colleges around them are required to think afresh about what they hold in common and how they, symbolizing the "old" ways, relate to those who claim to offer "new" and better ways.

According to those MultiEastern administrators interviewed, the faculty of Alpha College were divided on the question of the degree of autonomy to be given new federated colleges. The majority seemed to feel that university-wide standards should be determined by the traditions of existing programs, and that all new programs should conform to them. There could be innovation, but innovators should work within the general definitions set down for everybody. One interview yielded a comment containing the following estimate of attitudes: A third of the faculty in Alpha preferred one big liberal arts college for the university with a strengthening of existing departments, and with new colleges providing mainly social opportunities and personalized housing arrangements; a very small number favored nearly complete autonomy for new colleges, granting them freedom to innovate as they saw fit; and, finally, more than half of the Alpha faculty wished both freedom and responsibility for all new programs—freedom sufficient to innovate, responsibility to university-wide standards.

Two areas of conflict were admissions requirements for new college students—could such a program use nonintellective variables in the selection process?—and the matter of separate operating budgets for the new colleges. Administrators in the core unit, Alpha, were insisting on a shared budget plan, whereas administrators in Theta and the planning coterie of the first of the new colleges were asking for separate budgets to safeguard autonomy.

MultiWestern.   It has already been shown that the administrators of the major state university called MultiWestern were unapologetically committed to the conventional standard of institutional success. Here are additional comments on two of this university's campuses—one new, one old.

At Bay campus, it was expected by administrators that the success of the school's established programs at the graduate and professional levels—which were internationally renowned—would provide "quality control" for the new undergraduate colleges. The conventional criteria of excellence which had so successfully guided the campus in its earlier epoch were, therefore, applied to the establishment of Sigma College, Lambda College, and the others to follow. Yet these colleges were to be innovative and experimental— "the old ways, not the new, must defend themselves here." Bay's distinctions in graduate education and faculty guilds were not seen as serious threats to the achievement of change in the proposed undergraduate programs. But to the research staff, the fact that Bay campus was in the "big leagues," as one administrator put it, at the level of graduate education, did not assure that the new undergraduate colleges would immediately qualify for the "big leagues"—perhaps not by conventional standards, probably not by innovative criteria. The very distinction of the institution in one area could act to inhibit success in another. Nevertheless, administration interviews revealed no anxiety among the leaders, in 1966–67, about the ground rules and guidelines under which the university was operating to establish its new colleges. Nor did there seem to be any uncertainty about the adequacy of the conventional standards, even in a time of radical social change.

Things were not much different at MultiWestern's Valley campus. Aside from the traditional emphasis there on friendliness and the spirit of community, the distinctiveness of Valley was defined by administrators with the same measures employed elsewhere in the university. They were committed to achieving distinction for the campus by hiring a professionally oriented faculty, by securing motivated and hard-working students—as judged by standard criteria—and, at the level of their own responsibilities, by achieving efficiency, order, numerical and material growth for their campus under the terms of guidelines set by the statewide administration. Any disagreement would concern the means to be employed in the achievement of ends about which, it seemed, there was general agreement. There was not, in 1966–67, so far as project researchers could tell, any uncertainty in the thinking of administrators about the ends of education, about the assumptions, values, and goals of the university, about the role of that campus in the state's educational system, or about the meaning of institutional service and the forms that service should take. To the extent that fundamental values could be ascertained, and it was difficult here as elsewhere to get administrators to talk about them, it seemed clear that the traditional definitions of the nature of the university as a center of service to the public and to the values of the culture were accepted without challenge. Administrators were usually busy implementing, facilitating, organizing; thinking about education in quantitative terms. There were occasional moments when certain of these administrators wished for time to think seriously about the philosophy of mass public education, about the new youth movement with its new/old morality, about the possibility that today the university is obliged to stand in a new service connection—to serve as a center of countervailing power to the nation-state. But these administrators had no time for that, even as others saw no need for it. At Valley as elsewhere, few administrators were hearing the questions and almost no one was working on the answers.

Faculty and the Standard

Faculty, not administrators or students, are the most zealous guardians of the conventional criteria to which all academic interest groups are obligated. Certain items in the faculty questionnaire of the Institutional Character study show the high value that faculty— not only at the universities but also in the liberal arts colleges, not only on large campuses but also small ones—attached to research and writing, teaching in the area of academic specialization, pro- fessional meetings, and related interests.

Included in a group of questionnaire items dealing with features of academic life that have varying degrees of importance for faculty in American colleges and universities were these three: availability of research money and appropriate facilities, opportunity for research and writing, and teaching in the area of academic specialization. Faculty respondents on the MultiWestern campuses were asked to present their own opinion (coded "self" in Table 6) and their perception of the opinion that generally prevailed among their peers (coded "others" in Table 6).

One interesting detail is the consistency between the figures in the "Personal view" columns on the CIT and the figures in the "View of others" columns for the item dealing with money and facilities as research resources. Seldom was this balance duplicated in other questionnaire items of the research project. The more typical outcome was for there to be a considerable difference in self-perception and the view of others. It may be that money "talks" so forcefully that everyone hears. Faculty can be in doubt about what colleagues think concerning educational philosophy and other abstract subjects, but they accurately judge what others think about bread and butter concerns. Again, however, if this hypothesis can be accepted, priorities are revealed.

Attention is also called to a difference between certain data from Bay's Sigma College. Only 21 per cent of the faculty sample

Table 6

Faculty Views on Aspects of Academic Life, MultiWestern (in percentages)

	Valley Campus	Hilltop Campus, Gamma College	Hilltop Campus, Kappa College	Seaside Campus	Bay Campus, Sigma College	CIT
Availability of research money and facilities:						
Self						
Very important	70	50	31	58	21	51
Somewhat important	24	43	62	37	57	38
Others						
Very important	76	64	31	66	79	51
Somewhat important	13	29	50	28	14	34
Research and writing:						
Self						
Very important	77	79	81	76	100	66
Somewhat important	20	21	12	16	0	27
Others						
Very important	71	64	50	70	71	48
Somewhat important	18	21	31	17	14	36
Teaching in the area of academic specialization:						
Self						
Very important	87	79	81	85	86	83
Somewhat important	11	21	19	11	14	15
Others						
Very important	68	86	75	71	64	72
Somewhat important	20	0	6	19	14	17

NOTE—A "not important" response category was omitted from this table because of the comparative insignificance of percentages there.

there rated "availability of research money and facilities" as *very important,* but 100 per cent named research and writing as *important* for themselves. If this faculty were heavily weighted with humanists, who need relatively little in the way of money or research facilities, the difference would be understandable. But the Bay campus faculty was heavily skewed toward scientists, who need such things. This fact, coupled with the report that only 21 per cent of that faculty listed research money and facilities as *very important,* and set over against the fact that the Bay faculty were said to have gotten more research money per person than any institution in the nation, suggests the conclusion that faculty members are likely to rate high not what they have and value but what they don't have yet value.

Bay, the literature said, was a campus that proposed to challenge every assumption of higher education. If a professionally oriented faculty, one emphasizing research and publication and teaching specializations, was one of those assumptions that was to be challenged, these data indicate that it had not been challenged sufficiently to make a noticeable difference in the values of the Bay's Sigma College faculty or, if challenged, it had survived the challenge and defeated it. The Bay faculty showed themselves fully committed to at least these dimensions of the conventional criteria. The other campuses of MultiWestern were no different. Notice that the Hilltop campus faculty modified the intensity of commitment to research and writing a little, but they were not remarkably different on these scales from their colleagues elsewhere. This finding strikes an omnious note for those who have been pulling for a victory by the new colleges at Hilltop over the subject-matter divisions that have also been created on the campus, hoping that the grouping of faculty by colleges would reduce the pressures for research and publication and increase the possibilities of closer, more vital faculty-student relationships in the learning environment.

At MultiEastern, the report of the faculty at the college designated Alpha, and also at Theta, corresponded closely to the data from MultiWestern. The availability of research money and supportive facilities was *very important* to 76 per cent of the respondents at Alpha. Research and writing were equally important for 78 per cent, while 71 per cent thought teaching in the area of one's academic specialization to be *very important*. Faculty at Theta selected the same response on this item in 92 per cent of the cases. In this they were topped by only one other faculty sample in the study. The Alpha faculty response on this item was no less surprising: not only were they twenty percentage points below their sister college, but their 71 per cent, while high in terms of an absolute standard, was second lowest in the institutional sample. Project staff were surprised, therefore, on two counts: First, teaching in the discipline seemed more important in the college with the deepest roots in the liberal arts tradition, and in that college where more departmental bias might be expected, less was found. Second, the Alpha faculty sample, at a time when the university was intensifying its professional associations, showed somewhat less commitment to at least some of those values that are everywhere seen as a part of the conventional norms of professional excellence.

Although Alpha broke at least slightly away from one university faculty stereotype, it should be pointed out that in the other items mentioned, those dealing with the respondents' notions about the importance of research and writing, and about research money and facilities, the sample from Alpha fell back into the predictable pattern. Compared with the Theta College faculty and, indeed, compared with the composite institutional totals, they reflected the intensification of the research orientation at the university and acknowledged their own participation in that development.

Eastversity and Westversity were small in size compared to MultiEastern or MultiWestern, both were private schools not public, neither one could impress with the symbols or accomplishments of conventional success in competition with the larger, complex universities. Nevertheless, at both East and West the indices of excellence that we have regarded as evidence of the influence of the conventional superinstitutional standard were much in evidence. The opportunity for research and writing was *very important* to 57 per cent of faculty contacts at Eastversity's Beta College, the original undergraduate college of arts and sciences at East. Faculty regarding research and writing as *somewhat important* numbered 40 per cent.

Faculty at Westversity's older and more conventional undergraduate college, Delta College, listed research and writing *very important* in 32 per cent of the cases, with 58 per cent saying *somewhat important*. Interestingly, in the "view of others" column, only 5 per cent of the Delta respondents said research and writing were important for their peers, the lowest proportion for any institution in the study.

It is probably fair to infer that Delta faculty are still affected by an earlier era when the college was known as a place where teaching was everything and research figured not at all. This impression is further supported by the twelve respondents (32 per cent) who thought that research and writing were *not important* for colleagues. No other institutional sample offered a response this high on this item. But the 90 per cent of the Delta respondents who reported that research and writing had at least some measure of importance for them personally hints that professional considerations have influence. The conventional standard of institutional excellence has not been dominant at Delta, but it does have considerable authority with present faculty, and may be increasingly important for them at the level of aspiration.

On the item dealing with "teaching in the area of academic specialization," no faculty from Eastversity's Beta College stated that this arrangement was *not important* to them. Rather, 83 per cent called it *very important* and 14 per cent preferred *somewhat important*. The report from Westversity's Delta College was even more striking. Teaching in the area of academic specialization was *very important* to 95 per cent, *somewhat important* to 5 per cent, *not important* to no one.

A larger proportion of the faculty at Delta, Westversity, than at any other institution in the study, reported teaching in the area of specialization to be *very important* for themselves. This response probably suggests, on the one hand, the strength of the departmental orientation of this faculty; on the other hand, it may indicate the conscious or unconscious desire of the Delta respondents to identify themselves with mainstream faculty thinking as measured by national standards at a time when at least one of the cluster colleges (Omega) was innovating with cross-disciplinary contacts.

At West's cluster college, Omega, teaching in the area of academic specialization was *very important* to 44 per cent, *somewhat important* to 44 per cent, *not important* to 6 per cent. In the "view of others" column, the results ran 44 per cent *very important,* 39 per cent *somewhat important,* 0 per cent *not important.* Omega faculty regarded research and writing as *very important* personally in 50 per cent of the cases, *somewhat important* for 33 per cent, and 17 per cent said *not important.* They did not give research and writing the importance indicated by respondents in the total institutional sample (CIT), where major state university campuses were included. However, they did, especially when "self" and "others" data were drawn together for a composite picture, show a greater attention to these activities than colleagues at Delta.

There is apparently a mix of the conventional and the innovative in Omega. Faculty members there have been expected to break out of strict disciplinary guild affiliations, and the data presented suggest that Omega faculty have modified their thinking on this feature of professionalism. Almost all of them regard teaching in the area of specialization as somewhat significant for them, but less than half of the respondents regarded it as *very important.* On the other hand, Omega administrators and faculty, from the outset of the life of the college, regarded professional publications as a way to advertise the intellectual and academic stance of the college and to help faculty compensate somewhat for the professional risks they were taking in being involved with an innovative curriculum. They continue, these data show, to regard this facet of the conventional criteria as comparatively important.

Returning to Eastversity, it is evident that faculty at Beta College conform rather closely to the values of colleagues elsewhere on these subjects of general professional concern.

This emphasis in the Beta faculty on conventional educational standards is consistent with the assumptions, values, and goals for the general university that had been shown in administrative interviews. Not only did administrators state that the East faculty worked best within the regular disciplines and the conventional departmental structure, but they said also that, excepting Zeta College—where faculty were working across departmental lines effectively and without acrimony—there was no desire to reduce the strength of the departments. The departments still provided the best gathering places for energy and ideas, they argued, because at Beta, below the level of administration, the dispersal of people and the diversity of interests made it nearly impossible to establish a general sense of community.

Faculty advancement at East has been determined by success in four categories of concern—teaching, service on campus, community service, and professional life. The procedure has been for faculty to state their accomplishments in these areas; the department head would then make comments on the faculty member's performance, and these would be given to the faculty member to read and sign. Then the department chairman added his recommendations for salary and rank, and these too were shown to the faculty members. Here again, in the area of rewards and sanctions, in the way they are determined and reported, the professional and departmental emphases emerge.

The extent to which faculty identify theoretically with teaching in the area of specialization and with research and writing, regardless of their actual work situation (and this is the way the questionnaire items on these matters were put), is a measure of the authority these criteria exert on them. It does not necessarily follow that interest in these activities runs counter to the creation of an effective learning environment for students, although many perceptive educational observers claim to see a correlation between these faculty emphases and prevailing student complaints about intellectual fragmentation and scholarly withdrawal. It does follow, however, that faculty fidelity to these superinstitutional norms suggests that, at least as far as those faculty members are concerned, institutional distinctiveness will be identified with criteria that may not square with the stated educational philosophy and institutional objectives of the particular college or university.

One and perhaps two of the universities of the research project are avowedly research-oriented and professionally oriented institutions, while at least two others profess to emphasize teaching rather than research, and to give rather high priority to cross-disciplinary programs. Nevertheless, concern for the conventional criteria was considerable in these supposedly different universities. There was, perhaps is, sufficient discrepancy between the institutional objectives for students and the superinstitutional commitments of faculty at these schools to cause serious trouble.

On the questionnaire item asking respondents to comment

on the importance for themselves and other faculty of the "Availability of research money and facilities," 82 per cent at Delta, Westversity, considered these resources *important* for themselves while 18 per cent said *not important*. Faculty at Westversity's Omega College who thought research money and facilities were important totaled 72 per cent of the sample, with 28 per cent professing disinterest in these matters. When respondents evaluated colleagues, 50 per cent at Delta thought research money and appropriate facilities *important* for peers, while 37 per cent thought such considerations were *not important*. At Omega, 78 per cent said that faculty there regarded these professional resources to be *important,* with 11 per cent regarding them as *unimportant* for peers. On both the "personal view" and "view of others" the percentages of faculty at Westversity concerned for these services ran higher than the composite institutional totals.

Another item in the same list from which the above data were drawn provides another perspective on the authority of conventional criteria at Westversity's Delta College. Faculty were asked to comment on the importance of "An emphasis on teaching" in their own professional life and, again, to venture an opinion about the importance of teaching for their colleagues. About 82 per cent of the individuals at Delta who answered stated that it was *very important* for themselves. This is an impressive showing, at least to those auditors who have a high regard for teaching as a legitimate faculty function in contemporary colleges and universities. This figure puts Delta near the top of the participating schools and well above the CIT (61 per cent). Omega measured up equally well— 83 per cent.

It is when attention is directed to the "view of others" that what appears to be evidence of a change in value orientation comes to light. In judging their colleagues, 42 per cent of the Delta sample said that an emphasis on teaching was *very important* to them, 42 per cent thought it was *somewhat important,* and 3 per cent ventured the opinion that their colleagues did not regard teaching as important. Corresponding data from Omega were: 72 per cent *very important,* 17 per cent *somewhat important,* 0 per cent *not important*. What is noteworthy about the Delta response is that only half as many considered emphasis on teaching to be a very important consideration for colleagues. The CIT figures showed a parallel decline—61 per cent considered it *very important* for themselves and 32 per cent *very important* for others. Even so, in a university that has traditionally emphasized teaching, this discrepancy in Delta College data may suggest that whereas the faculty respondent felt the weight of the formal institutional commitment to teaching sufficiently to influence his personal response, he saw evidence of a developing variance in faculty values at the university, perhaps for himself as well as others, and he acknowledged this shift from the university's traditional attitude toward teaching when speaking of his colleagues. The ensuing value vacuum is increasingly being filled, in the opinion of the research team, by an emphasis on research, writing, and other features of the standard professional orientation.

The independent liberal arts colleges offered data from faculty respondents that definitely qualified the high level of support for the conventional criteria of excellence shown by faculty at the large state universities. However, the record of these colleges was not much different from that gathered in the smaller, private universities and was not, in the judgment of researchers, sufficiently different from that of the prototype universities to support the claim that America has a diversified system of higher education, one characterized by diversity at the level of values.

North College faculty to the number of 77 per cent of the respondents said that teaching in the area of academic specialization was *very important* to them personally, while 83 per cent regarded it to be *very important* to their colleagues. Forty-nine per cent said research and writing were personally *very important,* with another 43 per cent calling these tasks *somewhat important.* On the "view of others" side, 17 per cent of the faculty at North thought research and writing to be *very important* for their peers, while 63 per cent said these activities were *somewhat important* for associates. Teaching in the area of specialization was judged *very important* for colleagues by 83 per cent of the sample, 11 per cent saying *somewhat important.*

The outcome, therefore, shows faculty at North emphasizing the indices of professionalism in their evaluations of themselves while finding considerably less inclination in this direction on one of the measures—research and writing—among their faculty colleagues. It is not uncommon for human beings to associate others with what are regarded as the emphases of the past and oneself with those of the future.

Our justification for the claim that North is attracting an increasingly professionally oriented faculty is taken from the "View of others" column on these two questions. Social conditioning may cause one to give the "ideal" response, or the response expressing what one would do if moral considerations only were in question. But such idealizations are not necessarily a guide to practical behavior. Because the behavior of others is more observable than their thoughts, what the respondent sees in them may give more guidance on the practical realities of a situation. Thus, having noticed the sizable differences between the respondent's self-judgment and his view of others, and making some allowance for the possibility of distortion in both directions, project staff members have assigned considerable importance to faculty perspectives on professional colleagues. So judged, the North faculty seems to be strongly in favor of teaching in the area of specialization. This thesis is qualified by data from the research and writing category, where respondents reported that such professional activities were comparatively unimportant for their peers compared with themselves. But, by and large, researchers were impressed by the measure of agreement between conventional standards of excellence and the characteristics of the professional life of faculty at this institution, especially when the questionnaire item asking respondents about the importance, for themselves and others, of the availability of research money and facilities was added in. Forty-six per cent of the North respondents said these necessities for research were *very important* personally, while another 43 per cent choose the *somewhat important* category, and 9 per cent professed these matters to be *not important*. As for their view of others, 31 per cent said the availability of research money and appropriate facilities were *very important* to colleagues, with 57 per cent marking *somewhat important,* and 6 per cent *not important*. Thus the difference between the "self" and "other" evaluation, which had appeared quite marked, is greatly reduced by adding in this item.

Consideration has been given elsewhere to the tradition of

Midwest College emphasizing community with a Christian orientation and teaching by a committed faculty. However, the data on the questionnaire items dealing with specialization and professionalism, as collected from faculty at Midwest, put this group close enough to the record compiled at institutions with a professionally oriented faculty to suggest a challenge to the continuation and supremacy of Midwest's traditional values.

Seventy-nine per cent of faculty respondents said teaching in the area of academic specializations was *very important* to them, with 21 per cent electing the *somewhat important* category. The percentages changed very slightly when participants in the study spoke for other colleagues: 79 per cent *very important,* 18 per cent *somewhat important.*

When asked about the theoretical importance of research and writing, as opposed to actual conditions, 30 per cent stated that these matters were *very important* for them, while 21 per cent stated that in their opinion faculty colleagues would also regard research and writing as *very important.* Another 48 per cent felt these measures of professional accomplishment were, for them, *somewhat important.* The percentage jumped to 67 per cent in the "View of others" column.

The discrepancy between the percentages resulting when respondents were speaking for themselves, as compared to when they were appraising others, was shown again when the question about the importance of the availability of research money and research facilities was put before Midwest faculty. Speaking for themselves, only 9 per cent said these resources were *very important.* However, when respondents speculated about the attitudes of their peers, 21 per cent said that faculty colleagues would be of the same mind. With reference to themselves, 70 per cent said that money and facilities for research would be *somewhat important,* while 67 per cent thought these things would be regarded as *somewhat important* by other faculty of their acquaintance.

These data suggest the reverse of the situation at North College. There, where the research orientation for faculty has become established despite a heritage emphasizing teaching, respondents seemed free to identify personally with the new style, while showing that the college had not completely left the past through their hesitation to speak as "highly" for their colleagues. At Midwest, however, the emphasis of the college remained on teaching, with only the beginnings of a move in evidence toward professionalism. In this situation, faculty felt constrained to identify personally with the tradition, while acknowledging institutional changes under way by ascribing some of the characteristics of them to colleagues.

Southeast College and South College produced results similar to those found in the other colleges. Sixty per cent of the faculty in the sample at Southeast, and 54 per cent of those at South, stated that research and writing were, speaking personally, *very important*. However, while 13 per cent at Southeast saw these practices as *not important,* no one at South selected this response option. In both colleges percentages dropped sharply when respondents spoke for faculty colleagues. Thirteen per cent at Southeast saw their peers as likely to regard research and writing as *very important,* while the corresponding figure at South was 18 per cent. But at Southeast 60 per cent said colleagues would regard these professional activities as *somewhat important,* with 7 per cent reporting them *not important* for peers. At South, research and writing were called *somewhat important* by 68 per cent of the respondents when viewing others, and no one there put colleagues in the position of not regarding these matters as *important*.

Faculty samples at both Southeast and South spoke out strongly in favor of teaching in the area of academic specialization. At Southeast, 87 per cent said it was very important to them. The result at South was almost identical—86 per cent. Both groups saw less interest among colleagues in teaching in the academic specialization. Seventy-three per cent at Southeast put colleagues in this category, while at South 59 per cent were so inclined.

In both of these institutions administrators had supported subject-matter specialization for faculty and had no objection to the departmental organization of knowledge. Therefore, the strong support for teaching in the specializations by faculty at both places was a development consistent with administrative expectations as well as with prevailing emphases among faculties.

South College, as an innovative institution, had emphasized as the central feature of its curriculum a core program relating the humanities and social sciences. Faculty involved in teaching courses in this core, or in the science core, were not expected to abandon or even neglect their disciplinary specialization, but they were asked to come out to the borders of their field and to be willing, operating from their strength, to engage in relational learning.

With the emphasis on the core program—and every faculty member was expected to participate—the data from South on the item already presented dealing with teaching in the area of academic specialization are especially interesting. Researchers wondered whether South College faculty went particularly high in their support for the importance of teaching in the discipline because of the tendency of the core program, despite reassurances to the contrary, to draw men beyond their disciplinary boundaries. This faculty seemed to feel considerable tension, as revealed by the data and in conversations, between the cross-disciplinary tendencies of the "core" program and their own inclinations toward disciplinary and departmental specialization.

Student Expectations

The point with most students these days, it is often said, is not whether they will go too far in the direction of new goals and fresh means to them but, rather, whether they will go far enough. Despite the publicity given the 1 to 3 per cent minority of students who are truly revolutionary, or even the 10 to 15 per cent who may be regarded, in the avant-garde schools, as left-radicals, the majority of college students are seen to be conventional in values and practices. They may be expected, therefore, to support conventional procedures and the standard measures of excellence.

Because student data in the Institutional Character study were from entering freshmen only, student perceptions of the conventional standard of excellence could be only as formed by their earlier or precollege experiences and the values of parents, teachers, counselors and other adults, as well as student peer groups who may have influenced their thinking. Nevertheless, certain of the findings are instructive, both in showing the extent of the authority of conventional thinking with most students at entrance to college and also the extent to which changing values are affecting some of them. A significant minority of students were surprisingly independent.

At one point in the questionnaire given students at East-versity and Westversity, respondents were asked to choose be-tween paired features those they would associate with an ideal col-lege. Three of the items in the list of college characteristics relate to grading procedures (see Table 7).

Table 7

STUDENT OPINION ON GRADING PRACTICES AT AN IDEAL COLLEGE
(IN PERCENTAGES)

	Eastversity		Westversity	
	Beta College	Zeta College	Delta College	Omega College
Much competiveness for grades and recognition	31	31	43	25
versus				
Little competitiveness for grades and recognition	66	68	55	75
Students selected mostly on grades and admission scores	48	44	49	18
versus				
Students selected mostly on personal qualities	49	52	46	77
Courses given letter grades (A,B,C,D,F) ..	76	62	57	8
versus				
Courses graded "pass" or "fail"	22	38	42	92

The freshman class of 1966 at Eastversity's Zeta was much more like the freshmen entering Beta and Delta that fall, in attitudes toward conventional grading, than they were like the stu-dents entering Westversity's Omega. Omega freshmen, when com-pared with other students, were noticeably less interested in competition for grades, while they were clearly more interested in innovative admissions criteria and very much more interested in an innovative grading standard. Omega, it seems, had succeeded (1966) in establishing itself in the minds of students, and, presumably, with counselors and parents as well, as an innovative campus. Consequently, it drew larger proportions of students who were receptive to changes than did Eastversity's Zeta.

In the same question in which the student was asked to declare characteristics he associated with an ideal college by choosing between paired choices, two additional items reveal student attitudes toward conventional versus innovative arrangements. Hilltop's Kappa College freshman favored a college "experimental in most respects" (84 per cent) while students at Bay's Sigma College were also so inclined, but less noticeably so (66 per cent); the entering classes on the other two MultiWestern campuses stated a preference for a college "traditional in most respects"—Valley, 68 per cent, Seaside, 57 per cent. If the objection is raised that freshmen at Valley and Seaside may not have been personally opposed to an experimental educational program and that these data show only that they knew the campuses they were entering did not offer experimental programs, we call attention to the wording of the item: in choosing their ideal college, the students at Valley and Seaside declared a preference for one that is "traditional."

Student attitudes toward curriculum design were also tested in this study. Respondents were offered two statements that represented an open versus a structured way of organizing the learning experience. "Which of these statements," the question began, "comes closer to your own view?"

> Students should be given very great freedom in choosing their subjects of study and in choosing their areas of interest within these subjects.
> There is a body of knowledge to be learned, and the faculty is more competent than the student to direct the student's course of study, through required courses, prerequisites and the like.

On three of the four campuses of MultiWestern, Valley, Seaside, and Hilltop, more than half of the youth expressed a preference for freedom in choosing their subjects of study. At Hilltop's Kappa College, 66 per cent wanted this arrangement. Only at

Sigma College, Bay campus, did a preference for a more prescribed curriculum show up. There 66 per cent of the students indicated their willingness to follow faculty judgments. At Kappa, on the other hand, 32 per cent of the respondents favored the more traditional and structured curriculum.

At one of the liberal colleges, Midwest, entering freshmen voted 54 per cent to 45 per cent in favor of the more traditional proposition in which it is asserted, "There is a body of knowledge to be learned. . . ." These same students favored a college "traditional in most respects"—71 per cent to 27 per cent. However, this result was not representative of the student samples from the liberal arts colleges. Results across schools varied considerably on these and other items.

To conclude this brief probe of student views on conventional versus innovative ideas in higher education, responses from samples at Westversity will be mentioned: The conventional standard of institutional excellence, in its student dimension, features academic interests and plays down social activities. Thus, a prime consideration in the student's selection of a college or university should be, by conventional criteria, its academic reputation and provision for an individualized academic program. The student samples for project schools did show that more than half of the students in every sample except one emphasized "General academic reputation" as *important* in the selection of the college they had just entered. One of two colleges where the proportion fell below the 50 per cent mark was Westversity's Delta College. About 46 per cent marked this response option as important. Approximately 73 per cent of the entering freshmen at the other project college of this university, Omega, regarded the academic reputation of the college as an important consideration in their selection of it. Meanwhile, the 25 per cent of the Delta student sample mentioning an individualized academic program as important to them ranked this sample comparatively low (there were three other schools where the students gave slightly less attention to this variable). However, 58 per cent of the Omega respondents thought an individualized academic program important. They ranked highest in this connection.

Neither of the freshman classes at West gave priority to social aspects of college life in their selection of their college. In the

Delta sample, 18 per cent thought extracurricular activities important. About 1 per cent were of this mind at Omega.

Students on these campuses were also asked to select characteristics of their ideal college including certain social aspects. Seventy per cent of the Delta freshmen preferred a college with fraternities and sororities. At Omega, only 17 per cent stated this preference. Big-time intercollegiate athletics were considered a part of the ideal college scene for 74 per cent of the respondents from Delta, whereas 64 per cent of the freshmen at Omega said that they preferred a college in which intercollegiate athletics were not emphasized. Twenty per cent at Delta were attracted to a college with a "party school" reputation, but only 2 per cent of the Omega students were so disposed. Ninety-eight per cent at Omega thought they preferred a college with a scholarly academic reputation. It was the same with 74 per cent at Delta.

There is one disquieting implication in the data from Westversity. It is that the entering freshmen at Delta did not share faculty values, as compared with students at Omega. Delta faculty were, it appeared, giving attention to an intensified academic orientation for students as well as a more professional orientation for themselves. Meantime, the new freshmen were still interested in social activities, a less rigorous academic program, and various career orientations.

When asked to indicate the most important objective to be gained in college, student respondents at Delta and Omega showed considerable difference. Delta College freshmen were more vocationally oriented, 50 per cent stating that they came to college to master techniques applicable to their vocational intentions or field of special interest. This was true with 24 per cent of the students at Omega. Almost 50 per cent of the Omega youth said that they were intent upon acquiring the skills and mental habits necessary for critical and constructive thinking. This response option was selected by 21 per cent at Delta. Interest in general education and cross-disciplinary study was shown by 26 per cent at Omega who said that their goals included developing a broad general outlook and familiarity with a variety of subjects. Nineteen per cent at Delta shared these objectives.

Two colleges in the study ran higher on the vocational item

than Delta; all others were below it. Omega, with one other college, was least oriented in this direction. Only one student sample showed less interest than Delta on the "critical thinking" item, although two others were in a virtual tie.

The values of freshmen at Delta were also shown in a questionnaire item dealing with various considerations affecting the student's selection of his college. About 47 per cent of the Delta respondents said that an important consideration for them was "career reasons; that is, important for getting a good job, getting into graduate or professional school." About 28 per cent at Omega gave the same item this emphasis.

It is clear that many students at entrance to college have values and preferences that are essentially conventional. However, as mentioned, a number equally large seem inclined to change, innovation, and experimentation. But do faculty and administrators share their adventuresomeness? And to what extent are these themes or emphases influencing institutional life and shaping institutional character?

VI

Change, Innovation, Experimentation

There is now much huffing and puffing about effecting change in the institutions of higher education, but most of it is comforting spoofing on a grand scale, "sound and fury, signifying nothing." Innovations introduced or claims of experimentation do not reflect any change, as Paul Dressel has reported, in the basic philosophy, objectives, or assumptions of participating institutions:[1]

> . . . I am one of those persons who would hesitate to put down a list of institutions with innovations, because it has been my repeated experience to find that statements and writing about innovations on a campus did not correspond with reality when one is there for a few days. Again and again, as a consultant, as a representative of the North Central Association accrediting missions, and as a researcher, I have gone to campuses which have claimed to be distinctive, if not unique, and, once beyond

[1] "Academic Innovation Grows: Much of it called 'faddism,'" *Chronicle of Higher Education*, III, No. 11 (February 10, 1969).

the verbal facade erected by the administration and a few en-
thusiasts, have found very little in the way of evidence to cor-
roborate the publicity. . . . What I personally have observed is
that, once past statements of objectives and eulogies of programs,
one finds a great deal of sameness in what actually goes on in an
educational program.[2]

While our research dictates considerable agreement with
Dressel's findings—indeed the lack of substantive change correlates
with the paucity of value diversity—there is a qualification to be
introduced: many modest changes are occurring and, we think,
changes in degree may lead to changes in kind. Innovations, new
means to establish ends, are being attempted, and they can result
in experimentation, new means to new ends.

It is not inevitable that an innovative college or program be
never again so different as the day it opens, that every subsequent
change be back toward conformity to tradition, habit, and the
familiar. It is true that major innovations for educational institutions have been hard to initiate, harder still to transfer into the care
of those who did not come under the originator's persuasion, and
hardest to sustain over any considerable length of time, particularly
if the new venture involved holistic innovation. (People easily fall
back into the safe and easy roles that institutional organization has
encouraged.) Sustaining innovation is a bigger challenge than initiating it.

However, if historical precedent is to be taken seriously, and
it must be, then it is important to recognize that the flow of history
is fitful, sometimes effecting changes at a slow and meandering
pace, sometimes moving with such force and suddenness as to gouge
out new channels and redirect the stream of events. This has happened in the history of education, in American education. We need
consider only three instances: the establishment of Johns Hopkins,
in 1876, by its example and within twenty-five years transformed
the organization and emphases of most universities and many colleges; the spasm over Sputnik, 1957, resulted in curriculum changes
for elementary and secondary education, all within ten years; and
Berkeley, 1964, plus the resultant shock waves stretching across
the nation, overturned established thinking in five years, as the

[2] Paul L. Dressel, personal correspondence (March 12, 1969).

critic of the left-radicals, Lewis S. Feuer, has stated,[3] on such subjects as human relationships on campus, the definitions of authority and the implementation thereof, organization charts, and the public's attitude toward the institution of higher education.

What has gone before, what has been done before to produce change, is today joined and compounded by social change in the culture, the advent of the technological society, the new youth movement, and the feeling of anxiety that grips academic professionals. Changes have come in the past, and usually from outside the institutions. Now the pressures for change from the outside are joined and multiplied, in a way not true before, by equally insistent pressures within. Quantitative changes are under way that show promise of qualitative effects. Changes in degree are harbingers of changes in kind.

The changes, of course, are not all moving in one direction. There are cross-currents, making outcomes uncertain, assuring only that what is happening will make a difference. At the level of institutional governance, to illustrate, concern over fiscal inefficiency combined with campus turbulence, and the resultant charge that administrators have been unable to keep their houses in order, seem to be resulting in changes in the relationships between sponsoring bodies or the public of many institutions and boards of trustees, as well as between trustees and campus administrators. Legislative bills are being processed in many state capitols that are responses to campus unrest. Many of them would give the public greater control over policy formulation in state colleges or universities. Some would withdraw delegated authority, and circumscribe the already tenuous autonomy of institutions of higher education by the imposition of watchdog committees, fiscal controls, or citizen review boards. Almost all of them would "strengthen the backbone" of administrators against student dissidents. And trustees, in most cases, are expected to be, not buffers between the institution and the public, but conduits of public opinion, reaching onto the campus to see that the will of the sponsoring body is carried out.

Meanwhile, campus administrators are requesting and receiving from trustees and faculty a recasting of institutional organi-

[3] Lewis S. Feuer, "Berkeley and Beyond," *Change* (January–February, 1969), pp. 47–51.

zation charts so that their power is increased. Faculty, in most places, seem ready to cooperate with these changes because student demands offend faculty values and, worse, disrupt faculty activities. Faculty feel incapable of dealing with a situation so alien to their life style. Administrators, according to the new rationale, embody organizational expertise and public relations skills, so faculty may properly turn over to administrators the unpleasant duties associated with relieving the campus malaise. Thus, faculty are frantically unloading responsibilities that they once jealously vouchsafed to themselves. They apparently forget that with the transfer of duties goes power. So, administrators, who because of their influence on rewards and sanctions have always been powerful[4]—despite the popularity of a self-effacing, self-depreciating style ("I grease the wheels and get out of the way")—are now picking up new authority and increased clout in the area of governance. This is seen as a way of bringing dissident students to terms with established values and arrangements.

There are other faculty and administrators, however, who see that any solution to campus agonies that restores order by forcing youth to acquiesce to imposed authority could have adverse long-range outcomes. Because acquiescence means to comply without giving assent, the result of forced conformity could destroy the spirit of goodwill and cooperation that have been basic components in the educational tradition which advocates of a hard line seek to preserve. Because force breeds force, the "comply or be damned" solution to campus problems could lead to a more terrible outbreak by the youth later on. Herbert Marcuse has observed that the revolution which overthrows the prevailing repressive societal values will not likely come from the proletariat, because the working class is in a position of "voluntary servitude." But the revolution may come from affluent youth who, having tasted the fruit for which the blue collar whites and militant blacks are reaching, find it bitter, even poisonous, and, in their rage, violently uproot the tree of life itself. These youth from middle-class and upper-class homes cannot be ignored and, say many observers, must not be coerced. Force

[4] On the importance of presidents in policy formulation, see Edward Gross and Paul Grambsch, *University Goals and Academic Power* (Washington, D.C.: American Council on Education, 1968).

will lead not to the resolution of campus problems and the restoration of business as usual but to frustration and bitterness culminating in social revolution. People who think that there is evidence that a firm hand restores order, and there is some such evidence, had better beware the illusion of immediate success.

Just possibly, the youth who now seem to be so recalcitrant, so stubbornly rebellious, will break under the weight of imposed authority. New England Puritans said that a couple with marital trouble should be held together like two dogs on one leash; "After a time they will learn to go forward together, once they find that they cannot go apart." Perhaps this troublesome minority of students, if held forcibly in line long enough, will learn to march in step. Acquiescence can yield to the spirit of inevitability. But compelling youth to the point that they decide they had better cooperate with the inevitable is not likely to develop creative, assertive leadership for an epoch of massive technological and social change. It is more likely to produce servility and abjection. It would be like saving a marriage at the cost of losing everything the marriage was being saved for.

Because so many educators, and laymen, too, see the need to enlist youth in the decision-making processes of the institutions, all sorts of innovations in governance are now emerging. Most of the plans involve students in the formulation of policies dealing with the personal and social aspects of campus life, but hold them off or give them ceremonial or token representation on committees determining academic policies. In colleges where administrators have controlled everything—though they were usually benevolent despots—the move now is to involve or increase faculty representation; in institutions where faculty have controlled academic policies, there is a yielding to administrative participation. Neither development includes students. The words on the Establishment battle flag are "Professional judgments for the professionals."

This condition is illuminated by recent data from the Faculty Characteristics study directed by Robert Wilson and Jerry Gaff,[5] showing that about one third of their sample thought students

[5] Robert Wilson and Jerry Gaff, *Faculty Characteristics Study* (Berkeley: Center for Research and Development in Higher Education, University of California, 1969).

should have a voice (with vote) in academic decision-making, but only 9 per cent thought that students should have an equal vote with faculty in formulating academic policies. (When the question was student participation in social life decision-making, faculty were considerably more hospitable: 45 per cent of the Wilson-Gaff sample would accord students equal rights on committees and 21 per cent would leave students responsible for their own social regulations.)

The point in all of the preceding is that changes in governance are being effected, bringing about a redistribution of power. These changes, although at the level of structures and functions, have ramifications for the basic values, assumptions, and goals of the institution. Huffing and puffing may appear to have no immediate effect on the object of one's efforts, but it may eventually blow somebody's house down—particularly if the house is made of straw.

The interest in change is not limited to governance. There is also interest in extending the learning environment beyond the classroom to the community. Educators have had a tendency to limit the perimeter of learning to the campus environment. Numerous changes are under way now that promise to end that aberration. Colleges and universities in considerable numbers are providing some variation of the "interim term," with most of the plans committed to getting students and faculty off campus and into urban or rural settings for fieldwork. Overseas programs are a geographical extension of the same idea. Programs for the disadvantaged, tutorials, ethnic studies, and a score of other endeavors extend and enrich the learning environment for clientele with special needs. Para-educational programs in the military or industry are manifestations of a related concern—to extend learning not only geographically, or into different social classes, but over time and across age groups. Methuselah College on the Santa Cruz campus, University of California, has been one institutional expression of this "life-long learning" theme.

A related development is the national interest in extending learning opportunities to the point of "near-universal education." This change, advocates say, would be consistent with the American democratic tradition, especially in recent years when the idea has become dogma that advanced education equates not only with more salary and higher social status but with the good life in all of its dimensions. Very recently, however, doubts have been heard about the need or desirability of "near-universal higher education." Men of professional distinction, both in this country and abroad, are saying that there are some jobs for which we overeducate people, thus making them unhappy in their work situation. Also, from what is known of genetic variability, emotional and intellectual preferences, motivational diversity, and so forth, educators do many youth a disservice by creating a climate of compulsion in which they are made to feel inadequate if undereducated, that is, without a college degree. Perhaps not everyone should go to college—that is the theme more and more often heard.

Differences of opinion on this complex problem, as with so many of the other changes, lead in opposite directions. Some say that the current depreciation of the expansion of educational opportunity is intended to show that education could be less structured and should offer more experiential learning opportunities, directed to individual human needs and interests more than to social certification. They see this as a way to encourage standards but eliminate the conventional standard of excellence. On the other hand, those who propose further limitations on who goes to college, and where, may be saying that some people, the minority groups in particular, are going to have trouble measuring up to conventional criteria of academic accomplishment, or do not have the style or interests of academics, and hence should be kept out. Their point of view is opposed by innovators who argue that if today's college is not right for many of our youth—especially the culturally "different" young people—then it is not right for our society as a whole.

In addition to changes in governance configurations, or those extending the learning environment and educational opportunities, there are now various efforts under way to redefine or vitalize the concept of community for the institution of higher education.

Throughout this century when an emphasis on community within a college or university was giving way to a superinstitutional value orientation that not only supplanted but contradicted the nineteenth-century definition of community, educators have continued to talk in traditional terms, acknowledging, perhaps without recognizing the shift of emphasis, the need for a community of shared purposes. There has been a basis for a type of community—keyed on academic professionalism as defined by the academic/industrial elite, and on socialization as defined by American orthodoxy—but we have not had, except in rare cases, shared allegiance to distinctive institutional goals.

Now, however, there is concern in the society to get the concept of community, as perceived by society—emphasizing institutional autonomy in academic matters but institutional accountability to the society in social and political issues—renewed at colleges and universities. The institutions of learning have always been part and parcel of the society that sponsored and sustained them, particularly regarding moral and political considerations, and it should be, can be, no different today.

The new youth movement, albeit moving in another direction, is equally concerned for community. Although the new youth have talked about "doing your own thing," they see increasingly that a philosophy of rampant individualism makes community impossible. And community is important for individuals who would be enriched by shared experiences, and for institutions that would have character. Left-radicals are not content for the distinctiveness of a college or university to be set by professionalism, as a spin-off of technology; yet they are beginning to see that their commitment to radical subjectivism, as a spin-off of existentialism, is not capable of supplying a base for building community. Something more is required. One may speak about a community where individuals come together freely, of their own accord, but any such fellowship requires self-imposed limitations on personal freedom and then, inevitably, there will be group-imposed limitations on the freedom of others. There must be standards. There can be standards without community, but there cannot be community without standards. And these standards will affect not only the group, but others too.

Consider the case of the Afro-American minority in our society. The social movement in that minority is toward black separatism. The goal sought is black power as a prerequisite to social equality. The leaders in this movement cannot allow every black to do his own thing. They must have unity, community, or their program has no chance to prevail against white racism. At this stage in the development of black pride, the leadership of the black separatist movement cannot permit individualism. Not for blacks. For whites, however, they have a different ambition. Black militants would have those whites who believe themselves non-racist break away from the monolithic thinking of the white power structure and, as individuals, to stand against the white majority. Those blacks are using a variation on the old and time-honored strategy of encouraging unity at home and division abroad.

Just as whites of conscience cannot today remain within the vicious system of white supremacy and oppress blacks, so, in this developing confrontation, it is impossible for white people of conscience to live by their own inclinations. White liberals, for example, are now insisting that white people must sense and admit to feelings of corporate guilt for black suffering. They insist on shared responsibility for the historic abuse of minorities in this country and they will not settle for less than shared contrition.

Another example of the fact that there are always values, meaning standards held with conviction, that go beyond the individual, is seen in the thought of Herbert Marcuse, the controversial advocate of left-radicalism. Marcuse says it is the whole that determines the truth for the parts—not in the sense that the whole is prior or superior to its parts, but in the sense that its structure and function are the crucial determinants of what the parts can do. The modern technological society is today the behemoth, and it is so powerful that it is unlikely to be overthrown by any part of the whole, by any segment of society, no matter how large in number (except a segment that controls the arsenal of weapons and communications systems—which is the "government" itself). Furthermore, the sensitivities of the people have been dulled to the point where the individual is in a condition of voluntary servitude. To accept the rules of the behemoth's game is to agree to be ruled; the outcomes are fixed; even progressive movements are drawn into the service of their opposites. "Free expression" ends up absolving servitude.

Despite the odds against change, Marcuse writes about a society in which the present "negative constraints" on the individual are broken, perhaps by the new youth movement. Is the person set free, in the new age which is to follow, to do his own thing? Of course not. Marcuse's vision for the new society includes "positive constraints"—no neo-Nazi, for example, would be tolerated. You and I probably agree with Marcuse on that, which is precisely the point. We have some agreements about values that transcend and constrain the individual. As institutions are always accountable to a constituency or public, and thus are never really autonomous, so it is with individuals. The aims of education, then, must always make provision for both standards and community.

On the left as well as the right, there is concern for the renewal of community or for new definitions and models of the concept. Here, as with governance and the curriculum, changes are coming that will be as notable for their substance as for the rhetoric that attends them, as significant in their effect on the future as most innovations were ineffective in the past.

At the colleges and universities of the Institutional Character study considerable effort was being expended on behalf of innovation, if not experimentation. Indeed, the institutions were selected in part because they all had shown an interest in change, and the study was designed to determine the way change and change efforts were perceived by administrators, faculty, and students. It was expected that the effect of the institution's efforts in this connection would figure in the respondent's definition of institutional character. Two questions were asked: if the colleges and universities of the project are described as innovative, what differences will there be between that claim and the institution's stated philosophy or goals, and between the perceived commitment to innovation and the conventional standard of excellence?

Responses to Options

The schools of the study, with a few exceptions, had innovations under way in all three of the areas of concern to which attention has been given—governance, curriculum, and the search for community.

North College. At North College, for example, efforts to extend the learning environment included: SPAN, or the Student Project for Amity among Nations, which enabled students to travel to foreign countries during the summer on individual study projects; the Mexican Caravan; the Canadian-American Conference;

World Press Institute, bringing foreign journalists to the United States and to the college; and SWAP, or the Student Work Abroad Project. The 4–1–4 academic calendar made possible, among other things, an interim term opportunity for intensive study of European national cultures, art, economic problems, and languages.

There had been a special effort at North, as a part of its international program, to bring foreign students into the college community. When it was found that these students did not stay as long as had been hoped and were not successfully integrated into the life of the institution, North revised its program to make it worth while for the foreign students to come if only for a short stay of one or two years.

During the period of research for the Institutional Character study, special projects funded by the institution's chief benefactor numbered between sixty and seventy. Some had yet to be launched, several then in operation were floundering, others were regarded as very successful. The visiting scholar program, whereby several influential European scholars had been brought to the campus, was mentioned as a successful venture that would be continued.

One of the proposed programs would free twenty-three to twenty-five faculty per year, from a total of 122 faculty, to do research on campus during each academic year for the next five years. These faculty members would teach two courses each term and have the rest of their time free for research and writing. This was a way to accommodate the needs of the new research-minded faculty without resorting to an across-the-board reduction in the faculty teaching load. Under this plan, released time would be given selectively and without sacrificing the school's commitment to teaching.

The curriculum, too, had undergone some changes. An area studies program worked out with three other nearby Christian liberal arts colleges brought students and faculty together for integrated study at the upper division level. In one of North's publications, this was called "a unique contribution to American undergraduate education." Also, North offered an alternative to the conventional major by making provision for the student to substitute a "core concentration." The "core" consisted of two sets of six courses, one set within a department and one outside, to be approved by the departments concerned.

Most of the student's academic program, however, was organized and judged conventionally. Departments remained strong and carried the expected range of courses. A residence requirement, the letter-grade formula (though there was a pass-fail option), midterm and final examinations, and other standard arrangements predominated. The visitor got the impression that the college preferred to change like the automobile industry—by extending the line of products and services, improving quality, and innovating within the predicted taste range of the trade.

An example of the North way with innovation was the organizational provisions the college had worked out for the participation of students in governance. In 1966–67, academic administration was in the hands of the faculty, with considerable power delegated to a faculty advisory committee (six elected faculty members). The faculty had also set up an academic affairs council (later to be disbanded), with two committees advising and reporting to it—the in-class advisory council and the out-of-class advisory council. Students sat on both of these committees, with the academic dean heading the in-class and the dean of students the out-of-class committee. From North's perspective, this rather elaborate arrangement was seen, no doubt, as evidence that the college was innovative at the point of student participation in policy formulation. The arrangement provided an educational experience for student representatives and gave them a role in academic and social deliberations. From another and critical perspective, however, the academic affairs committee appeared to serve as a buffer between faculty and students, with the powerful faculty advisory committee and the faculty senate effectively insulated by this device from student influence. The students had only a tertiary role, safely removed from real power. By introducing students to academic policy formulation the college had gone beyond what was being done in most institutions of higher education. However, North had innovated safely. The college was doing enough to satisfy its desire to be innovative without doing so much as to jeopardize its commitment to conventional excellence.

To the outside observer, the innovations of the college, including the varied and numerous programs with an international flavor, were variations on familiar themes. Nothing suggested that anything else was desired by faculty. Nor, indeed, on the basis of surface manifestations was anything different desired by the majority of students. They were hard-working, professionally oriented youth with middle-class values. They had not advocated, and perhaps could not be expected to advocate radical innovations in education—Marcuse notwithstanding.

On the administrative level two surprises emerged that may have been the most radically different features of North College. They illustrate how a college, like a corporation, particularly if the business ethic governs its operation, may react innovatively to external opportunities or to an internal problem. When it appeared that the then academic dean of the college might be hired away to become president of another liberal arts college, North responded innovatively. The dean was a highly respected academic leader, finding favor with all segments of the college community. Therefore, the president of the college created the position of executive vice president and provost and put the dean in that chair, and, by this action, had one vice president for financial affairs and another for academic matters, the executive vice president and provost serving the latter function. The innovative feature that carried this arrangement beyond general practice in American higher education was that the former dean was authorized to report on academic life directly to the board of trustees through its education committee. The president, in making the arrangement, noted that senior officers in corporations today often share policy-making responsibilities.

Another innovation—this one in response to an external opportunity—deals with the way policy decisions were made on the allocation of money from the school's principal benefactor (whose generosity was making possible so many changes). The gentleman's contacts with the school were confined to the president and the executive vice president and provost, with his personal representative playing an increasingly important intermediary role. This arrangement limited the number of persons involved in the transactions through which so much of the life of the college was being affected. Ideas flowed from the president or the executive vice president and provost, or both, to the benefactor, were approved by him, and then presented to the faculty or appropriate segment of the college community. Because the benefactor's views on the nature of the college and the characteristics of its program had been entirely conventional, as were those of his emissary, college officials had the difficult task of trying to write proposals that would satisfy him and, at the same time, shape proposals appropriate to the future of the college and acceptable to the values of its faculty.

The executive vice president and provost said that several times he would have consulted faculty committees on new program ideas had there been time and if he could have been sure that they would facilitate things and not turn obstructionist. The sensitivity of the situation was not caused primarily by the benefactor's attitude; he has been called the "perfect angel" because, while he had standards and would not support programs that conflicted with them, he never threatened to withdraw his support from the college because of the existence there of variant standards or programs that he did not favor. Nevertheless, to the time of this research project the college had not ventured far from the benefactor's values, partly because of an essential compatibility in these matters and partly because of the feeling in the college community that long-range benefits of this money to the college would more than compensate for immediate and partial compromises. Therefore, one of the most innovative aspects in the life of North College has been the way the administration, the executive vice president and provost particularly, worked to reconcile the interests and preferences of a conservative benefactor and board of trustees on the one hand and a more liberal faculty on the other—a faculty which while not radical in social and political values was sensitive about its academic autonomy. It took consummate skill to persuade faculty to accept programs that they did not plan.

Midwest College. Midwest College and South College shared most of the innovations in effect at North. Midwest had made provision for foreign study, including a student exchange program, an Institute in American Studies for Scandinavian Educators, and a Latin American Studies program. (A Norwegian-American museum is located in the town and has been a source of pride and historical information for local citizens and college people.)

Midwest's curriculum also featured an interim term (January of each academic year); a tri-college interim term abroad; interdisciplinary programs such as the Freshman Core history of western civilization, literary masterpieces of the western world, and an introduction to Christian theology; and social service intern work in various part of the country—including Sauk Center, Minnesota, of Sinclair Lewis' *Main Street,* where students could do intern work in the Reformatory for Women.

As a member of the Central States College Association, Midwest's students and faculty had opportunities for field research projects, study tours, and cultural and artistic enrichment programs going beyond the resources of individual institutions. Through these activities, the members of the college could extend their experiences beyond those available in the isolated geographical locale of the college.

South College. South College had carried the curriculum core concept further than had any other project institution. It was a four-year feature in the social sciences and humanities, with a two-year science core running on a parallel but separate track. In 1966–67, according to a report from the dean, 70 per cent of the total faculty were leading discussion sections at one level or another of the four-year core program. Eighteen from different disciplines were to work in the first-year class sections, fourteen in the second year, eight in the third, and five in the senior year. The aim at South had been to arrange for a faculty member to teach two courses in his own discipline plus participation in the core, where he would lead a discussion group about twice a week and give perhaps five lectures per year. Here innovation linked with professionalism. A faculty member participating in the core program, the program which transcended departments, lectured there in his specialization. As the dean put it, "We're not asking him to be an authority in all things, but to impart from his discipline information that is pertinent to problems, works, and periods under study." The trick, of course, as the dean at South understood, is to impart that information in ways that will have impact or meaning for students who do not end up as workers in the professor's field of knowledge.

Southeast College. Southeast, the only college in the research project that was predominantly black, and the college that may have been most in need of innovations and alternative options, appeared to be least interested. The only evident agitation for change was from students interested in participation in governance.

Students were not serving on academic policy committees at the time of the study—not even on the student discipline committee. Punishment for student social violations was meted out by faculty committees of the same sex as the student offenders. Students were pressing for representation on major policy committees, including the Council for Administrative Affairs and the Council for Academic Affairs, although certain administrators denied that students were interested in such participation. The mood of most administrators seemed to be to limit students to advising or consultative services. The general attitude, one not entirely shared by the new college president, was that faculty and administrators were the specialists in academic governance and that students had the freedom to learn. Students might become involved in social matters, but control of the academic life was the domain of senior members of the community.

Whereas certain administrators were emphatic about Southeast students being unready for the responsibilities of leadership, certain students felt they had not been given sufficient responsibility to encourage the development of leadership. For example, students had been assigned the task of setting up an annual budget for student government, but when their respresentatives took specific proposals to college administrators, what they had done was challenged repeatedly. Students concluded that their work was not taken seriously and that they were not regarded as competent to carry out what they had been asked to do.

There is, of course, nothing very new about such tensions, particularly in areas of governance where it is easy to misunderstand what is delegated and what is retained. But the project staff saw little interest at Southeast in new solutions to such old problems. There was no general emphasis on innovation. A particular program in one of the departments might carry innovative features —small freshman laboratory sections in biology, with senior faculty working there even at the sacrifice of time with upper division students—but, by and large, neither in the curriculum nor in social organization were comprehensive innovations attempted. Emphases were elsewhere, mainly on the conventional standard of institutional excellence.

Considerable attention has already been given in previous chapters to the organization of cluster colleges at Westversity and to the various innovative emphases at Eastversity. Attention will now be given to innovative developments at only two project universities, MultiEastern and MultiWestern, and particularly to administrative perspectives.

MultiEastern. Confusion seemed to exist at MultiEastern at to whether the university, despite its plan to establish three innovative undergraduate colleges, wanted to be known for efforts at educational change. Comments were made by students and faculty that no clear-cut leadership in the area of innovation had been shown by key administrators beyond the initial acceptance of the federated college plan. Although steps had been taken to move the university toward an organizational arrangement within which colleges might become centers of innovation, there were no assurances that if individual colleges actually turned out to be different, that is, to have differing values as well as different procedures, they could get the support necessary for their success. There were some signs, one interviewee said, that attempts to establish a new and distinctively innovative college were already suffering opposition and that it was likely that the university's financial realities and conservative academic traditions would unite to bring this project to terms with tradition. Yet, on the other hand, assurances were heard from administrators that the first of the new colleges was being given every freedom essential to the success of the innovations proposed thus far. Faculty and administrators associated with that planning were not interested in having the college tagged as radically innovative or experimental, but they were determined that it would have a contemporary curriculum and provide opportunities for individualized student programs while satisfying the university's exacting standards.

It was the university's intention, one administrator reported, to set all-university standards for admission and graduation and yet to permit undergraduate divisions of the university to establish their distinctions within these broad definitions. There would be ample opportunity within MultiEastern's standard for individual colleges to create a distinctive identity.

There seemed to be no fear that the most creative, energetic faculty and administrators in the university would congregate in the new colleges, leaving only atrophied old guard at Alpha and Theta colleges. Both the older units, visitors were told, would develop their own distinctiveness under the federated plan.

In another interview it was suggested that faculty might find more opportunity for innovation in "traditionalist" Alpha than at either Theta or the later establishments. The new colleges would tend to think holistically and, therefore, all participants would be required to conform to programmatic emphases. At Alpha, conversely, individual faculty members were free to structure their courses, and particular departments or academic subunits within the college could innovate without impinging on others. This "freedom" meant opportunities for even more radical changes than would be possible elsewhere. However, project staff wondered whether the faculty person likely to be hired into a college not noted for innovativeness would be the sort to attempt radical changes or, if the desire for change were to strike him, would his colleagues long tolerate an unexpected and perhaps unsettling dissimilarity?

Another point of uncertainty at MultiEastern was whether Alpha would become the core college with several other colleges clustered around it serving mainly as housing units within which students could gain a sense of identity and human fellowship, or whether there would be essential parity for all colleges and considerable autonomy for each one. Some administrators seemed confused on this issue, perhaps waiting for guidance or still weighing alternatives; others were obviously partisan. The central administration, in staff opinion, favored diversification of programs and personalities. The right of the several colleges to mark out a place for themselves, and the autonomy necessary to do so, had already been decided. Administrators were not so much concerned that the new colleges would get too strong or too separatist as they were concerned that such programs would not have sufficient drawing power in the university to get the faculty needed to assure first-rate standing. The danger, administrators said, was not that the new colleges might overrun Alpha or Theta but rather that they might not muster enough support, particularly respect and professional acceptance, to assure equality for the new programs in the university community.

MultiWestern. The Hilltop campus of MultiWestern has been, from its opening in 1965, self-consciously innovative. Publications have emphasized this intention, and administrators interviewed stressed it. Certain interviewees stated that they shunned the use of the word "experimental" because of its tentative and unsettling connotations, but everybody agreed that Hilltop had been organized to innovate. The pass-fail grading system instituted by the first of their colleges, Gamma, was often mentioned as illustrative of the audacity of the innovations proposed or under way. The very organization of the colleges, each with a character of its own, was the most frequently mentioned indication of innovation.

When the goals or aims of Hilltop campus were examined, researchers were impressed by the lack of change rhetoric or radical statements. One administrator who was queried on this point replied that the educational objectives of Hilltop were not particularly different, nor more radical, than those in better institutions of higher education across the nation, but this campus had an opportunity to achieve these objectives to a degree not characteristic of other colleges and universities. The opportunity to start afresh and the shared resolve of faculty and administrators would be decisive.

Most of the ten administrators questioned at Hilltop did not care to speculate on how radical the campus might become. Visitors got the impression, even as one administrator said, that the issue had not been joined, that the possibilities had not been tested. Only one provost, at the time of the study, had shown any radical academic inclinations and, given the determination of the chief campus administrators to hire as provosts only men of already established national reputation, it was unlikely that the situation would change. Later leadership would necessarily be limited, in great measure, by precedents set by predecessors. However, one key administrator insisted that leadership for the faculty and administration could be found that would combine interest in research and teaching, in tradition and change. He said, "So long as we can get both talents, why settle for one?" Another administrator argued that the creative capabilities of faculty and administration at Hilltop may have been dulled early by the sheer necessity of "getting the show on the road," by organizing classes and colleges. Therefore, the present status of the colleges, he said, should not be regarded as representative of potentialities or, necessarily, of future probabilities. The faculty might give more time to innovations with their classes later on, after the organizational work was completed. Then they might turn out some radically different programs.

However, another administrator said that it should surprise no one that course titles at Hilltop were conventional or that the academic programs of the colleges were developing along conventional lines. Nothing different could or should be expected. All faculties these days are professionally oriented, researchers were told, and may be expected to organize their work accordingly; there was no possibility that Hilltop or any other campus could act independently of the traditions and procedures existing among academics.

The long-range *Academic Plan for [Hilltop], 1965–75,* emphasized the creation of a physical environment that would provide a setting well suited for educational innovation. The challenge was to experiment with new methods of instruction, study, and communication and to build a campus that would be up to date in the twenty-first century. At the inaugural ceremonies, May 3, 1966, the campus chancellor called Hilltop an "experimental campus."

However, from the first, and perhaps increasingly over time, this forthright commitment to radical change had been qualified. The Hilltop campus was expected to adhere to statewide policies and procedures, hence the criteria for employment, at the level of both faculty and administration, have been largely conventional, seldom innovative. The same was true of student admissions policies. The organization of administration has been conventional; a few new offices and titles were introduced, but most of the positions are those of the statewide system (for example, assistant vice chancellor for humanities), and no serious challenge to the university's hierarchical organization has been raised. As one administrator put it, in correspondence with project staff:

> Because this campus is launched within [MultiWestern], we must accept as "given" many things that come along with

that context: provisions of the state constitution and laws, definition of roles in the Master Plan, regental by-laws, regulations
of the Academic Senate, and at least a modicum of customs and
traditions. In exchange we get financial support, a share of the
general endowment, instant accreditation, assumed equality standards.

And this leader concluded, showing a determination to combine the
old and the new:

I think the price is not too much to pay, and I think the
terms of reference permit both innovation and experimentation.

Two other administrators interviewed did not want to be
regarded as innovators because they professed to have no particular
interest in innovation per se. What they wanted was a rigorous intellectual experience for Hilltop students, not "gimmickry." If transforming the superficiality of much of America's higher education
into something intellectually rigorous was innovative, then, of
course, they were happy to be called innovators.

Two or three administrative officers said that they were
quite willing to allow radical innovations in one college but were
not eager to have other and later colleges obligated to adhere to the
same emphases. These administrators were concerned lest the image
of the total university campus become identified with an innovation
in one of its colleges. For example, they thought it possible that the
faculties of later colleges might not want to take up the pass-fail
grading arrangement of Gamma College. Administrators emphasized the importance of protecting freedom for later colleges to innovate in their own way, even in ways more radical than those
devised by early planners.

Experiences with other avowedly innovative colleges in the
study, and data gathered from other studies, suggest that after five
to seven years innovative colleges reach a critical period when the
rationale that motivated the pioneers is no longer evident and the
expectations of newcomers, both faculty and students, may vary.
The consequence is factionalism within the community, usually
resulting in the separation of "traditionalists" and "innovators," a
development threatening stagnation as further changes become
difficult to achieve. With the loss of a sense of community, attention
is focused on whatever subcultures emerge or on various manifesta-

tions of individualism. At this stage of development, perhaps even more than at the outset of the program, strong leadership is needed. The contending forces in the innovative colleges may balance each other off, the attendant sense of frustration causes withdrawal, and, therefore, a "third force" is needed to reconcile factions, to point a direction and get things moving again. It is crucial that this third force, be it from administration or a coterie including representation from administration, faculty, and the student body, have a sense of purpose and be willing to provide leadership.

At Hilltop, the central administrators, particularly the chancellor, have shown a remarkable consistency of purpose. The campus would be innovative, they said, and the collegiate emphasis, the opportunity for independent study, the pass-fail grading arrangement, were all expressions of that commitment. But the colleges of this campus would also be firmly established in the Multi-Western system, and the supremacy of the conventional standard of excellence was proof of that commitment.

The "middle path" of Hilltop was vividly illustrated in 1966–67 by a campus controversy over student social regulations, dress rules, and the like. Students noticed that the administration seemed to think that students had sufficient self-discipline academically to engage in independent study, and, indeed, this was an innovation featured by campus publications, but that there was no parallel delegation of responsibility concerning personal and social matters. Students thought that though they were being set free academically, they were circumscribed socially. Administrators, however, refused to yield to student pressure for the individualization of student behavior patterns. They argued that just as academic standards would prevail at Hilltop, so there would be social standards. The achievement of community required shared commitments, and the university, not the individual, would finally decide the basic nature of that community. Administrators, it seemed, saw themselves as the spokesmen and interpreters of the university's values. The university had, in fact, definite academic values—it did not hesitate to discriminate academically, for example—but, socially, the university was much less definite, less certain of its values. Hilltop administrators had little reason to believe that there was a consensus of opinion in the university as to what constitutes good taste and moral behavior, and in arrogating to themselves the right of judgment, they may have been putting the university's signature to their own values.

In several of the administrative interviews, on the other campuses of MultiWestern as well as at Hilltop, the disappointment of adults with current student values was evident. Administrators at Hilltop stated that the achievement of a spirit of community or a sense of shared enterprise was basic to the success of all else on campus, but that students today were so highly individualistic, even anarchistic, that it was impossible to establish the unity of purpose with the collective involvement of all parties in the total program the first planners had envisioned. They were somewhat dismayed by the personal styles of some students. Several administrators were "Anglophiles" and they were a little wry about the lack of social grace and basic courtesies in the behavior of the youth. It was clear that, in the opinion of these planners, Hilltop students were more experimental in their personal behavior than was desired or expected for this innovative campus.

The prospects for substantive student participation in academic governance at Hilltop were probably hurt because the students, at least a conspicuous minority of them, were sufficiently variant in their personal behavior patterns to both disappoint and confuse certain administrators. These administrators would have been happy to involve students in planning, at least in advisory capacities, perhaps as voting participants in policy formulation, had the students given evidence of being firmly committed to the social and ethical values of the educated adult society. But when so many of the youth became critical of societal values, including the values of the chief agent of socialization, the school, administrative leaders at Hilltop, at least in 1966–67, seemed more determined than they would otherwise have been to retain the conventional, hierarchical organization of the institution. One evidence of reaction to student "excess" was seen in the considerable modification in provisions for student government at Kappa College as compared to the first college, Gamma. With the burst of enthusiasm, energy, and idealism that usually accompanies new beginnings, the Gamma administration had left the organization of student government in the hands of students. Starting with the Gamma Assembly, a rather pure form of community government, students spent most of the first year oscillating between anarchy and oligarchy. When Kappa opened things were different. Entering students were presented with a provisional form of student government, worked out by the provost and a committee of junior college transfer students. Thus, under this plan, at least for most of the first year, Kappa would have a structural provision for orderly government and an arrangement within which a more traditional form of student government could get a head start. Innovation was welcome, but not experimentation. However, in 1966–67, Gamma emerged with a sense of community that, everyone agreed, was much more noticeable than that at Kappa.

Many explanations for the greater measure of collegiality in the first college were offered. Some said that the architecture of Kappa had an opposite effect to that of Gamma. Whereas the Gamma buildings were grouped closely and thus created a centripetal effect encouraging the spirit of community, the somewhat more sprawling layout of buildings at Kappa had a centrifugal effect. This viewpoint is especially interesting in view of the fact that the buildings of Westversity's Omega College, which also were tightly grouped in quadrangle fashion, were thought by students and faculty there to offer much too closed a stance, to be so centripetal as to necessitate measures that would encourage centrifugal influences to somehow open and relax the atmosphere of the college. Another explanation of why the Kappa community had not become unified and was called the "cafeteria college" was that nearly half of their first student class had transferred from Gamma College and were either sorry to have left the Gamma community or were hostile toward Gamma—either way, their attention was not easily centered on Kappa. A third factor involved the personality and style of leadership in the colleges. The provost at Gamma was a charismatic leader.

While granting the significance of all these influences, project staff wondered if the early attempt to establish community government at Gamma, with all of the fumbling hesitation and confusion that attended the effort, was not another important factor in the creation of a noteworthy sense of unity in that college. This explanation was not heard in 1966–67. Kappa, after all, was in its first year. But, on the basis of later visits to the campus, researchers are prepared to make the claim that the early experimental efforts at Gamma, which at the time seemed threatening to the ideals of the campus, were in fact more consistent with those ideals than certain later modifications that tended to threaten the collegial spirit in the name of order.

Other evidence that the students at the Hilltop colleges may have contributions to make in governance, if the campus is to be innovative, will come out in the review of data from the student questionnaire. One other incident, a report of which came from administrative interviews, will be mentioned here as another measure of student interest in change and their willingness personally to accept the risks involved in it.

The pass-fail grading plan, a controversial innovation from the outset, but especially because the action of the academic senate in the first year of organization seemed to impose it on all colleges, was modified in 1967 to permit the boards of studies to decide whether, in their areas of academic responsibility, the pass-fail arrangement or conventional letter grades would be used. The board of study controlling courses in government and political science voted to use letter grades—to protect, the faculty said, the student's transfer and graduate school standing. But students enrolled for courses in this department appealed to the faculty to reverse its action. They argued that the faculty's caution threatened the innovative nature of the Hilltop campus by compromising one of its most distinctive innovations; as for the risk to the students' future, the students declared their willingness to bear that themselves.

This development is akin to one at Westversity's Omega where, under student encouragement, the three-point grading scale that had been introduced as a modification of the conventional five-point grading formula when the college opened was changed to "satisfactory/unsatisfactory." Here, again, student action helped to assure the full thrust of an innovation.

One of the ways to test the commitment of administrators to change is to look for innovation in the administrative structure of the institution—in the positions, titles, job descriptions, and other definitions by which they derive their authority and security, and by which the authority structure of the campus is defined. Application of this test to the Hilltop campus revealed the ambivalence of the situation there—the mixture of old and new, tradition and innovation.

The Hilltop plan had its warp and woof. The colleges represented the warp. Faculty were to be associated with one or another of the colleges. Each college had a provost, whose job it was to establish the college as an entity with a sense of purpose and community. This university campus was, however, also organized into three major subject-matter divisions—natural sciences, social sciences, humanities—and this feature was the woof of the organizational fabric. A vice chancellor headed each of these divisions, and faculty at all the colleges were identified with one or another division even as they were with an individual college. Within divisions, there were the boards of studies, each with a convener. These boards served as surrogate departments, with the convener a chairman-equivalent. Boards and divisions protected the subject-matter specialization of faculty. Thus, at Hilltop, an innovative organizational mesh accommodated traditional arrangements—but in a loose weave, and with the design changed. The colleges were established first, given a start, before the divisions got under way. The colleges had been given a chance to establish their identity and win the loyalty of faculty and students even as the university had shown itself to be committed to the collegiate plan.

But, of course, professional rewards and sanctions in twentieth-century American higher education are tied to teaching, research, and publications within departments and by specializations. Hilltop was not willing to break with that tradition, therefore the boards of studies and the divisions seem likely to eventually win out, despite the head start given the colleges. Hilltop faculty live now in a house with two doors, and they have been moving freely through the collegial, innovative door as well as the departmental, traditional door. The provosts stand at one, the vice chancellors at the other. Provosts were leaders in academic matters in 1966–67, but since that time vice chancellors have been appointed and are now at work. The title given these guardians of the university's traditional academic concerns is well known, the title of provost is new, ill-defined, untested. The academic senate regarded provosts as something like deans at the time of the study, but they had neither legal nor traditional authority. They succeeded by their wits.

In the early days of campus planning, the ambiguity of the provost's position in the hierarchy was probably an advantage. Free of the delimitations of regular job descriptions, the provost could provide leadership in a situation where faculty and administrators were just gathering strength and were sufficiently unsure of themselves to extend "senatorial courtesy" to anybody who seemed to know what he was doing. But it is not difficult to foresee a day when the Hilltop division of MultiWestern's academic senate—and, so far as could be determined, no serious effort was made in the beginning days to block the formation of the senate at Hilltop—will become so strongly established, and so much aware of its connection and continuity with the other university campuses, that the leadership of provosts in the academic realm may be ended. Provosts could become lackeys of the faculty, carrying out routine and ceremonial duties. Under such conditions, it would be impossible to find strong, able persons for this position, and the innovative intentions of the collegial plan would then be at the mercy of the divisions and the senate, bodies not likely to be advocates of change.

Faculty now have divided loyalty—to the college and to the senate. They cannot be advanced through the academic ranks without the approval of the provosts, and that provision was meant to assure the faculty person's active participation in his own college. But it is also true that the faculty member cannot be advanced in MultiWestern except through success measured by conventional criteria of excellence. The colleges are at a disadvantage if the faculty person discovers he does not have time to give to activities that advance the interests of the college, such as involvement with students or the implementation and refinement of college innovations and, concurrently, to activities such as research and publications that advance him in his guild. The college is local, the guild is national. Faculty were likely to think one way when sitting as the governing body of a college, it was noted, and another way when sitting at the Hilltop division of the academic senate, because the emphases were so different. Perhaps they are irreconcilable.

Yet the innovative nature of the campus had not hurt student or faculty recruitment. The campus had five student candidates for every opening in the colleges at the time of the study, and administrators were deluged with faculty applicants. Some students at Hilltop might feel that the faculty had not taken advantage of the opportunities for innovation, while some faculty might find certain aspects of the Hilltop program too innovative for their taste; but, by and large, Hilltop was succeeding at being different without being radical. Despite all qualifications and cautions, this campus was mixing organizational innovation and conventional arrangements to a degree not found elsewhere in the study. And, despite formidable problems, including the threat of failure, the effort of Hilltop to be an innovative campus contributed significantly to the fact that both students and faculty there were noticeably different from other samples. Something significant was happening at Hilltop, something that seemed to affect students, faculty, and administrators sufficiently to create on that campus a quality that can be called institutional distinctiveness.

The other avowedly innovative campus of MultiWestern participating in the research project was Sigma College of Bay campus. This was the campus proposing to divide an eventual 27,500 into twelve colleges of about 2300 students each. Three or four colleges would be grouped together to provide as a unit most of the benefits of a university. Each college, however, was to be distinctive—in architecture and program.

When research personnel interviewed chief administrators on the subject of innovation, they found that these leaders emphasized that the development most likely to be the distinctive feature at Bay would not be the clustering of the colleges, as unique as that arrangement was, but rather the combining of truly distinguished graduate programs and a faculty oriented to graduate level work and academic specializations, with an effective undergraduate program in the liberal arts characterized by a total relationship between students and their renowned faculty. The innovations that interested administrative representatives were those that would bring this high-powered faculty into contact with lower division students without jeopardizing the professional commitments of faculty to research and publication and yet would assure students of a shared learning experience that would fulfill their best expectations of a liberal education.

The emphasis at Bay had been on hiring distinguished

faculty and giving them freedom to follow their own interests. Thus, since it has also been a part of the policy to hire the department chairmen first, these distinguished department chairmen inclined to develop the department according to their own experiences, values, and professional preferences. Several administrators acknowledged that there were problems in innovation associated with this policy. But they fell back when pressed to their buoyant and persistent optimism—the optimism of new beginnings—that somehow they would find faculty who were interested in teaching and educational reform, in a philosophy of education for a new era as well as in research and publication; even though, as they admitted, other campuses of MultiWestern would presumably have been equally pleased to have such men but had not been able to find and hold them in sufficient numbers to achieve substantive innovations and effect marked change.

Actual innovations at Sigma, the only college in operation at the time of the study, included breadth and sequence curriculum requirements for all students, the setting aside of units of credit as graduation criteria in favor of a prescribed number of courses, including a three-quarter math sequence and five quarters with courses in the humanistic tradition. The college, however, was conventional in having the curriculum organized by departments, in the structured class arrangements and course content, and in the use of conventional letter grades.

Ideas featured in the planning under way for the second college, Lambda, had to do with the restructuring of courses, a greater emphasis on cross-disciplinary contacts, and a more open, elective system of course selection than was true at Sigma. While Sigma had a prescribed lower division curriculum in the liberal arts, with the student going over into a major for his upper division program, Lambda students could have greater lower division flexibility and a chance to develop a "specialization" in the junior and senior years, rather than being identified with a typical major.

One area in which it was evident that Lambda planners were drawing on the experience of Sigma, with the intent of departing from it, was in facilities planning. The Lambda provost and early faculty were working at the time of the study to bring the thinking of the architects more in line with their own educational philosophy and program emphases. There had been a four-day meeting during which the provost had spelled out at great length for the architects the purpose and expectations of the Lambda curriculum. As a result, a consortium of architects was established to take advantage of the insights and ideas of one particular architect who had best caught the faculty's educational intentions. From this time on, a closer and more purposeful working relationship had been established. Also, a student committee was drawn into the planning of the residence halls, and they made significant contributions to this endeavor.

These developments emphasize a problem that all new colleges face. The lead time requirement for facilities construction means either that buildings are constructed with little or no knowledge of the uses to which they will be put, innovative or not, or a faculty-administration planning team must be hired so early that few institutions can afford to have them around long enough to reach agreement on the functions and philosophy of the proposed college in order to give guidance to those responsible for the design and construction of facilities. One of the most innovative features of this campus of MultiWestern has been the creation of a "staging area" where a new college could be housed for two years while the facilities for that program were still under construction elsewhere on the campus. Thus, at least some faculty and most administrators for the new college can be on hand early enough to exercise influence on facilities planning.

Yet again, this innovation pertains to structural and organizational considerations, and there was very little evidence in 1966–67 that administrators at Bay were interested in radical curriculum changes or new value orientations for colleges that had been declared to be free to challenge every educational assumption and condition.

One of the most complex and enduring questions regarding the prospects for innovation at Bay has to do with the range and authority of administrative leadership. The impression gained by project interviewers was that university administrators on this campus did not believe that they were in a position to provide significant leadership in academic affairs. The curriculum was in the hands of faculty, and the administration was important only as a conciliator and adjudicator of faculty aspirations or faculty factions. Caught between statewide regulations on the one hand and the autonomy of a strong-willed faculty on the other, administrators were not sanguine about their ability to effect curriculum changes. And yet this campus had been given encouragement by the university president to innovate, decentralization was expected to make it possible, and this campus had from the beginning declared itself to be well disposed to change in all areas of its life. It sought to establish an image of ferment, criticism, and openness to new ideas. As a provost promised, "It will not be a comfortable place for those whose minds are made up." Whence was leadership for such change and innovation to come? From faculty? But their interests and traditions were in graduate education, in specializations, in those very arrangements and experiences that had in recent years come under so much justifiable criticism, and away from which it seemed necessary to move. Such leadership must come, at least in large part, from administrators who alone would have a sense of the whole, yet the curriculum was, apparently, an area closed to them.

Certain Bay administrators did, in fact, sense the need for leadership in academic matters, and they acknowledged the likelihood that the campus administration would have to lead the way if changes were to be noteworthy. With this concern in mind, a decision had been made in 1966–67 to bring administrators more actively into the planning of curricula for new colleges. They had been involved very little at Sigma, somewhat more with Lambda, and it was said that there would be joint faculty-administration committees for the planning of later colleges.

The role of the provosts in the administrative hierarchy of MultiWestern was a particular area where clarification was needed. Their power and authority were being circumscribed by the faculty on one side and the university administration on the other: They had to measure up to the criteria of academic professionalism to be acceptable to faculty, meaning teaching experience, research, and publications; but they were also required to have administrative skills, political sensitivity, and the "integrative" talents necessary to succeed with central administration and the general public. Since

they were the administrators closest to students, they had to be able
to represent student interests and, if necessary, act as buffer between
students, faculty, and central administrators.

At Bay campus and elsewhere, there had been a rapid turnover of provosts; the complexity of their task plus the ambiguity
of the limits of their authority and responsibility for leadership were
contributing factors. But there was another problem, one to which
most provosts were partners. Opportunities for administrative leadership had not been exploited because most administrators in key
positions, including provosts, came from highly structured situations
where their rewards and sanctions were specified and they, consequently, proceeded to impose past conditions on new opportunities.
Rather than regarding the ambiguity of the new situation as an
opportunity for leadership, they inclined to draw back waiting for
the old, familiar lines of authority and responsibility to emerge and
give them guidance. There has been not an excess but a paucity of
audacity.

Another possible source of leadership for innovation at Bay
and elsewhere is the student body. But, at least in 1966–67, the
majority of administrators interviewed at Bay were strongly opposed
to student involvement in planning and implementing academic
programs. Students are conservative, provincial, and self-satisfied,
it was said; they concentrate on personal affairs and professional
study, and it was a myth to see them as true activists. It was popu-
lar, said one administrator, for some students to take on the
"Berkeley style," but he had no use for them. He also said that students had little contribution to make on committees charged with
the formulation of academic policies, and to put them there would
only create sham and unnecessary obstructions. A student "uprising"
on compus in 1965 was cited by two administrators as illustrative
of the fact that students are unlikely to understand the multiple
facets of committee work and, furthermore, student activism was a
development entirely harmful to the campus. This incident had
caused some faculty to change from a position of advocacy for student involvement to one of conservatism emphasizing faculty autonomy in academic planning. Yet two other administrators were more
favorably disposed to students and thought the 1965 student agita-

tion had forced administrators to think of ways to better the undergraduate collegiate program.

Another limitation on prospects for change was shown in the criticism made by certain Bay administrators on innovations attempted at Sigma. The college's breadth and sequence requirements were being criticized—the breadth requirement with its heavy concentration in science was said to be drawing a certain type of student into the college, many of whom were getting stuck in the language requirement; more than half the students had not satisfied the language proficiency examination that was prerequisite to junior standing, yet these students had been advanced to junior standing. Most of the seniors scheduled to graduate in 1967 had not passed these written and oral language examinations, and it seemed likely that various language tracks would have to be set up (in math and science there were already three tracks—an honors track, a high, and an ordinary track). The point here is not the merits or deficiencies of specific innovations. Rather, the concern is over the fact that some Bay spokesmen gave the impression that innovation would be welcomed on that campus only within the limits of assured success. The quickness with which criticism and impatience arose suggested a low tolerance for innovations that irritate or for those that do not facilitate conventional thinking.

What, then, would be the role of innovation and experimentation on this new campus? First it was pointed out by one administrator that innovation had been possible within MultiWestern before the president's decentralization plan of 1964 and that, on the other hand, there was no more likelihood of change since 1964 than there had been before. The findings of this research project support that comment. Despite the emphasis of the printed materials that "the old forms, not the new, must defend themselves here," which might suggest radical intentions, conversations with administrators gave evidence that the conventional standard of excellence was well established at Bay and that the new ways, not the old, would have the burden of proof.

Neither MultiWestern's Valley campus, nor the one called Seaside, was committed to innovation and change to the degree expected at Hilltop and Bay. At both of the more conventional campuses, however, attempts were being made to explore on a small scale most of the innovations being offered on more holistic terms and with considerable fanfare elsewhere. At Seaside, in addition, one dramatic innovation was under discussion in 1966–67, one that did come into being later on—a "college" especially designed for creative students. The first announcement stated that this college would be ". . . a separate academic unit, separately staffed and administered, with a special curriculum and a specially selected group of students." The innovative nature of the program, and this is one proposal that came to light during the study that showed promise of being innovative to the point of being truly experimental, was revealed in the following quotation from a brochure announcing the college:

> Each student will be enrolled on the evidence of a capacity for intellectual pursuit, discovery, and reformulation of a particular art or science. Each course in the College curriculum will offer the student, not an exposure to a predetermined quantity of fixed subject matter, but an occasion for exploring and modifying a field of knowledge.

Other innovative features in this special curriculum were the lack of prerequisites for courses, the absence of upper or lower division designations for courses, and, indeed, the fact that there would be no specifically required courses. Instead, each student was to be required to take a minimum of two courses in each of the six curriculum areas. The grading and credit system was also innovative. A student could receive any number of units—from zero to six—for each course, the exact number to be reached by agreement between student and instructor. One hundred eighty units would qualify the student for graduation. No grades, as such, would be given. However, for courses taken in the regular academic departments on the Seaside campus, students were expected to maintain a 2.0 grade point average.

Here was an innovative idea that came from the faculty and was organized largely by faculty initiative. A professor of English who had been a sharp critic of university policy had been drawn into the chancellor's office to work on the campus master plan, and this innovative college was the product of his thinking. Administrators showed no resentment about these developments. Indeed, as at Bay, the prevailing opinion was that the faculty academic senate was so strong that academic changes must come from faculty thinking or by planting the idea with faculty so as to preserve the appearance of faculty initiative and faculty control. Administrative leadership must be subtle and indirect to be persuasive. There was considerable enthusiasm among administrators on this campus in 1966–67 for the organization of yet another innovative college in which nearly 500 students would receive a first-rate program of general education, but administrative contacts insisted that the idea could succeed only if it were lodged in the minds of key faculty leaders who would shepherd it through the academic senate. These administrators emphasized not only that campus political realities were such that an administrator's success was contingent on his ability to subordinate himself to faculty, or at least appear to, but that they also sincerely favored a strong senate and were happy to be regarded as the facilitators of faculty policy.

A former chancellor was credited in administrative conversations with bringing students into participation in policy formulation at Seaside. While agreeing that a start had been made toward innovations in this area, there was no agreement on the roles students could or should currently play. Some spokesmen felt that students were apathetic toward educational reform, at least in 1966–67, and that there had not been a significant number of students involved in activist programs, political, social, or educational. These administrators tended to insist that the earlier efforts had not been successful and that they had failed because students were not qualified for involvement in academic policy formulation. Other administrators, and they tended to be at comparatively lower ranks, were optimistic about student abilities and felt that what had been started by the departed chancellor was still an important influence and certainly a harbinger of things to come. At most of the colleges and universities of the study, those administrators more removed from student contacts were less likely to urge student involvement in governance than were those administrators working actively with students. Here is one area of life where familiarity, if that means human contacts, does not breed contempt.

The independent and off-campus housing arrangement, where approximately one third of the Seaside students live, was seen by some administrative interviewees as an "albatross" to the academic aspirations of the campus. The dynamics of the situation in the special housing area were said to be anti-intellectual. This off-campus concentration of students has no direct counterpart elsewhere in the university, and was seen by several interviewees as contributing to the "fun and games" image of the campus. One of the innovations at Seaside has been the attempt to introduce an academic dimension into the off-campus housing milieu by getting the financers of a high-rise complex of dormitories to include 1500 square feet in these facilities for academic utilization.

Other efforts to combat the anti-intellectual image of the campus included an academically centered orientation program for entering freshmen—that is, faculty lecturing on substantive topics and working with fraternities and sororities to improve the academic influences on campus. The development of the "Greeks" at Seaside in recent years was defended by one administrator because of the willingness of these houses to contribute to the intellectual development of their members. Finally, an academic ethos was being encouraged by arranging visits to faculty homes, setting up student-faculty discussions on campus, and trying to bring certain faculty into residence on campus. These are all modest innovations compared to what is happening at some colleges and universities. With the exception of the college for creative students, the faculty at Seaside campus, as at Valley, has not shown much interest in innovation.

Faculty Attitudes

In the introduction to this chapter the claim was made that faculties in American colleges and universities were, although held to the standard, sufficiently aware of forces bringing change in the society, and sufficiently anxious about the adequacy of conventional procedures and traditional values on campus, to be interested in the subject of change, innovation, and experimentation for higher education and, indeed, in provisions whereby specific changes might be facilitated. Several items in the faculty questionnaire were intended to elicit data on these themes.

On the matter of faculty attitudes toward educational changes in the context of change in the society, one item read: "Radical technological changes in our society necessitate radical changes in the educational experiences offered our youth, not because the past was bad, but because the future will be different." Results from the colleges and universities of the project are given in Table 8.

Table 8

FACULTY VIEWS ON STATEMENT: "RADICAL CHANGES IN SOCIETY NECESSITATE RADICAL CHANGES IN THE EDUCATION OF YOUTH" (IN PERCENTAGES)

INSTITUTION (N)	RESPONSES		
	Agree	Can't Say	Disagree
MultiWestern			
Valley (151)	60	8	25
Hilltop-Gamma (14)	57	36	7
Hilltop-Kappa (16)	69	6	19
Seaside (94)	49	11	32
Bay-Sigma (14)	35	36	21
MultiEastern			
Alpha (51)	53	8	22
Theta (25)	60	24	12
Westversity			
Delta (38)	50	16	26
Omega (18)	56	0	22
Eastversity			
Beta (42)	60	7	28
Zeta (5)	60	20	20
North College (35)	57	11	26
Midwest College (33)	67	12	18
Southeast College (15)	74	20	7
South College (22)	87	4	9
CIT (577)	59	11	23

The general conclusion drawn from these data is that the weight of opinion among faculty is clearly on the side of change, in both the universities and the colleges of the institutional sample, with the innovative colleges, whether independent or within a university, leading the way. Faculty members at the Negro institution, although it was a conventional college, were also active advocates of change.

A second item in the questionnaire that drew out faculty attitudes toward educational change read: "Course work should be more relevant to the social and political realities in the world outside the campus." Data gathered in this item indicated that the general commitment to change in the educational experience of youth was modified noticeably when the issue became change in actual course offerings. Change in the general context is always easier to agree to than change in the classroom. About half of the respondents agreed with the item's assertion, while about one third disagreed, and the remainder chose the "can't say" column or did not answer. Leadership in the advocacy of change in course offerings, to make them more relevant to social and political realities in the world outside the campus, remained with those faculty at innovative campuses or colleges. However, it should be noted that at the most conventional places a strong minority of the respondents favored change of this sort.

There were high "can't say" percentages in several institutions. This may have been due to an identification by some respondents with the liberal arts tradition, understood as an ideal and as activities that should properly stand apart from the pressures of time and place. Recently, however, some authorities claim, faculty have been coming to see that the liberal arts ideal is not compromised by efforts to involve it in social and political realities. Such a change in stance may be perceived in this study in the reports from newer campuses—a change toward greater participation by the colleges and universities in the formulation and implementation of values and objectives for the general culture of the society because of a change toward greater self-consciousness about the basic values and objectives of the institution of higher education itself.

This change in institutional objectives was proposed in an item reading: "Colleges and universities, as institutions, must assume a larger, more important role in setting the goals and programs of our society." Seventy-one per cent of the faculty participating in the study favored this proposition. Only 17 per cent explicitly disagreed. There was no significant difference in the opinions of those at older and more conventional institutions as compared to those at the newer and innovative colleges. The data suggest that faculty everywhere, as with other human beings, seldom hesitate to seize the opportunity to advocate a leadership position for themselves or their institutions. However, faculty respondents in large majorities did in effect say that the institution of higher education should be in a position of societal leadership, after having said (Table 8) that changes in the society necessitate changes in colleges and universities. These responses, taken together, certainly move faculty toward the viewpoint that their institution should be an agent of social change.

However, when these findings are compared with those dealing with the need for curriculum change, the conclusion can be drawn that despite all the nuances of meaning possible in the preceding statements, and all the variables involved in the populations considering them, respondents were more willing to have the institution of higher education change society than they were interested in changing the institution in response to society's needs. But this was 1966–67; openness to change on the part of faculty, especially regarding the nature of educational institutions in contemporary society (an openness that according to these data was beginning to be evident, though still qualified and hesitant), has grown considerably since that time as the magnitude of social and economic problems has become better known.

Another item in the faculty questionnaire of the Institutional Character study offered academic traditionalists an opportunity to stand up and be counted: "Too much emphasis is presently being placed on innovation and experimentation in higher education. Existing standards and arrangements are sound, and these should be achieved and utilized—not replaced." As might be expected, faculty in the innovative colleges had little sympathy for this statement. No more than six per cent agreed to it at these colleges. At the more conventional places, support for the idea that too much emphasis is being placed on innovation ran as high as 40 per cent (Westversity's Delta and Southeast College), yet most faculty at most institutions disagreed, indicating thereby that they were not generally opposed to the current emphasis on innovation. (The rate of disagreement with the item averaged about two thirds.) The comparatively high percentage agreeing with the questionnaire statement at Delta College, Westversity, may indicate the extent to which these respondents, and perhaps others elsewhere, gave their replies within the context of local conditions; some Delta faculty may have been reacting to the presence in the university of Omega College, feeling that this cluster college tended to overplay the importance of innovation. However, given the spirited efforts on behalf of innovation in the university during recent years, the surprise may be in the fact that the reaction was not greater.

When attention in the faculty questionnaire focused on personal rather than more general considerations, most respondents still showed an interest in innovation. One item read: "Please scale your faculty colleagues, as personal observation allows, on their attitude toward innovation and experimentation in the curriculum of your college by checking one response for each item." There were five response options, ranging from *most* to *very few,* from which respondents were asked to choose one in considering statements such as "Seem to favor change for change's sake," "Willing to participate personally in experimental ventures," "Not hostile to innovation but unwilling to get involved personally," and "Hold to the principle that nothing new must be tried for the first time."

When faculty were asked to rank their colleagues on whether they were "willing to participate personally in experimental educational ventures," the report from the total sample (all schools) showed that 20 per cent thought that *most* of their colleagues were so inclined. Twenty-three per cent said that *about half* would be willing to get personally involved, and 43 per cent said *some.* Nine per cent marked *very few.*

The extent to which structural provisions for innovation, such as the creation of a semiautonomous college, may help to encourage prospects for change by drawing in faculty who are willing to be identified personally with innovation is suggested by data showing that *most* of the faculty at South College, Eastversity's Zeta College, Westversity's Omega College, and Gamma and Kappa colleges of Hilltop campus, MultiWestern, were thought by 50 per cent or more of their faculty colleagues who are respondents to be so inclined. At only one of the newer, innovative colleges—Sigma College, Bay campus, MultiWestern—did less than one half of the respondents say as much. There 36 per cent thought *most* of their colleagues would be personally willing to innovate. That percentage was higher than all but one of the more conventional institutions in the study.

On another dimension of this same questionnaire item, dealing with the statement "Not hostile to innovation but unwilling to get involved personally," the general data showed that 18 per cent of our respondents thought this statement true for *most* of their colleagues, 30 per cent thought it an accurate representation of the position of *about half* of their peers, while 35 per cent thought it true of *some*, and 11 per cent said this statement was appropriate for *very few* faculty colleagues.

When attention is directed, again, to a comparison of faculty samples in conventional versus innovative schools, about 20 per cent of the respondents on the conventional university campuses felt *most* of their colleagues would be of this mind. At the innovative colleges on university campuses this judgment was made by 14 per cent or less. The independent liberal arts colleges were in about the same position as the innovative colleges at universities. Meanwhile, at the other end of the range of choices, those schools where respondents felt that *very few* of their colleagues would be "Not hostile to innovation but unwilling to get involved personally" were clearly the innovative colleges. The earlier point about structural provision for change helping to create a climate of opinion compatible with it is sustained by these data.

A comparison of the findings on these two questionnaire items shows that, predictably, faculty respondents thought that a somewhat higher percentage of their professional colleagues would be willing for others to do what the colleagues themselves preferred not to do. Again, the new and innovative colleges ran considerably ahead of the older and conventional places, suggesting that structural provision for change produces at least a surface commitment to this institutional goal and pointing up the general congruence between statements of purpose and the stated interests of faculty.

At another place in the testing instrument, a question similar to one already reported was raised. Faculty were asked about the importance for them personally of "an opportunity for experimentation and innovation." Then respondents were asked to speculate about the attitudes of their colleagues on the same subject. The composite institutional total showed 66 per cent saying that such an opportunity was *very important* to them personally. The percentage of faculty so inclined in the newer and innovative colleges ran more than 20 per cent higher than in older, more conventional schools. But, regardless of setting, the respondents identified personally, and by decisive percentages, with the idea of innovation. When the *very important* and *somewhat important* columns are combined, 94 per cent of the faculty are shown to be attracted to the idea of openness toward prospects for such change.

The respondent's view of his colleagues' attitude toward innovation and experimentation is regarded by some researchers as a less idealistic representation of faculty thinking and a more practical indication of the prospects for change than is the self-evaluation. On the item under consideration, enthusiasm reflected in the "personal view" was considerably moderated in the "view of others" section of the question, yet, still, the majority of faculty identified their peers as receptive to change. Thirty-five per cent, as compared with the earlier 66 per cent, thought colleagues would regard an opportunity for experimentation and innovation to be *very important*. Forty-eight per cent, rather than 28 per cent, elected the *somewhat important* column when judging colleagues on this subject.

It is impossible to know how respondents defined experimentation and innovation; some may have thought of it as meaning freedom for the professor to organize and conduct his classes according to his own desires, however conventional, while others were thinking in more programmatic terms. Nevertheless, respondents affirmed that an opportunity to change the provisions within which teaching and learning may take place was important to them personally and to most of their colleagues.

Opportunity was given faculty to state their attitudes toward certain fairly explicit forms of innovation. One, for example, asked for responses to the statement, "There should be less emphasis on grades, units of credit, and rigid course requirements." (Faculty were asked to apply the assertion to their college or university.) This statement was approved by 63 per cent of the respondents, while 28 per cent disagreed. The general tendency, when specific institutional data are considered, was for faculty at conventional places to be more favorably disposed to change in this regard than were faculty at the innovative colleges. This fact encourages two inferences: first, that proposals for innovations reducing emphasis on the norms of quantification at conventional colleges have good prospects for initiation and, second, that faculty in colleges where innovations of this sort are under way are somewhat apprehensive about how far such changes can go without completely removing the constraints of order. To illustrate both points: At the Valley campus of MultiWestern, a conventional institution, 64 per cent of the respondents agreed that there should be less emphasis on grades, units of credit, and rigid course requirements. At Hilltop campus, however, only 21 per cent of the respondents at Gamma College and 24 per cent at Kappa felt this way. Faculty there, at first glance, appeared to be mainly opposed to change in these areas, but the difference was probably due to the fact that Gamma and Kappa had a pass-fail grading arrangement already in effect, plus other innovations, and they apparently thought things had gone far enough in the direction of changes of this sort while at Valley campus no general institutional changes in these areas had been effected.

After allowing for the ambiguities created by wording, and for the effect of local emphases in the answers given, the conclusion that remains unassailed is that a definite majority of faculty on the older, conventional campuses, and a sizable minority to a clear majority on the new, innovative campuses favored less emphasis on certain conventional indices of student accomplishment and institutional excellence.

A modest form of innovation, one used at many colleges and universities, is cross-disciplinary teaching. Two sections of the faculty questionnaire had bearing on the subject; respondents were asked about: (1) "the theoretical importance of cross-disciplinary teaching," and (2) the "importance of interdisciplinary faculty contacts and teaching opportunities."

Cross-disciplinary teaching and interdisciplinary contacts for faculty, although encouraged at many colleges, must be regarded as innovative arrangements in this day of tight disciplinary specializations and departmental segmentalism. It is, therefore, significant that both teaching opportunities and provision for such contacts were deemed important by most faculty respondents in project colleges and universities. Three fourths of the faculties involved elected *very important* (27 per cent) or *somewhat important* (45 per cent); only one fourth thought it *not important*. This was an item for which there was no sharp distinction between old and new, conventional and innovative institutions. The two places that might be regarded as exceptions were South College, where the core program had encouraged cross-disciplinary contacts, and Omega college, Westversity, where the curriculum had been organized by divisions rather than departments. Sixty-four per cent at South and 78 per cent at Omega regarded cross-disciplinary teaching as *very important* to them personally. Although at these schools and elsewhere the interest that faculty claimed for themselves was not attributed in anything like the same measure to colleagues, the percentages in the "others" columns were sufficiently strong to support the contention that there is a developing interest in innovation, and in cross-disciplinary or relational teaching and learning particularly, on different kinds of campuses.

Innovations in governance configurations, as stated earlier, are more and more in evidence at American colleges and universities. In 1966–67, however, faculty of the Institutional Character project were divided on the extent to which students should participate in academic policy formulation. One item read:

> Should students at your college participate more significantly than they do at present in the formulation and implementation of academic policies, i.e., in establishing the content and organization of courses, on academic policy committees, by student-formed and student-led seminars?

(It should be remembered that responses were given in the context of local conditions. Conditions in project schools included provision at several project colleges for students to serve in advisory or consultative roles on academic considerations but, at the time of the study, in no cases were students full voting participants with faculty in the formulation of policies controlling academic life in the institutions.) Sixty-two per cent of the faculty respondents said No, while 34 per cent said Yes, to the idea of whether students should participate more actively in academic policy formulation. At most places academic professionalism or social paternalism—protecting faculty by one value orientation and students by the other—seemed to be the main reasons behind the stated preference for the continuation of conventional governance arrangements. But the fact that 34 per cent favored further change in already changing institutions is a development not to be forgotten. The extent to which the traditional paternalism of Southeast College was under critical evaluation at the time of the research project is shown by the identification of 73 per cent of the respondents, the highest in the total sample, with the concept of an improved role for students.

Faculties at most institutions these days are much more favorably disposed toward the idea of granting students control over, or at least active participation in, the determination of institutional policies affecting social and personal behavior than they are on the academic side of governance. This difference between faculty attitudes on academic versus nonacademic policy formulation involving students is shown by comparing the preceding data with that to follow, in which the issue is *in loco parentis*. In one section of the questionnaire headed, "Here are some ideas about higher education in the context of change. Check the category that best indicates your personal view on these matters," there was a subsection reading: "The concept of *in loco parentis* is unnecessary and undesirable because students should have the freedom and responsibilities of adults." Respondents in universities, especially those associated with innovative colleges within universities, were most likely to support this uncompromising statement that was the questionnaire item. Fifty to 70 per cent agreed, whereas around 25 per cent tended to disagree. The same was true at most of the liberal arts colleges. Only at Midwest College was there a marked difference. There, 61 per cent disagreed.

A slight majority of faculty at the MultiWestern campuses sided with the idea that the concept of *in loco parentis* ought to be changed. But, as previously stated, faculty there and elsewhere were hesitant about bestowing freedom and responsibility on students in the academic realm. Apparently many faculty were not opposed to change, nor indeed to change in areas affecting the student's learning experience (remember the research showing that most of the student's learning takes place outside the classroom). However, they are opposed in greater numbers to changes in academic governance, to changes that would enlarge student freedom and responsibility by involving them as young adults in academic policy formulation.

The final area of inquiry for faculty views on the subject of change, innovation, and experimentation deals with initiatives for change in innovative colleges and universities. Faculty were asked: "Where have the initiatives come from for recent changes in your institution?" In the composite institutional totals, faculty and faculty administration showed first place, each with 25 per cent of the vote. Administrative came next with 15 per cent. No college or university sample gave more than 7 per cent of its votes to students or more than 7 per cent to external influences (state legislature, constituency, national agencies).

Administrators interviewed at several universities said that faculty controlled academic policy formulation to the extent that leadership for change by administrators was nearly impossible. However, data show that while faculty see themselves as a strong influence in the initiation of change, they know they are far from alone in providing leadership. Administrators have tended to depreciate their role in institutional leadership—yet they have been crucial in providing leadership for the more innovative colleges and universities of this study—while faculty have often overstated their own importance, encouraged to do so by administration. Leadership has been in fact usually shared. Since faculty claim the powers of initiation, those interested in effecting change in institutions of higher education should put this faculty claim to the test. Given responsibility for the success of innovation and experimentation, they might become leaders in the achievement of change as well as the self-proclaimed initiators of it.

Student Perspectives

Turning now to student data on change and innovation, freshmen at MultiWestern campuses and North College were asked "Should students participate significantly in the [selection of] content and organization of courses, academic policy decisions, and matters of this sort?" Many respondents showed the becoming humility most faculty would like to see in entering students, but a strong percentage of these youth gave a foretaste of the assertiveness that has since come to characterize the new students: 46 per cent of those at Valley campus said Yes, at Seaside the affirmative response came from 45 per cent, and at Bay's Sigma College 42 per cent were in support of student participation in academic policy formulation. At Kappa College, Hilltop campus, 56 per cent, the highest percentage of students favoring student participation in academic governance, was recorded. This finding was representative of results from other student questionnaire items, particularly on the subjects of change, innovation, and experimentation.

At one point in the questionnaire, student respondents at MultiWestern were asked to choose from paired features those emphases they would associate with an ideal college. Three items in the list of college characteristics related to grading procedures (see Table 9). The freshman class of 1966 at Bay's Sigma College was much more like freshmen entering Valley and Seaside that fall, in attitudes toward conventional grading, than they were like the students entering Kappa College at Hilltop. Yet Bay, as with Hilltop, was to be an innovative campus. Hilltop's Kappa College freshmen were markedly less interested than students at Bay in competition for grades, while they were somewhat more interested in innovative admissions criteria and very much more interested in an innovative grading standard. Hilltop, it seems, had succeeded in establishing itself in the minds of students and, presumably, with counselors and parents as well, as an innovative campus. Consequently, it drew larger proportions of students who were receptive to changes of the sort described in the preceding tables than did Bay. Eighty-six per cent at Kappa College, Hilltop campus, indicated that this had been a criterion in their selection of the college, indeed 59 per cent said it played an important role, while the opposite was true at Valley campus and at Seaside, where about three fourths of the freshmen said it was not important in their choice. As for students at Sigma College, Bay campus, just under half said that an opportunity to participate in experimental educational programs was not important while just over half said it was a factor; the majority of these did not list it as *important* but as *somewhat important*. Thus although Bay as well as Hilltop students had a more pronounced interest in innovation than Valley or Seaside, these data show that the image of innovation had affected students entering Hilltop campus in a measure that set it apart.

Table 9

STUDENT OPINION ON CHARACTERISTICS OF AN "IDEAL COLLEGE,"
MULTIWESTERN (IN PERCENTAGES)

	Valley Campus	Hilltop Campus, Kappa College	Seaside Campus	Bay Campus, Sigma College
Much competitiveness for grades and recognition	32	16	41	44
versus				
Little competitiveness for grades and recognition	66	82	54	52
Students selected mostly on grades and admission scores	58	43	61	65
versus				
Students selected mostly on personal qualities	39	54	34	30
Courses given letter grades (A,B,C,D,F) ..	36	12	50	47
versus				
Courses graded "pass" or "fail"	62	85	45	50

On the question in which the respondent was asked to declare characteristics he associated with an ideal college by choosing between paired choices, two items in addition to those already reported revealed student attitudes toward change and innovation:

College traditional in most respects
    versus
College experimental in most respects
Little emphasis on independent study
    versus
Much emphasis on independent study

At Valley, 68 per cent stated a preference for a traditional college.

At Seaside, 57 per cent of the freshmen made the same choice. At Kappa College, Hilltop campus, students reversed the emphasis, 84 per cent stating a preference for a college with an experimental emphasis. Students at Bay's Sigma College also gave their emphasis to experimentation, though less markedly (66 per cent). If it is concluded that students at Valley campus and at Seaside had shown comparatively little interest in an experimental program, not because of any personal educational conservatism but simply because they knew the campuses they were entering did not offer experimental programs, these latest data show that in choosing their ideal college, students at Valley and Seaside still declared a preference for one that is traditional. It should also be pointed out that entering students at Valley and Seaside strongly favored independent study for their ideal college, despite also wanting one traditional in most respects. Perhaps this feature would be one respect in which their ideal college would not be traditional, for this feature is not often emphasized in the majority of American colleges and universities. Nevertheless, though all of the MultiWestern student samples stated a preference for independent study, the Hilltop freshmen once again accepted the innovative option by a larger proportion than did others (91 per cent).

Another feature that drew strong support from freshmen in all four of the MultiWestern campuses was a teaching and learning arrangement featuring group discussions rather than lecture classes: 68 per cent favoring discussion groups at Valley, 73 per cent at Seaside, 76 per cent at Sigma College, Bay campus, and 83 per cent at Hilltop's Kappa College. Again, students at the newer campuses were most attracted to that approach to learning which is for this country the more innovative.

Of greater interest, perhaps, is the broad support that group discussion, like independent study, received across campus lines. In the opinion of researchers, the high level of receptiveness shown by students toward independent study and discussion groups makes them ideas with which advocates of change might begin to work. This is especially true since both ideas are calculated to increase student involvement in the learning process and, as a corollary, to personalize the learning experience. Independent study should have appeal for faculty who want to get on with their own research and writing, because the burden of responsibility in this plan is on the student (for independent study should mean that students take the initiative for their own education while faculty act as resource persons), as well as for faculty who work well in the individual conference setting, while discussion classes should have appeal for faculty who would like more direct, informal student contacts in a group context.

Student attitudes toward an innovative approach to general curriculum design were also tested. Respondents were offered two statements that represented an open versus a tutelary way of organizing the learning experience. "Which of these statements," the encompassing question began, "comes closer to your own view?"

> Students should be given very great freedom in choosing their subjects of study and in choosing their areas of interest within these subjects.

> There is a body of knowledge to be learned, and the faculty is more competent than the student to direct the student's course of study, through required courses, prerequisites, and the like.

Student opinion was quite divided at MultiWestern campuses. At Hilltop and Bay the outcomes were reversed, 66 per cent at Hilltop favoring the "open" curriculum and 66 per cent at Bay favoring the prescribed one. Fifty-two per cent at Seaside and 57 per cent at Valley supported the notion of student freedom and involvement. The curricular emphasis at Bay may have been responsible for the student attitude there. If so, it means that innovation will need to come by faculty initiative.

The institution other than MultiWestern with the most experience in cluster college development, participating in the Institutional Character study, was Westversity. There, as with the Multi-Western situation, comparative analysis of the student data shows that the cluster college concept as a structural provision to encourage change can be successful. Although student admissions for Delta College and Omega College were processed through the same office, and despite evidence that the announcement of the cluster colleges had not greatly extended the range of contacts which the university had build up with counselors, parents, or students over the years, the level of expectation for entering freshmen at Omega, the cluster college, was significantly different than that found among Delta freshmen. The differences were very noticeable in the sections of the student questionnaire dealing with change and innovation (though not limited to these topics).

By and large, Delta students did not expect to find their college characterized by substantive curriculum changes, nor did they show any special interest in having Delta so characterized. Three fourths of the Delta students considered their ideal college as one "traditional in most respects" rather than "experimental in most respects." This was the highest proportion of any entering class in the study to side with the traditional. Omega students voted strongly the other way; 86 per cent declared a preference for a college experimental in most respects. They were the most experimentally inclined of all samples.

The traditional-experimental issue was raised, though with a more particular focus, in a question dealing with the considerations that figured in the student's selection of his college. Only 3 per cent of the students at Delta, the lowest percentage in the study, said that an important consideration in their coming there was an "Opportunity to participate in experimental educational programs." Thirty-eight per cent of the entering Omega class indicated the opportunity for participation in such programs was important to them. Only one other college in the project had a freshman class that gave greater attention to this variable.

However, significant proportions of students at both colleges showed an interest in specific forms of innovation. In the questionnaire item dealing with the characteristics of an ideal college, when students were asked about the importance for them of lecture classes versus group discussion classes, every respondent at Omega voted for group discussions. At Delta, 66 per cent voted in favor of discussion type classes and 32 per cent favored lecture classes. This was again a comparatively conservative response by the Delta sample. No other student sample gave as high a proportion of their support to lecture classes. However, nearly 77 per cent of the Delta respondents stated a preference for a college emphasizing independent study, compared to 98 per cent of the entering freshmen at Omega. On pass-fail versus letter grades, the Delta student sample was divided, with 57 per cent favoring letter grades and 42 per cent preferring pass-fail. In this respect, the Delta freshmen were closely akin to students at the other college and university campuses of the study. It was only in the new semiautonomous cluster colleges that students favored the innovative grading method. At Omega, for example, where a form of the pass-fail system is used, 92 per cent of the entering class voted for pass-fail.

A significant number of students in Delta were at least curious about curricular changes, but they had no illusions about what they were getting into at their college. Delta was not regarded as having innovation as a mark of distinctiveness. The reverse was true at Omega. Again there was the curiosity and also the predisposition, but by and large Omega's entering class was better informed of prospects for innovation than was true at Delta. When asked how much they knew at entrance about "The availability of specialized, independent courses of study," 33 per cent at Omega, the highest proportion of any project sample, professed to know a lot about these matters and 56 per cent said they knew at least a little. At Delta 17 per cent claimed considerable knowledge in this realm and 64 per cent thought they knew a little.

This comparatively high degree of knowledge about and identification with the unique features of Omega by its entering freshmen could have been due to the controversial nature of the program. Precisely because it was radically innovative, students may have taken the time to learn more about it and, at entrance, were better informed. Their choices, in most cases, appeared to be deliberate. This conclusion is based in part on data from a questionnaire item in which students were asked whether anyone had discouraged them from coming to the college of their choice. Some 44 per cent of the Omega freshmen said Yes, and 56 per cent said No. At Delta the figures were 36 per cent Yes and 64 per cent No. Omega had the highest percentage of freshmen encountering opposition, whereas the Delta percentage was about comparable to findings at other places. The greatest number of arguments raised against Omega, according to student data, dealt with its being "Too expensive" (34 per cent), "Too much academic pressure" (19 per cent), "Type of people attending" (14 per cent), or "Geographical location" (13 per cent).

At Westversity, in the comparison between the colleges here called Delta and Omega, the extremes of the study on the continuum of tradition-experimentation, and on other measures, were found. The explanation for this phenomenon was the cluster college concept and, no doubt, the innovative stance taken by Omega that set it apart and made it different.

A general impression emerging from study of student data involving all of the participating colleges and universities of the Institutional Character study, and supporting the findings of other researchers, is that somehow—by the work of counselors, the accuracy of printed materials, the students' intuitive skills, the grace of God—there is remarkable congruence between the expectations of entering students and what the institution they are going into promises to provide. Perhaps student respondents in this study were identifying with the characteristics of their college. If so, it is encouraging to realize that students know so much about what they are getting into.

Summary by Schools

South College. On the basis of faculty questionnaire data and administrative interviews, South College has been straightforward in its declarations about innovation and its plans were, at the time of the study, understood by nearly all faculty and accepted by a majority of them.

The formal organization of the college—offices and job descriptions, the authority structure and official relationships—was not nearly as innovative in design or conception as the curriculum. The actual performance of administrators might be quite innovative, but people worked, formally, whatever the informal dynamics, within a conventional structure. Thus, the record of South College shows that innovations can be grafted onto an old-fashioned administrative trunk if the leaders in administration favor the changes and do not, therefore, reject the graft.

The crucial variable at South had been its leadership. Purposeful leadership in administration was joined with leadership in key faculty positions sharing the same aims. The combination has produced a college of character testing certain innovations that may have positive consequences for many liberal arts colleges.

North College. Study of North's literature and insights gained through administrative interviews gave project researchers the impression that eighty-three-year-old North has been attempting for the last seven or eight years to do what South College, founded in 1960, has attempted during the same period. These two colleges, with the same denominational affiliation, have experienced growth in numbers and quality, have been concerned to secure a teaching faculty with guild qualifications and scholarly interests, have offered variations of a core program and putative emphasis on international studies, have drawn cheerful, hard-working students, and have had strong-willed, energetic administrative leadership.

This comparison does, however, overlook certain significant differences. North has more money, better facilities, a stronger board, a more highly developed international program, more award-winning students and more nationally viable faculty members. South has a stronger religious orientation, a more comprehensive core program, a greater interest in innovation and, at the time of the project, a more aggressive, less democratic leadership. These gradations of difference are just what one might expect when comparing an older with a newer institution. What is surprising is that the newer school has closed the gap to the point that comparisons can be made.

Despite the good match at North between student desires and general institutional promises, there is a difference between what the students would like and what they are likely to get from the faculty. Data show that if there is a basis of support for innovation at North it is more likely to be among the students than the faculty.

The educational philosophy and the broad institutional objectives of North College have not been matters of principal concern to the academic community as a whole during the recent years of transformation. There was no evidence that administrators, faculty, and students were carrying on a dialogue about institutional goals. Everyone assumed that everyone knew what the goals were but, at a time of considerable change in the size and perhaps in the character of the faculty, and certainly at a time of change in the intellectual and social disposition of the student body, this assumption was shaky at best. The nature of the institution supposedly known to all was, according to administrators, that North would remain a Christian liberal arts college and that it was becoming an innovative one. But North seemed to be no more or less Christian than hundreds of other colleges whose Christianity is largely residual, nor did researchers find much basis for the growth of a new image of North as a particularly innovative institution. The money the college has received makes it possible for this school to do more than most of its competitors are doing and to do it, in some cases, better. To this extent the college is innovative. But North is developing, expanding, refining essentially familiar themes. Where much has been given, much is expected. What North might have done would have been to look less to certain elitist colleges for models and, given its resources, brought people and programs together in new academic configurations.

From the evidence, the research team concluded that North College does not care to be experimental and is interested in innovations only so long as they advance the school toward the goal of conventional institutional excellence. It may be North's fate to achieve such excellence just at the time this standard is being abandoned as unworthy by those colleges North had hoped to impress.

These observations, containing explicit or implied criticism, are not aimed at urging North toward more political or social liberalism. The college has been a conservative school moving slowly, and perhaps wrongly, in a liberal direction. Perhaps it should be unapologetically conservative. North has a conservative constituency and funding base, although the students and faculty have of late been somewhat more liberal politically and socially, if not academically. Yet they are far from radical and the majority are probably most at home with conservatism. Administrators at North seem to feel compelled to promote social liberalization, largely because of the presumed need to provide a compatible setting for a new liberal faculty. However, it should not be difficult, with North's salary schedule, to find conservative faculty. Indeed, some evidence suggests that even faculty liberals tend toward conservative values after they have been on campus a while and begin to think about conserving their privileges.

Concern for diversity in American higher education indicates the need for a wide spectrum of political, social, and educational perspectives represented by, not only in, colleges and universities—

at the level of values as well as organizational forms. There must be alternative institutional models. North could innovate with traditional themes and arrangements, and do so from a Christian perspective too seldom represented these days in academe. The challenge for this college, whether it takes a conservative stance or not, is to bring all of its considerable resources, financial, intellectual, and spiritual, to bear on a united effort that will result in the constituency, administration, faculty, and students defining for that community the nature of academic excellence for a time of radical social change.

Midwest College. On the campus of Midwest, academically average students with above average religious motivation and a definite concern for vocational preparation come into the presence of a competent, hard-working teaching faculty that is beginning to change its ideas about what constitutes a satisfying professional life without as yet changing its conventional thinking about the rights and privileges of students. The administration has been in recent years making provisions for the faculty that are of importance to them—better salaries, reduced teaching loads, more mobility, and national exposure—as well as interpreting the new faculty ethos to students while waiting for students to develop a new ethos on their own.

The students, meanwhile, seem to be developing ideas about student participation in academic governance that had not yet been expressed, at the time of the project visits in 1967, to the administration. The generally shared concern for community, the willingness on the part of the faculty to innovate and on the part of the administration to encourage and accommodate demands—these and other ideas gathered through contact with Midwest—mean that innovation will be used to increase the student's involvement in his own learning experiences, to reconcile contending factions within the college, to alleviate differences and, finally, to integrate them.

Southeast College. At the time of the Institutional Character study, Southeast was in such a period of uncertainty concerning yet unspecified changes that neither students nor faculty could understand more than a small segment of the situation in which they found themselves. There were not only educational and political problems but the problems of personal and group identity one would expect to see at a Negro institution in today's America, revolving around such concepts as "The Negro versus the black man" and assimilation or integration versus separatism or pluralism.

Students from essentially conservative homes were vaguely aware of social and academic changes with which they rather wanted to become identified and yet their values were still conventional. Their responses on the questionnaire items reveal the tension implicit in that situation. Faculty responses were even more divided; faculty members sometimes contradicted their own statements and disagreed strongly with each other. They were personally uncertain about the emphases the new administration was bringing to the college and the way they would relate to whatever it was, and they had become sufficiently divided into subject-matter enclaves, or into young-old, liberal-conservative categories, that they were unable to assess accurately the institution's philosophy of education or the values and goals of their colleagues.

However, by the end of the project's association with the college, the new administration was asserting itself, a sense of direction seemed more evident, and students and faculty were showing a concern for both purpose and program that was to the project staff a harbinger of institutional vitality and relevance for the future.

Eastversity. There were cross-currents of opinion at East sufficient to suggest that the character of the institution was changing, but they were not sufficient to provide any clear understanding of future probabilities. Despite some interest in innovation, data seem to put Beta College in the mainstream of the values, forms, and styles of American academics. This could be precisely where the faculty of this college want to be. They may prefer for the innovative thrust of the university to be confined to Zeta College or to other special, perhaps peripheral, components of the university. Thus, in their view, to suggest that the university does not stand out as an innovative institution may lose force in that it is seen by faculty to be invalid to expect innovation from a unit of the university that is not and does not aspire to be innovative. However, the university, as a university, has declared itself to be committed to experimentation, innovation, and change. Furthermore, many respondents indicated that Beta, perhaps more than Zeta, was the innovative college.

Not all data from Beta showed faculty there as being as conservative as faculty in institutions where no claim to innovation is made. Beta faculty came out rather strongly in support of a statement that blamed faculties for the failure of innovation at the undergraduate level. The Beta response pattern was either an exercise in *mea culpa* or an expression of dissatisfaction with a situation that frustrates change. The statement was by David Riesman:

> In the United States . . . the major tide seems to be running heavily against innovation at the undergraduate level, less because of student conservatism, although this is a factor, than because faculty members are in such demand that they can set their own terms. Generally the terms include a reduction of hours spent with undergraduates, whether in the classroom or as advisors, and an unremitting effort preferably to teach postgraduate students and, failing that, to teach only advanced undergraduates—and to teach these in turn as if they were being prepared for graduate work.

Those expressing agreement with the quotation totaled 71 per cent in the Beta sample. About 21 per cent said they disagreed. Eastversity ranked high among the institutions of the study in giving an affirmative answer. The composite institutional total showed 60 per cent agreeing and 32 per cent disagreeing. The highest percentages in support of Riesman's point came from Alpha and Theta colleges of MultiEastern (76 per cent each), both comparatively conservative institutions.

Despite the potential for divisiveness inherent in conditions just discussed, the prospects for an intellectual community at Eastversity seemed as good as in more secluded, residential, cohesive institutions. When asked about the importance of a sense of community, nearly half (45 per cent) of the Beta College faculty respondents said they regarded it as *very important,* while 33 per cent said community was *somewhat important,* and only 19 per cent replied *not important.* Unlike the results on many other items, on this question respondents answered rather similarly for colleagues: *very important,* 36 per cent; *somewhat important,* 48 per cent; and 10 per cent, *not important.*

Faculty were asked whether more effort should be made in their institution to bring students and faculty together in unstructured, personal encounters. Over three fourths of the Beta respondents said that they agreed or strongly agreed with this idea, while only one sixth disagreed. This was a better showing than the entering students at this college gave when asked how important in selecting Eastversity was the notion of a "Closely-knit college community," and a "Chance to know students and professors." Some 39 per cent said they were *important,* with another 39 per cent regarding such features as *somewhat important.* About 20 per cent thought them *not important.* These matters were more important to Zeta College freshmen (65 per cent), but these respondents did not show the enthusiasm for community that was true in other new and innovative colleges. The 39 per cent in Beta College marking these qualities *important* was second lowest of all entering class samples in the study. Does this perhaps mean that freshmen at East realized that commuting students and faculty would have little time to contribute much in these matters?

If the spirit of community is achieved in the new Eastversity, it will be distinguished from that which characterized campus life in the early days by the diversity of participants. Homogeneity is giving way to heterogeneity, yet most faculty and students seem united in their concern for community. While entering students did not emphasize community as a factor in selecting East, they did rank a "Closely-knit college community" very high when asked to list the characteristics of an ideal college. Ninety-one per cent of the respondents in Beta and 89 per cent in Zeta expressed such a preference.

The sense of community existing at East is based, said certain administrators, on two things—first, the university's struggle for survival and, second, close student-faculty relationships that have developed in many departments. What will produce the spirit of community at East in the future? The answer to that question cannot now be known because the direction and thrust of the university, that which gives character or distinctiveness to the place— whether philosophy and purposes, conventional criteria of excellence, or forms of innovation and experimentation—have not yet been made manifest.

MultiEastern. The meaning of the federated college plan, and of the university's inclination to innovation for the students of the several colleges, were matters only vaguely known to students in

1966–67. They were curious about announcements concerning the first new college, especially its commitment to coeducation, but they had not participated in the academic planning for the program and were not inclined to extend themselves beyond immediate interests and problems in their own college. Student views were solicited by administrators when planning for the facilities of the new college was under way (and according to one report, they were very helpful), but neither students nor administrators seemed to realize that if the new colleges at MultiEastern were truly innovative there would be significant ramifications from that fact for all phases of student life in the university.

Perhaps the so-called February uprising of students (1967), a mild student revolt, was an expression of a subconscious awareness that vast changes were pending. Reports suggested that while students involved were not protesting specific plans for the new colleges, they were expressing a desire to be better informed about university developments and to become more active participants in university planning. They sensed that the federated college plan implied major changes in MultiEastern's future, and because the announcement of the plan—which had triggered the turbulence— did not convey the point that everything about it was tentative and subject to change, students felt they had not been consulted about decisions vitally affecting them. They acted "in typical [Multi-Eastern] style," visitors were assured. Having demonstrated publicly to make their concern visible, students then expressed confidence in the administration and retired from the scene, leaving with the expectation that their views would thereafter be sought and incorporated. Another interpretation of the February uprising was the agitation was confined mainly to Theta College where some students and certain younger faculty were expressing their anxiety that Theta would, under the federated plan, lose its identity.

One of the most exciting aspects of the MultiEastern story is the way in which such developments, starting as functional details, quickly led into the most fundamental considerations and required attention to first principles, to matters as complex as the administrative reorganization of the university. Thus is illustrated how a modest interest in innovation can lead to considerably bigger things. At MultiEastern, basic issues have emerged from modest beginnings. It remains to be seen whether this university will press on to a position of innovative leadership for American higher education.

Westversity. Most American institutions of higher education have judged their mission by quantitative norms—grades, units of credit, and other conventional criteria—and Westversity's Delta College has been no exception. But now, as with so many colleges and universities, Delta must think anew of the character of its mission, and it must do so in qualitative terms. The college literature asserts the liberal arts ideal, but the program of study has been vocationally oriented. Students were, and are, self-satisfied, pleasant, socially and politically conservative, academically placid; good, clean, middle- to upper-class youth who think most of the time about how to get ready for daddy's business and with whom to set up their own homestead.

Omega College students incline the other way. They rank high on the Omnibus Personality Inventory scales showing intellectual disposition; they rank low in practicality, orderliness, and conventional social and personality characteristics. Perhaps the most important finding from this study is that the extremes of the various measures appeared on the same campus.

The faculty at Delta seem to be increasingly committed to the conventional standard of institutional excellence: They want better students as judged by standard criteria; they are concerned for faculty specialization, degrees, research; and they want administrators who defend academic freedom and raise money. The Omega faculty, meanwhile, may not be able to sustain the fundamental commitments that originally characterized that community. They may not want to do so. At the time of the study, faculty there seemed to be dividing into factions and interest groups or taking refuge in various forms of privatism. There was a strong possibility that the Omega faculty would end up in the condition from which the Delta faculty was beginning to seek ways to extricate itself. Since this study was completed, the character of Delta seems to be changing; it is too early to know whether the change is more than a temporary response to national pressures, to the enthusiasm and leadership of a new academic vice president for West and a new dean for Delta, and to support for curriculum reform from a major educational foundation. Also, the prospect looms that the Omega faculty will join colleagues at Delta in adhering to the conventional criteria of institutional excellence. If this happens, both faculties might come to define their colleges in terms that are alien to the university's historic goal—liberal education—as well as to West's contemporary commitment to innovation and change.

MultiWestern. One of the open sections of the faculty questionnaire called for participants to write out, without multiple-choice items being provided, their answer to this question—"What do you think are the most distinctive features of your college?" At the Valley campus of MultiWestern 20 per cent of the sample gave no reply. Ten per cent said that the most distinctive thing about Valley was its image, style, or ethos—probably a reference to the community spirit or attitude of friendliness about which administrators spoke. Five per cent said there was nothing especially distinctive about the campus, but nearly half of the respondents offered multiple distinctions covering a wide area, from facilities to personnel.

The Bay faculty sample, representing one of the new campuses, divided as follows: The largest percentage among the single category responses (21 per cent) went to "new programs," or to specific forms of innovation. More than 60 per cent gave answers similar to the Valley group, but with new curriculum developments listed frequently. Fourteen per cent at Bay did not answer.

Responses at Seaside were more widely scattered than at the other campuses of the university. The largest cluster of answers in a single category had to do with the growth rate of the campus, and the impact of that growth (7 per cent). Four per cent, the second largest grouping, said there was nothing especially distinctive about Seaside. The largest proportion of answers (56 per cent) were in the multiple-response category. There, various aspects of professional life were mentioned. The no response rate on this item for the Seaside sample was 20 per cent.

Faculty samples from Hilltop's Gamma and Kappa colleges, especially from the latter place, were clustered largely about "innovation and experimentation" or "new programs" and in the multiple response category, emphasizing the holistic or inclusive nature of the change emphasis there, or professional considerations.

Fourteen per cent at Gamma and 25 per cent at Kappa did not answer.

As suggested by these data, and as made manifest by findings from other questionnaire items referred to earlier, the ideal of professionalism motivates all campuses of this university. It provides the norms by which institutional character at MultiWestern is defined, achieved, and changed.

Value convergence to the point of conformity has resulted in isomorphism—the condition of being, or wanting to be, identical in form or substance despite a different ancestry. So Seaside has come from a teachers college and liberal arts tradition, but is bent now on becoming a general university campus, featuring standards set by graduate and professional specializations. Valley, from farm status and agricultural center, is now becoming a general university campus. Bay, starting at the graduate level, is extending the values of its professionally oriented faculty into new undergraduate programs originally intended to avoid the very problems the graduate professional mentality helps to create. Hilltop, still the most innovative, created to be different, but apparently unable to innovate in its relations to statewide planning and unwilling to innovate in its relationship with the university's conservative academic senate, will eventually embrace 27,000 students and may become just another general university campus complete with a house plan for undergraduates and a full complement of graduate and professional programs.

One consequence of isomorphism is that discrimination is rampant in the university, not toward those of a different color or socioeconomic status but toward those whose qualities are not defined or validated by the conventional criteria of academic excellence.

If that consequence closes some good people out, a second one ties good people down. Isomorphism, in the professional ghetto which is the university, threatens substantive diversity. MultiWestern's structures and functions encourage variations on a common theme in a day which calls for the harmonization of seemingly dissonant voices and the effective expression of multiple themes.

VII

Faculty:
the Different and
the Like

In the preceding chapters, colleges and universities of the Institutional Character study were described and evaluated according to their regard for educational philosophy and institutional goals; the conventional standard of excellence; and change, innovation, and experimentation. In this chapter, faculty data have been sorted to determine how variables other than affiliation with a particular institution figure in the determination of professional values and the emergence of institutional distinctiveness.

The total sample ($N = 577$) was divided, first, into two groups called "Junior" and "Senior" faculty as determined by the critical seven years or tenure hurdle. Junior faculty, one to six years of service, numbered 234, while Senior faculty, seven or more years, totaled 332. Respondents were also sorted by academic rank across all schools, by undergraduate teaching load, and by record of publications (articles). Additionally, the sample was cut according to the established divisions of the liberal arts: the humanities (including fine arts), the social or behavioral sciences, and the physical and natural sciences. Representative academic disciplines in the humanities ($N = 200$) were English, philosophy, religion, art, music, languages, history, journalism; in the social and behavioral sciences ($N = 116$), psychology, sociology, economics, political science, geography, anthropology; and the natural and physical sciences ($N = 167$) included biology, chemistry, physics, mathematics.

Comparative data were also compiled on faculty in various types of institutions. By use of these tables, researchers extended evaluations beyond those available from the composite institutional total (the CIT) and pursued various subgroupings of faculty by type of schools. Two classifications were decided upon. The first was a comparison of those institutions which could be said to be characterized by inclusive innovation—"Radicals"—and those which featured the conventional criteria of excellence—"Standard Bearers." Grouped as Radicals (faculty $N = 75$) were South College, the university colleges coded as Zeta (Eastversity) and Omega (Westversity), and MultiWestern's Hilltop campus colleges, Gamma and Kappa. Standard Bearers (faculty $N = 436$) were North College; the two colleges of MultiEastern, Alpha and Theta; the core college of Eastversity, Beta; the same at Westversity, Delta; and two campuses of MultiWestern, Valley and Seaside. Since neither of the preceding categories was appropriate for a few of the institutions in the study, two colleges—namely, Southeast and Midwest—and one campus of Multiversity—Bay—were not included in the Radicals versus Standard Bearers analysis.

The second classification compared the new colleges—"Newcomers"—with colleges that had been in existence prior to the organization of the newcomers as a part of the sponsoring university. These were called "Elder Siblings." Both of these groups were then compared to the small liberal arts colleges—"Libarts." Included as Newcomers (faculty $N = 73$) were the new private cluster colleges in actual operation at the time of the project, Zeta (Eastversity) and Omega (Westversity), and the new colleges of Multi-

Western, four in number but located on two campuses—code names
Sigma and Lambda (Bay campus), Gamma and Kappa (Hilltop
campus). Alpha College and Theta College of MultiEastern and
Eastversity's Beta College and Westversity's Delta college comprised
the group of Elder Siblings (faculty $N = 158$). The four independent Libarts colleges (faculty $N = 104$) were South, Southeast,
Midwest, and North.

In the Newcomers versus Elder Siblings versus Libarts comparison, as with Radicals versus Standard Bearers, not all of the
institutions in the study were included. The group called Newcomers overlaps with the group of Radicals. Similarly, the Elder
Siblings overlap but do not include all the Standard Bearers. The
Libarts colleges are represented in both the Radicals and Standard
Bearers; thus every institution in the study is included in at least
one of the two major classifications. Table 10 shows the correspondence of college or university code names to institutional
categories.

Table 10

FACULTY SAMPLES BY TYPES OF INSTITUTIONS

Standard Bearers .... North College; Alpha and Theta colleges,
MultiEastern; Beta College, Eastversity;
Delta College, Westversity; Valley campus
and Seaside campus, MultiWestern

Radicals .... South College; Zeta College, Eastversity;
Omega College, Westversity; Gamma and
Kappa colleges, Hilltop campus,
MultiWestern

Libarts .... North College, Midwest College, Southeast
College, South College

Elder Siblings .... Alpha and Theta colleges, MultiEastern;
Beta College, Eastversity; Delta College,
Westversity

Newcomers .... Zeta College, Eastversity; Omega College,
Westversity; Gamma and Kappa colleges,
Hilltop campus, and Sigma College, Bay
campus, MultiWestern

The chi square test was used on the data for these various cuts. In sorting questionnaire item data, responses were eliminated which involved comments placed in the margin qualifying the answer to such an extent that it was unclear whether the faculty member wanted his response coded one way or another. For the most part, this elimination of data did not affect the chi square sufficiently to change the interpretation. Also, when a faculty member did not respond to the question, or gave a variant reply, he was not included in the analysis. This made the interpretation of the significant difference easier as the responses were on the same scale (for example, *very important, somewhat important, not important*). Certain items were not tested because the response options were not scaled on such a continuum. With data modified in these ways, those differences which appear are differences between all those faculty members responding to the question by using the response categories available in the questionnaire.

The item analysis to follow will, unless otherwise specified, report only those differences significant at the .01 level of confidence. Comparative faculty data analyses to be reported are (1) Radicals versus Standard Bearers and (2) Libarts, Elder Siblings, and Newcomers. Faculty comparisons to be reported here are: (1) between Senior and Junior members, and by academic rank with Instructors grouped with Assistant Professors and Associate Professors grouped with full Professors; (2) according to the divisions of the liberal arts —humanities, social sciences, natural sciences; (3) by professional articles published: zero to three, four to ten, eleven and more; and (4) by teaching load, zero to eight hours and nine to sixteen hours.

Differences by Institutional Type

Educational Philosophy and Institutional Purposes. One key item on the Faculty Questionnaire ran:

When you were negotiating for your present job, was attention given through the correspondence, during the interviews, or in casual conversation, to the educational philosophy and objectives of the institution, particularly as compared to the details of the particular task for which you were being considered? (Please check one)

............Institutional objectives were treated at length, indeed at
       greater length than the particulars of the job.
............About equal attention was given to institutional objectives
       and job description.
............The institutional philosophy and educational purposes were
       mentioned, but in a tangential or ancillary way.
............The emphasis was clearly on the work of the department
       and the way my own training and interests would relate
       thereto.

Newcomers generally said that institutional objectives were treated
at greater length than the particulars of the job. Libarts said about
equal attention was given to each. Elder Siblings said that emphasis
was clearly on the work of the department.

Seventy-three per cent of the Radicals compared to only 6
per cent of the Standard Bearers reported that in job negotiations
institutional objectives were treated at greater length than the particulars of the job. Fifty-four per cent of the Standard Bearers and
just 1 per cent of the Radicals reported that the emphasis of the
interviews was on the work of the department.

Another key item in the Faculty Questionnaire posed this
question:

What proportion of the present faculty do you consider to be
seriously concerned, pro or con, with the formal institutional
purposes that are intended to give direction and character to your
college?

............Almost all
............Well over half
............About half
............One-fourth or so
............Very few
............Such things are not the concern of the faculty

(Note: Only the first response options were used in the analysis.) Newcomers judged that *almost all* of their colleagues were
seriously concerned with institutional objectives; Libarts felt that
well over half were so concerned; Elder Siblings said that *about half*
of their colleagues were of this mind.

A third item ran:

Do your colleagues express much loyalty for the history and
traditions of this institution?

(If you are a faculty member at a new college established within the general framework of a university, apply this question to that university.)

............About as much as faculties in similar institutions elsewhere
............More than in similar institutions elsewhere
............Less than in similar institutions elsewhere

Newcomers and Libarts tended to report that their colleagues expressed more loyalty for the history and traditions of their institution than was the case with the Elder Siblings. Newcomers saw their colleagues as generally expressing more loyalty than faculties in similar institutions elsewhere (Libarts wavered between "about as much" and "more than" but were different from Newcomers only at the .05 level). Elder Siblings felt that the situation at their institution regarding loyalty was about the same as elsewhere.

Radicals said that their colleagues expressed more loyalty for the history and traditions of the institution than faculties in similar institutions, but Standard Bearers thought that their colleagues expressed about as much loyalty as faculties elsewhere.

Conventional Standard of Excellence. Item 12 in the Faculty Questionnaire was a complex question inquiring into faculty attitudes toward the theoretical importance of a number of faculty activities. The heading and the first item, with response options, ran as follows:

Following you will find a list of many interests and responsibilities that engage the efforts of faculty members in American colleges and universities. Please rate them, first, in terms of their theoretical importance for *you* . . . then rate them according to their theoretical importance in the thinking of your present *faculty colleagues.*[1]

Professional meetings and attendant responsibilities

Personal View	*View of Others*
............Very important	............Very important
............Somewhat important	............Somewhat important
............Not important	............Not important

All three groups—Newcomers, Libarts, and Elder Siblings—saw professional meetings and attendant responsibilities as *somewhat*

[1] The body of Question 12 will hereafter be abbreviated as "The theoretical importance of . . ."

important. The only difference was in the self-ratings between Libarts and Newcomers where the Libarts rated the item higher.

This item was again given a rating of *somewhat important* by the Radicals and the Standard Bearers, but the Standard Bearers put more emphasis on it than did the Radicals in the Personal View section. The responses of the two groups were nearly identical in the View of Others section.

A second item in Question 12 asked about the theoretical importance of research and writing. In the self-ratings of this item, all three groups said that research and writing were *very important.* Newcomers gave this item more importance than Libarts did, however. Newcomers maintained their lead in the Others section by saying that this responsibility was *very important* for colleagues while the Libarts and the Elder Siblings lowered their ratings to *somewhat important.* Again, the only difference significant at the .01 level was between Newcomers and Libarts, but the Newcomers did differ from the Elder Siblings at the .05 level.

Standard Bearers regarded research and writing as *very important* for their colleagues and themselves. Radicals agreed that these opportunities were *very important* for themselves, but they rated them as only *somewhat important* for colleagues.

Change, Innovation, and Experimentation. Question 2 of the Faculty Questionnaire was another multi-item question inquiring into faculty attitudes. The heading, first item, and response options went as follows:

> The following are features of academic life that have a varying degree of importance for faculty members. Please rate them, first, in terms of their importance for *you.* Then rate them in terms of the importance you believe they have for faculty colleagues in your institution. (Please check.) [2]
> . . . an opportunity for experimentation and innovation.

Personal View	*View of Others*
............Very important	............Very important
............Somewhat important	............Somewhat important
............Not important	............Not important

[2] The body of Question 2 will hereafter be abbreviated as "The importance of . . . ," thereby differing from Question 12 which has been abbreviated as "The theoretical importance of . . . ."

An opportunity for experimentation and innovation was regarded by all three groups as *very important* for themselves, yet Newcomers said *very important* significantly more often than Elder Siblings. When speaking for Others, only Newcomers said *very important*—both Elder Siblings and Libarts said *somewhat important*. But Newcomers and Libarts were both significantly higher than Elder Siblings on this section of the question. Faculty respondents in colleges designated as Radicals placed more importance for themselves and for colleagues on an opportunity for experimentation and innovation than did Standard Bearers. The Radicals called it *very important* throughout while the Standard Bearers called it *very important* in the self-ratings, but only *somewhat important* in the View of Others.

Question 15 was constructed in a similar way:

Here are some ideas about higher education in the context of change. Check the category that best indicates *your personal* view on each of these matters.[3]

Too much emphasis is presently being placed on innovation and experimentation in higher education. Existing standards and arrangements are sound, and these should be achieved and utilized —not replaced.

..............Agree
..............Can't say
..............Disagree

Newcomers, Libarts, and Elder Siblings *all* disagreed that too much emphasis was being placed on innovation and experimentation. But the Elder Siblings' disagreement was not as strong as that of the Newcomers or the Libarts, however.

Similarly, while the Radicals and the Standard Bearers both tended to disagree that innovation and experimentation were overemphasized in higher education, the disagreement was not so strong among Standard Bearers as among Radicals.

Question 19 continued this explanation:

Please scale your faculty colleagues, as personal observation allows, on their attitude toward innovation and experimentation

[3] The body of Question 15 will hereafter be abbreviated as "Personal view of the idea that . . . ."

in the curriculum of your college by checking one response for each item:[4]

Seem to favor "change for change's sake"
..............Most
..............About half
..............Some
..............Very few

Fifty-nine per cent of the Standard Bearers and 46 per cent of the Radicals reported that *very few* of their colleagues seemed to favor change for change's sake, but the Standard Bearers were more confident that this was not the case at their institutions.

Another item under Question 19 asked about the proportion of colleagues willing to participate personally in experimental educational ventures. Newcomers felt that *most* of their colleagues were willing to participate in experimental educational ventures; Libarts estimated that *about half* of their colleagues were so inclined; Elder Siblings said that *some* of their colleagues would do this. These differences were significant at the .01 level. The majority of respondents from Radical institutions felt that *most* of their colleagues would be willing to participate personally in experimental educational ventures, while the majority of those from Standard Bearer institutions felt that only *some* of their colleagues would be so inclined.

An item under Question 19 asked about the proportion of colleagues not hostile to innovation, but unwilling to get involved personally. Elder Siblings reported more often than Libarts or Newcomers that this was true of their colleagues. *About half,* they said, were not hostile to innovation, but would likely be unwilling to get involved personally. The Libarts said that this was true for *some* of their colleagues. Newcomers differed from Libarts at the .05 level of confidence when they said that either *some* or *very few* of their peers were so disposed.

Standard Bearers felt that *about half* to *some* of their colleagues could be described as being not hostile to innovation, but unwilling to get involved personally. The majority of the Radicals felt that only a *very few* or *some* of their colleagues held such an

[4] Question 19 will be abbreviated as "proportion of colleagues . . . ."

attitude. Another item asked about the proportion of colleagues who hold to the principle that "nothing new must be tried for the first time." All three groups said that *very few* of their colleagues held to this notion. Elder Siblings reported that this was the case with more of their colleagues than was true for Newcomers. Eighty-seven per cent of the Radicals, compared to 66 per cent of the Standard Bearers, felt that *very few* of their colleagues believed that "nothing new must be tried for the first time."

When faculty were asked to judge the proportion of colleagues who believed that "if it is not necessary to change, it is necessary not to change," all three groups felt that this was true for only a *very few* of their colleagues. The estimate of the Newcomers was significantly smaller than that of the Elders or the Libarts, however. Seventy-five per cent of the Radicals felt that only a *very few* of their colleagues believed that "if it is not necessary to change, it is necessary not to change." Forty-eight per cent of the Standard Bearers said the same, but the two groups were found to differ statistically.

The Faculty Questionnaire data showed some differences in attitude toward specific innovations. An item under Question 2 asked about the importance of interdisciplinary faculty contacts and teaching opportunities. Libarts and Newcomers saw interdisciplinary faculty contacts and teaching opportunities as *very important* for themselves. They were significantly different in this regard from Elder Siblings who rated these contacts and opportunities as *somewhat important*. When speaking for their colleagues, Elder Siblings again rated the item less favorably than Libarts or Newcomers, but all groups saw it as *somewhat important*. Radicals considered interdisciplinary faculty contacts and teaching opportunities to be *very important* for themselves but *somewhat important* for colleagues. They placed more emphasis on this item than did Standard Bearers, who rated it as *somewhat important* for themselves as well as others.

What of the theoretical importance of cross-disciplinary teaching? The Elder Siblings did not consider cross-disciplinary teaching to be as important as did Newcomers and Libarts. The Elders rated it as only *somewhat important* for themselves while

Libarts wavered between *somewhat important* and *very important* and Newcomers said *very important*. The relationship between the three groups was the same when they spoke of their colleagues, but the ratings were lower—Newcomers and Libarts saying *somewhat important* and Elder Siblings saying *not important*. Radicals placed more emphasis on cross-disciplinary teaching than did Standard Bearers. The self-rating of the Radicals was *very important* while that of the Standard Bearers was *somewhat important*. When rating colleagues both groups said *somewhat important,* but the Radicals were still more favorably disposed toward this innovation.

On the theoretical importance of tutorials and other one-to-one student-faculty learning arrangements, there were no significant differences between Newcomers, Libarts, and Elder Siblings in the Personal View responses, although the majority of Newcomers called it *very important* while the other group said *somewhat important*. In the View of Others section, all three groups generally called tutorials *somewhat important,* but Newcomers gave the item a more favorable rating than was the case with Elder Siblings. Radicals rated tutorials and other one-to-one student-faculty learning arrangements as *very important* for themselves but *somewhat important* for colleagues. They nevertheless placed more importance on this item than did the Standard Bearers who rated it *somewhat important* consistently.

Professional Activities.   An item under Question 12 asked about faculty attitude toward the importance of opportunities for professional advancement. When speaking of themselves, the majority of the Standard Bearers felt that opportunities for professional advancement were *very important,* while the Radicals split their sentiments between *very important* and *somewhat important*. But the difference in emphasis between these groups was not significant except in the View of Others section. Here, the Standard Bearers placed more emphasis on the feature than did the Radicals.

On the importance of an emphasis on teaching there was no difference among Newcomers, Libarts, and Elder Siblings in the Personal View section of the question, all tending to call it *very important*. But when speaking for their colleagues, the Libarts group put more importance on this than the other two groups. Radicals placed more importance than Standard Bearers on an emphasis on teaching.

One item under Question 12 asked about the theoretical importance of student advising and counseling. Libarts put more emphasis on student advising and counseling than either the Elder Siblings or the Newcomers. In the View of Others section the difference between the Libarts and the Elder Siblings remained. All three groups generally judged it as *somewhat important* for colleagues. Both Radicals and Standard Bearers split their ratings between *very important* and *somewhat important* in the Personal View section of this item. When they rated their colleagues, Radicals put more emphasis on student advising and counseling than did Standard Bearers, but both groups called this *somewhat important*.

The University in the Societal Context. An item under Question 15 asked about faculty agreement or disagreement with the idea that the concept of *in loco parentis* is unnecessary and undesirable because students should have the freedoms and responsibilities of adults. The Newcomers showed stronger agreement than the other two groups with the idea that *in loco parentis* is unnecessary, but all three groups generally agreed with the statement. Both Radicals and Standard Bearers agreed with this idea, but among the Standard Bearers there were more respondents who disagreed than there were among Radicals.

Another item explored faculty attitude on the idea that course work should be more relevant to the social and political realities in the world outside the campus. The only statistically significant difference on this question was between Radicals and Standard Bearers. Both groups agreed, but the Standard Bearers' agreement was not so strong as that of the Radicals.

Miscellaneous Subjects (Personal, Social, Intellectual). Faculty were asked whether it was true that at their institution not enough emphasis is placed on shaping the student's moral and ethical values. Newcomers, Elder Siblings, and Standard Bearers all denied that this was the case in their institution. Elder Siblings showed less disagreement than the other two groups, however. The difference between Radicals and Standard Bearers on this question was sharp. Again, both groups disagreed, but among the Radicals only 17 per cent agreed, while the corresponding figure among Standard Bearers was 42 per cent.

Faculty were asked how—apart from any formal religious affiliation—they would describe themselves in the area of religion? The response options ran as follows:

..........Deeply religious

..........Moderately religious

..........Largely indifferent to religion

..........Basically opposed to religion

The Libarts declared themselves to be religious more often than the Newcomers or the Elder Siblings. They most frequently said they were *moderately religious* but several said they were *deeply religious*. Elders wavered between rating themselves as *moderately religious* and *largely indifferent to religion*. Newcomers most frequent said they *were basically opposed to religion,* but they did not differ significantly from the Elder Siblings.

Differences According to Faculty Characteristics

Rank. When Junior (one to six years) faculty were compared to Senior (seven or more years) faculty, significant differences were found on only two items. The first of these read: "Too much emphasis is presently being placed on innovation and experimentation in higher education. Existing standards and arrangements are sound, and these should be achieved and utilized—not replaced." Both groups generally disagreed, but Juniors showed stronger disagreement than Seniors.

The second area of differentiation was on the concept of *in loco parentis:* "The concept of *in loco parentis* is unnecessary and undesirable because students should have the freedoms and responsibilities of adults." Juniors showed stronger support for this idea than Seniors, but both groups generally agreed.

When instructors were grouped because of their small number ($N = 16$) with assistant professors, and associate professors were combined with full professors, the results were the same as when grouping faculty by the number of years of full-time teaching, except at one point. On the item that asked faculty about the importance to them of an opportunity to influence department policies, the higher ranking faculty placed more importance on such opportunities than did instructors and assistant professors.

On all other items in the areas mentioned and in the areas of educational philosophy and general institutional purposes, the Standard, and miscellaneous personal, social and intellectual values, there were no statistically significant differences between Junior and Senior or between the academic rank divisions of faculty.

Academic Disciplines. When the faculty sample was sorted by the classical divisions of the liberal arts—humanities, social sciences, and natural sciences—differences were significant on only three items. All three groups agreed to the statement which read: "Radical technological changes in our society necessitate radical changes in the educational experiences offered our youth, not because the past was bad, but because the future will be different." Yet the social scientists and the natural scientists showed more agreement with this than did faculty in the humanities. The groups also differed in the extent of their agreement with the following statement: "Course work should be more relevant to the social and political realities in the world outside the campus." Social science faculty members showed more agreement with this than humanities faculty or natural scientists. The natural scientists, in fact, showed only a tenuous agreement.

A difference at the level of personal, social, and intellectual values was found in faculty responses to a quotation on relativism:

> For some decades now, in the humanities and in the social sciences, they [faculty members] have been preaching the dogma of relativism—ethical, historical, axiological, epistemological. On most of our campuses the dogma gets its most unequivocal expression in courses in philosophy, history, anthropology, and sociology. One finds it also in political science and in the fine arts. But when these evangelists of relativism are suddenly threatened in some value which they themselves deeply cherish, they are at once absolutists. It does not occur to them that the academic freedom and the pursuit of truth, which they so ardently extol, have been made meaningless by their own pronouncements. It is not a tyrannical administration, nor reckless students, nor scoundrelly regents that have shaken their strength. It is they themselves who have cut out the ground under their feet.
>
> —Robert E. Fitch

Humanities faculty and natural scientists generally felt that this statement was correct, but social scientists did not.

Data stratification did not reveal any other differences in the themes mentioned above or in the realm of educational philosophy and general institutional purposes, the Standard, specific innovations, or professional activities.

Number of Publications. Faculty were separated into three categories according to the number of articles reported published: those who had published three articles or fewer, those who had published from four to ten, and those who had published eleven or more. For the most part, differences that were found concerned the relative importance of teaching and research, the importance placed on research increasing with the number of articles published.

Three items exemplary of this trend follow: One item concerned the importance of the "availability of research money and facilities." Faculty members who had published three or fewer articles called this feature *somewhat important*—a significantly lower rating than that given by those who had published either four to ten or eleven or more articles. Both of these latter groups called the availability of research money and facilities *very important*.

A similar item asked faculty to judge the importance for themselves of research and writing. Those faculty members who had published eleven or more articles placed more importance on these matters than did faculty who had published either from four to ten or from zero to three articles. (Likewise, those who had published from four to ten articles were more concerned for research and writing than those who had published three or less, but this difference was significant only at the .05 level.)

A third item concerned the relative importance of an emphasis on teaching. All three groups rated this as *very important,* but the group publishing the least found it to be more important than did the other two groups.

On the importance of an opportunity for experimentation and innovation, the data show that such an opportunity was more important to those who had published eleven or more articles than to either of the other two groups. The difference between those who had published eleven or more articles and those who had published three or fewer was significant only at the .05 level, however, and all three groups declared this to be *very important*.

The specific innovation of student participation in academic governance was received differently by those who had published fewer than four articles than by those who had published eleven or more. All three groups answered *no* when asked: "Should students at your college participate more significantly than they do at present in the formulation and implementation of academic policies, that is, in establishing the content and organization of courses, on academic policy committees, by student-formed and student-led seminars?" Those faculty who had published least were not so negative as those who had published most.

Faculty stratified by the number of articles published showed no statistically significant differences on the other items of the Faculty Questionnaire.

Teaching Load. Faculty respondents were divided in another section of the cross-cuts into two groups determined by undergraduate teaching load. The first group consisted of faculty members who reported that they taught eight or fewer hours per week of undergraduate classes; the second group consisted of those who reported teaching from nine to sixteen hours.

The group teaching fewer classes differed in predictable ways from the group teaching more. Faculty spending fewer hours in the classroom concerned themselves more with research and the group spending more hours teaching concerned themselves with teaching rather than research. In similar vein, those faculty members teaching less than nine hours of classes placed more importance on research money and facilities than those who taught more. The results were similar for responses to the item that concerned the importance of research and writing. The first group again put more emphasis on these features than did the second.

In the area of change, innovation, and experimentation, the two faculty groups were at odds over only one specific innovation. Those who taught fewer than nine hours of classes placed less importance on interdisciplinary faculty contacts and teaching opportunities than faculty in the other group.

With respect to items under Question 2 of the Faculty Questionnaire dealing with the importance of professional advancement and the importance of an emphasis on teaching, there were some differences. "An opportunity for professional advancement" was *very important* for faculty teaching fewer than nine hours but only *somewhat important* for those teaching more. "An emphasis on teaching" was more important for faculty who taught more often than for those who taught less often. Both groups, however, declared this to be *very important*.

When stratified by undergraduate teaching load, faculty differed not at all with respect to general attitudes toward change, innovation, and experimentation; the means for implementing innovations; their ideas of the university in the societal context; and on various personal, social, and intellectual values.

Different and Like

These cross-cuts on faculty data, whether by age categories, publications, academic specializations, teaching load; whether old or new schools, conventional or innovative, show that faculty are more alike than dissimilar in their attitudes toward educational assumptions, values, and goals; the criteria for institutional excellence; and the prospects for professional or institutional change.

There are, to be sure, important gradations of difference when the professional groups are compared on certain items; that is, younger faculty are less inclined than older to support the concept of *in loco parentis,* with its corollary of parietal rules, and social scientists are more likely than people in the humanities or natural sciences to think that the institution of higher education should be more responsive to social change. However, over against these gradations, on item after item there were no statistically significant differences among faculty while comparative data analyses made clear their overwhelming degree of likemindedness. Differences that appear were often a matter of degree: A small majority in one group and a large majority in the other had chosen the same response, the conditions of statistical significance were satisfied— the two or three groups could be declared as "different"—but the question remained as to whether the difference was sufficient to claim that an alternative set of values had been presented. On the other hand, it should not be concluded that the differences that do exist on campus, or that appear to be emerging there, are unimportant. They may prove to be the first fruits of a bumper crop of changes leading to substantive differentiation in American higher education.

It can be said, however, that most colleges and universities, administrators and faculty alike, have become the victims of their own rhetoric, suffering the consequences of their own use of language, because they have claimed the presence of diversity that was not there and, worse, they have professed loyalty to diversity they did not practice. It may be a matter of error compounded by hypocrisy.

When faculty were invited to indicate their agreement or disagreement with the Robert Hutchins assertion "The duty of the faculty is to formulate the purposes and programs of the university. The duty of the regents [trustees] is to interpret and defend them," respondents from Newcomers, Libarts, and Elder Siblings institutions all agreed with the quotation. However, faculty in the Elder Sibling group said, in response to another item, that only about half of their colleagues were seriously concerned, pro or con, with the institutional purposes that were supposed to give direction and character to their colleges or universities. At yet another point, they said that when they were employed negotiations had been focused on the work of the department, not on general institutional objectives. Clearly, for one reason or another, large numbers of faculty and administrators have not been giving themselves very seriously to those areas of concern which faculty have claimed to be their proper domain. They may not have done so because of technical or legal barriers, frustration, negligence, or the press of competing loyalties, but the result has been a takeover by a superinstitutional value orientation—professionalism, with a loss of value diversity.

However, if attention is given more to those cross-cuts of faculty by types of institutions—Newcomers, Libarts, Elder Siblings, or Radicals and Standard Bearers—than to data from the various professional groupings—years of experience, teaching loads, specializations, publications—there is reason to speak of improved prospects for change. There was, for example, marked differentiation between faculty at the new cluster colleges as compared to faculty at the older colleges of the same universities in such areas as awareness of institutional purposes and loyalty to those purposes. This may be evidence of an available mechanism, the cluster college concept, that encourages correctives to the aforementioned problems of ignorance and evasion.

The Newcomer colleges as well as the Radicals showed tendencies to break away from the dominance of the conventional criteria of excellence and to become institutional probes of alternative futures. They were more interested than the Standard Bearers in change, innovation, and experimentation.

The Libarts group also emerged with points of distinction, as in their commitment to student advising and counseling. Usually, however, these colleges stood between Newcomers and Radicals on the one hand and Elder Siblings and Standard Bearers on the other. They were not trailing behind, as those who position institutions by the conventional marks of excellence would have us believe, but they were somewhere in between, behind the leaders of change but in front of those former pace setters who have allowed the burden of their "honors" to make them fall behind.

Those persons who favor the standardization of higher education in this country, believing that there are certain assumptions about the role of educational institutions to which all schools should aspire if not adhere, and believing that there is or can be agreement on what constitutes liberal education, the sociology of learning or how teaching and learning should be structured, may take comfort from the data of this study which seem to show that the overwhelming majority of faculty are so much alike. The standard of conventional excellence continues to be well represented.

Those persons who favor diversification in structures and functions, yet also of values and styles, to the point of creating viable alternative tracks to the achievement of conventional standards of excellence, or who favor change to the point of transforming established thinking about education, certification, and socialization, may take comfort from the emergence of colleges in established universities, here called Newcomers and often Radicals, where evidence seems to be accumulating that structural and organizational provisions for change do help to effect it, that faculty can be found whose values on important issues are different, or, if not that, who are at least open to change because they are in an atmosphere where they are constantly reminded that their institution has a will to be different.

VIII

Beyond Conformity

Every college or university has character in the sense that it has characteristic programs or activities by which the institution can be identified. Indeed, these administrative and organizational differences, plus their quantitative and qualitative effects, have been the basis for the claim that America has the world's most diversified system of education. But does diversity in structures and functions mean diversity at the level of basic values? Given the range in types of institutions and the variety of roles for individuals within them, it would seem likely that value differentiation as a consequence of role differentiation would be a conspicuous feature of college and university life and an integral part of the diversity claimed for the system. However, it is precisely this "obvious" outcome that was not supported by the findings of the Institutional Character research project. Beneath diverse structures and functions we found uniformity in educational assumptions and sociopolitical values across major interest groups and in various types of institutions.

This general conclusion will be emphasized throughout this chapter because of its far reaching significance: American higher education has been characterized by conformity where diversity is needed, that is, at the level of values. External variety and surface change have concealed the conformity and rigidity in fundamental values even as false confidence that differences in external forms and appearances must result in varied internal assumptions, or, from another theoretical perspective, that differences in structure and function are always manifestations of differences in values, have diverted attention from that prerequisite to significant change—examination of the deep values.

Values have been present and operating, though poorly understood and seldom examined, at a time when major changes in the institution of higher education were needed but could not be effected without conscious attention to values. As Sir Walter Moberly stated over twenty years ago, the question is not whether educational institutions will have assumptions or basic values, but whether those things which motivate and direct practices will remain as unexamined presuppositions and unacknowledged commitments or will be consciously and persistently reviewed, then reaffirmed or, when necessary, changed.[1]

Certain developments in contemporary society have made essential a deliberate evaluation of the philosophy and basic value orientation of American colleges and universities. One is the rapid rate of societal change. Because the institution of higher education is a service institution, a conception of its nature to which nearly everyone assents (even educators who opt for it to be a center for independent thinking do so in order that it may "serve" society by criticism and creativity), attitudes and functions that characterize the institution must be reviewed for their relevance. Only so can the educational services offered to society be kept congruent with society's needs.

The second feature of contemporary life that has necessitated institutional self-analysis is the emergence of the new youth movement. These young people have forced colleges and universities to examine their structures and functions—governance configurations, service roles, teaching and learning theories, political relationships. The new youth have been challenging not only the utility of in-

[1] Walter Moberly, *The Crisis in the University* (London: SCM Press, 1949), p. 62,

stitutional arrangements but the adequacy of the institution's basic ideology. No longer can professors or administrators assume support in the student body for what academics have traditionally proposed to do, any more than for what they have actually done or the way they have done it. There is now no consensus and there is greatly reduced confidence. The institution of higher education is required as never before to prove the viability for the future of its structures and functions and, even more, its assumptions, values, and goals.

If the institution is to be validated, it seems essential to ask: Are there functions that set the institution of higher education off from others? If not, why not? If so, what are they? How does the structure of a college or university support or inhibit, form or deform its functions? What are the ends on behalf of which the means operate? Out of the amalgam of purposes, organizations, and activities does anything really distinctive emerge? Can it be said that there is something that gives direction, vitality, or moral excellence to what goes on in the institution?

Getting answers to these questions requires examination of general institutional purposes and, we feel, the emphasis today must be put on that task. But it is important to examine means as well as ends. Christian Bay has written:

> . . . every college, ideal in design or not, soon becomes an institutionalized social system in which a fairly stable system of compromises is established. This latter system, with varying degrees of success, reconciles educational ideals with the variety of incentives and motives of the persons who occupy the significant roles inside and outside the college.[2]

Nevitt Sanford accepts the necessity for the study of goals as well as social processes but also warns of what may result:

> The study of objectives must be continued. We do not know enough about the relationship of means to ends; it may be that means that now appear to be necessary to the attainment of one goal actually tend to prevent the others that we deem no less essential.[3]

[2] Christian Bay, "A Social Theory of Higher Education," in N. Sanford (Ed.), *The American College* (New York: Wiley, 1962), p. 987.
[3] Nevitt Sanford, "Research and Policy in Higher Education," in N. Sanford (Ed.), *The American College* (New York: Wiley, 1962), p. 1031.

Because present institutional arrangements may be self-contradictory and in conflict with institutional purposes, and because institutional purposes, assumptions, and goals seem to have escaped critical analysis and may not be clear or vital, this and similar studies have focused on the interface between ideology and action. If traditional norms are to survive in colleges and universities, program anomalies must be removed and distortions reduced. If suspected contradictions are found in organization or performance, with assumptions weak or irrelevant, new goals and arrangements for the future must be devised. In all of this both form and content are crucial factors, as is the interaction between them.

Studies of institutional change have tended to concentrate on inducements—contributions, showing the importance of rewards and sanctions for achieving innovations and urging that change leadership be skilled in incentive management; or researchers have emphasized the organizational monolith and have advocated breaking it into more manageable subunits where "goal factoring" and "means-ends chains" can be established, with leadership concentrating on proximate objectives and operational criteria. Thus a complex organization may be changed by bits and pieces, by tending to the parts that make up the whole.[4] Successful innovation, from either theoretical approach, is dependent on the innovator's ability to manipulate an otherwise dominant environment.

But as Schiff and others have noted, not enough emphasis in research or in the literature of organizational theory has been given to the role of fundamental administrative outlooks or basic professional ideologies. For this lack there has seemed to be good reason. General statements of direction involve value assumptions that seldom yield manageable hypotheses and never result in clean empirical data. "Their almost metaphysical character," says Schiff, in an illustration of academic understatement, "is perhaps disconcerting to students seeking more manageable analytical categories."[5]

Because the Institutional Character study centered on fundamental outlooks and basic ideologies, emphasizing the what and

[4] Ashley Schiff, "Innovation and Administrative Decision-making: A Study of the Conservatism of Land Resources," *Administrative Science Quarterly*, 2(1), 1966, pp. 1–2.
[5] *Ibid.*

why of institutional life more than the how, when, and where, the
methodology for the study included provisions for what Erik Erikson
called "disciplined subjectivism." The project's research was not
empirical throughout, unless the term is allowed to include observation and experience as much as experimental or quantitative data
(and of course the word can quite properly be used that way).
What was emphasized was research defined as "disciplined inquiry": research carried out with an awareness of its historical context and methodological limitations; with norms, values, or biases
clearly stated; language and concepts purposefully employed; and
results open and available for analysis by other scholars.

Too much research these days, in our opinion, errs on the
side of "data fixation" (Kenneth Boulding) within discrete projects
that are manageable in terms of research methodology but meaningless for institutional policy making. While the following statement
from Will Durant is extreme and divisive, it conveys the reason
researchers in this project sought to maintain an open stance toward
relevant, albeit complex, issues. Durant warned forty years ago that
". . . inductive data fall upon us from all sides like the lava of
Vesuvius; we suffocate with uncoordinated facts; our minds are
overwhelmed with sciences breeding and multiplying into specialistic chaos for want of synthetic thought and a unifying philosophy."[6]

The crucial variables for this project in determining an institution's integrative value system have included educational philosophy—those traditions, myths, assumptions, articulated goals,
and inarticulate desires that go into an ideology; the structural or
organizational norms by which the educational environment today
is organized—the main feature of which is the conventional standard of excellence; and finally, various forms of innovation or experimentation as expressions of change. They have been studied in
relation to each other and with special attention to the effect of any
perceived form of institutional distinctiveness on the person, whatever his role or place in the school.

Researchers hoped by interviews, observation, and the use
of questionnaires to determine how institutional character was perceived and what it meant for the lives of people associated with the

[6] Will Durant, *The Story of Philosophy* (New York: Simon and
Schuster, 1926), p. 102.

academic community. Would institutional character be defined in essentially quantitative terms and by structural and organizational forms or in more qualitative terms and by axiological categories that might not be evident in the institution's organization chart but were crucial to the lives of people who populated the categories and acted out the roles? Would there be differences between institutions, at the level of basic values, sufficient to satisfy the diversity in attitudes, abilities, and interests to be found in the extended range of people, young and old, who are now seeking the benefits of higher education?

In the first chapter it was stated that whereas the diversity of form and function in higher education had been heretofore regarded as the chief distinguishing characteristic of the American system of education,[7] that system seemed to be shifting toward diversity in values, toward programs and institutions characterized by substantive differences in norms, styles, and outcomes. Differences quantitative. it was suggested, showed promise of becoming differences qualitative; differences in degree were on the way to becoming differences in kind. The challenge for educators was to become aware of such distinctions and, indeed, to accept them as a positive good. Now, in the conclusions, it is necessary to acknowledge that there was no widespread evidence, in any of the prime interest groups at colleges in the Institutional Character study, of commitment to value diversity to the point that such differences would not only be tolerated but encouraged, could not only survive but actually prosper. Some students, faculty, and administrators showed interest in the creation of a system of higher education where various institutional models featuring different assumptions, values, and goals would be active and respected, but they were exceptions. Yet they were harbingers of change. Diversity in values as well as in organization and structure was a matter of growing curiosity and concern during the time of the study and seems just now, in 1969, under the pressure of various developments on campus and off, to

[7] See Talcott Parsons and Gerald Platt, *The Academic Profession* (preliminary report) for a statement of praise for the supposedly differentiated system of higher education in this country. Also the Study of Selected Institutions, to be published by the Center for Research and Development in Higher Education, University of California, Berkeley.

be emerging as fact—not as an option for sentimentalists but as a necessity for national survival, not because of past practices but in spite of them.

Absence of Holistic Planning

Most administrators and faculty in the project samples were giving little attention to and seemed to have only a minimal interest in the educational philosophy of their institution. They had no coherent rationale, no compelling vision for the college. Consequently, they found it difficult to answer questions about institutional goals or to describe their school's integrative value system.

There are several reasons for the inability or unwillingness of faculty and administrators to think and plan holistically. Often their condition is caused by a lack of practice, growing out of a lack of interest, and resulting in a lack of skill. Faculty, oriented to disciplines and guilds, think of institutional goals in terms of their associations and priorities. Research tends to confirm the frequently heard assertion that faculty are more likely to feel loyalty to their professional guild than they are to the institution in which they work. Administrators, also specialists, are busy with their particular functions and, therefore, have no time or preference for general goal formulation. Daily pressures force long-term considerations of this sort off their agenda. Therefore, like faculty, they are uncertain and uncomfortable when asked to take up the integrative, generalist role presidents and deans once played so actively.

In other cases, unwillingness to get involved in institutional goal formulation is due to a feeling of futility. Faculty and administration see the prospect of endless controversy in these matters and have no hope of ever achieving closure. Educators have not been able, viewed historically, to show the superiority of one educational philosophy over another; the idealists, from Plato to Hegel, took a stand for the primacy of trans-historic verities, for universals or absolutes, while the realists, from Aristotle to Mill, made the case for the dignity of men and ideas in and of this world. In more recent time came the perennialists—Hutchins and Barr; the progressivists—James and Dewey; the analytic philosophers—Wittgenstein and Russell; the existentialists—Kierkegaard and Heidegger. All these schools of thought and these philosophical theoreticians have been persuasive, yet they have failed to persuade, in the sense of winning a dominant position in the field. Because educators have been unable to prove the superiority of one educational philosophy over another, or to incorporate several explicit philosophies in a given institution without fratricidal warfare, it has seemed expedient to many administrators and faculty to play down the whole business. A vacuum seemed better than a whirlwind.

Three comments should be made concerning what has transpired: First, the pressure of difficult problems has never been, in academe, an acceptable reason for the abandonment of the search for true answers. In the natural sciences, complexities have been reason for the intensification of efforts to resolve them. Should not scholarship be as disciplined and persistent in the moral subjects as in the nonmoral? Is it appropriate, then, that the quest for value certitude should be abandoned on the ground of rival claims and attendant difficulties?

A second comment develops a point made earlier. The absence of open commitments forming an integrative value system does not mean that there are no values or philosophical assumptions operating in the institutional context. This research does not support the contention that a value vacuum exists on American college and university campuses. There is, to be sure, a lack of conscious involvement in or collective resolution of these issues today; but, as always, for institutions as for individuals, an educational rationale with attendant "behavior supports" is operating at all times. Nowhere do men teach just anything; everywhere they exercise selection, taking one thing, rejecting something else. And philosophical norms, consciously or unconsciously espoused, provide criteria for selection, continuation, and change.

To illustrate: colleges and universities have emphasized a "philosophy" featuring cognitive rationality. The superiority of communicating knowledge by rational processes has long been assumed by academics. Approaching the emotions by the mind has been favored over coming to the mind by the emotions. The goals have been scholarly objectivity without running off into dogmatic absolutism, intellectual relativism without yielding to individual subjectivism.

There has also been general commitment in institutions of

higher learning to certain class and caste values. Discrimination—racial, attitudinal, stylistic—has been and is rampant. Rewards and sanctions, the departmental organization of learning, professional specializations, the distribution of power within the institution—all these structures and functions have supported class or caste distinctions.[8]

It is mistaken to say, therefore, that there are no shared values on American campuses. There are fundamental norms and various preconceptions that have made possible the program diversity that so much enamours us while encouraging a value conformity that may now be our chief threat. (Because most faculty and administrators have not been "stalkers of meaning," the educational philosophy of the school has been determined willy-nilly by the pressure of external circumstances or methodological biases, by hoary tradition or anticipatory opportunism.)[9]

The paucity of conscious attention to institutional values and an excess of conformity to superinstitutional academic and social values does not mean that this state of affairs must inevitably continue. This is the third comment. Although administrators, faculty, and most students were poorly equipped and personally reluctant to talk about institutional goals, it became evident that certain developments in contemporary life, including those mentioned earlier, were prompting new concern for the purposes behind institutional programs. Social unrest, technological change, and especially the new youth movement, plus anxiety on campus about the relationship of institutions of higher education to these social forces, now compel educators young and old to think contextually if not holistically.

Evidence of propensity to change was most apparent among

[8] Warren Martin, "Education as Intervention," *Educational Record,* 50(1), 1969, pp. 47–48.

[9] Senator J. W. Fulbright has warned, as have others, of the consequences for the modern university when it strikes an "arrangement of convenience, providing the government with politically usable knowledge and the universities with badly needed funds. . . . The price can be the surrender of independence, the neglect of teaching, and the distortion of scholarship." Fulbright has been especially concerned about universities betraying their fundamental purpose, which purpose is, he says, in the words of James Bryce, to "'. . . reflect the spirit of the times without yielding to it.'" (*Chronicle of Higher Education,* Vol. II, No. 8 [December 21, 1967], p. 3.)

students. Entering freshmen showed concern for the social relevance
of the program of the institution of higher education and seemed
to have no trouble accepting the old-fashioned idea that a college
or university should be based on heady idealism. Not that most
students were daring or adventuresome with values or theory; except
for a small minority in most schools and a large minority in a few
schools, students were conventionally oriented. Nevertheless, comparatively, they were in the vanguard of an emerging concern for
educational philosophy and the basic purposes of higher education,
and their concern is having an effect on faculty and administrators.
While students were the first to turn again to the normative questions, talking increasingly about what Dostoevsky called in *The
Brothers Karamazov*, "the eternal questions," the questions of
". . . what do you believe or don't you believe at all?"[10], their insistent questioning is forcing older members of the academic community to give provisional answers to student questions if not final
ones, certitudes if not answers of absolute certainty. The realization
seems to be growing that where there is no philosophical framework, faculty as well as students lack an institutional standard
against which to test themselves. Faculty need such a standard because they are at the stage of life when, as Erik Erikson put it, the
issue is integrity, just as students need it because they are at the
stage in life where, as Edgar Friedenberg has shown, the issue is
self-identity. Neither faculty nor students can decide such issues in
a void. (A measure of the peril in higher education today is the
fact that at a time when institutions as well as individuals are expected to have character, the experiences, habits, and paradigms of

---

[10] Dostoevsky used the phrase "the eternal questions" to refer to
fundamental issues about the nature of reality. But questions of that order
and social questions are, as the following quotation asserts, "the same questions turned inside out."

> . . . Talking about nothing but the eternal questions . . . what
> do you believe or don't you believe at all? . . . of the eternal questions,
> of the existence of God and immortality. And those who do not believe
> in God talk of socialism and anarchism, of the transformation of all
> humanity on a new pattern, so that it all comes out to the same, they're
> the same questions turned inside out . . . .

F. Dostoevsky, *The Brothers Karamazov* (New York: Modern Library,
1950), p. 277.

most educators have not prepared them for this kind of leadership. Thus, it is not at all certain that they can do what the times require.)

The observation of an emerging concern for establishing fundamental values in the schools must be qualified not only with respect to students vis-à-vis faculty or administrators but also with respect to types of institutions. Interest in achieving a sense of shared purpose was more evident in the smaller colleges. In these places there was concern for precision in declaring goals and an awareness of their effects. At the older and larger institutions, conceptualizations about the nature of the university were either ignored or scorned by all interest groups while roles, functions, and structural forms were emphasized. The larger the institution, especially if under public control, the more educational philosophy and broad integrative objectives were written off as meaningless rhetoric or were thought of by respondents as matters beyond the control of administrators or faculty and set by the state, the constituencies, or impersonal forces within the institution. But this qualification needs further refinement. In the semiautonomous, innovative colleges operating within large universities, knowledge about and concern for educational philosophy and integrative institutional objectives within that subunit and concerning the relationship of that program to the total enterprise was most evident of all.

In the preceding chapter, comparative data analyses of the "Radical" colleges (four out of five were semiautonomous, innovative subunits within established universities) versus the "Standard Bearers" were given on the item in the faculty questionnaire dealing with the attention given during job negotiations to educational philosophy and institutional objectives compared with departmental considerations and professional specializations. Seventy-three per cent of the respondents in Radical colleges compared to only 6 per cent in the institutions designated Standard Bearers reported that general objectives were treated at length. Meanwhile, 54 per cent of the faculty from Standard Bearers and 1 per cent of the Radicals said that the emphasis during job interviews was predominantly on the departmental specializations.

Students, faculty, and administrators in new colleges, including colleges under public auspices, become by the very nature of their situation quite self-conscious about educational assumptions, goals, and values, especially if their programs are located in close proximity to and in competition with other units of the same university. Their involvement with these concerns can act as a prod toward the achievement of institutional character. The establishment of new colleges within the general structure of the existing institution provides a mechanism for confronting value questions and probing alternative answers.

Lack of Diversity

Contrary to the thinking of most educators, but in line with project findings alluded to earlier, substantive value diversity is not characteristic of American higher education. Diversity in organizational, methodological, and structural matters had led to confusion about diversity in values. So much has been made of differences between public-private, university-liberal arts, rural-urban higher education that it is believed that because people organize themselves differently they must be different in ideals and aspirations. A necessary distinction between operational diversity and value diversity is often missed—between what people do and what they aspire to be, between practices and the picture dominating their imagination.

That academics fill diversified roles is unmistakable. That they are affected by those roles is equally certain. But our data suggest that behind professional roles is a shared ideology by which institutional outcomes are judged and by which individual worth is measured. The attitude a man brings to his work influences how the work will influence him. This is a variation of the insight emphasized by left-radical students when they speak of power being in the eyes of the beholder.

For academics today the undergirding ideology is professionalism or, as it is called, the "professional orientation," for which the autonomous research scholar is the paradigm. Faculty may be separated into departments and specializations, or by methodological preferences, but they are united in wanting to be professionals. Administrators, too, have differing functions and perspectives. Academic administrators differ in emphases from, say, personnel deans. But behind these operational differences is a great similarity in basic values. They, like faculty, have areas of competence. They want professional acceptance. At the level of academic aspiration, values merge.

There is a distinction between faculty and administrators regarding sociopolitical values. Administrators, more than faculty, are inclined to cling, when pressed, to the sociopolitical values of the societal status quo. A study of critical incidents on campus in project schools showed that administrators accepted without serious question the fundamental assumptions of the Western liberal tradition which, after all, underlie liberal education. These assumptions have to do with man as a rational being; with community, consensus, and order; with certain ideas about the family, home, property, race, work, nationalism, democracy, free enterprise, science, and technology. The consequences of these commitments are that administrators think of change in terms of traditional conceptualizations of issues and of reform consistent with established values. They are not inclined to favor radical alternatives or think of reform leading to the transformation of conventional values, of evolution culminating in revolution. There was no substantive value diversity—political, social, or moral—among administrators. They were more uniform in their thinking than faculty or students. The conclusion may be depicted in a pyramidal model of value diminution. Most open to value diversity were students; they are represented by the base line of the pyramid. There was less openness among faculty, and least among top administrators. Thus, value diversity diminishes as one climbs the institutional pyramid.

When one looks at surface manifestations of campus life, at roles played and behavior manifested, there appears to be in American institutions of higher education a great deal of diversity —in programs, styles, objectives, even values. Those things that are valued, roles or relationships in the personal, social, or professional realms, are confused with values. Value diversity is claimed on the basis of the multiplicity of things valued by individuals and groups.

But values, properly understood, operate beneath surface choices and act as criteria or normative standards. Beneath choices that are valued in the personal life is the normative value of self-interest; beneath social attitudes and actions is the basic need for social acceptance, the value base for that which is valued; behind professional roles and functions is the deep value, professionalism.

> . . . it is not the fact of preference or choice but the standard in accordance with which it was made that really matters. And when this point is brought out into the open, the critical or normative aspect of the value situation is disclosed at the same time. For the value aspect resides in the criterion determining the critical response.[11]

Without getting into the issue of how people acquire their basic values—is it something in the family history, a matter of metabolism, a generic strain?—or into whether the justification for human values is ultimately rational or irrational,[12] or further into the unending disputes over Platonic "categories" and Aristotelian "realism," we assert that the commitments of faculty, administration, and students show a lack of diversity and an excess of value conformity.

One of the most significant research projects reported in 1968 was the study by Edward Gross and Paul Grambsch entitled *University Goals and Academic Power*.[13] These researchers sent out a questionnaire listing forty-seven goals for American universities to 16,000 administrators and faculty in sixty-eight universities (1964). Each respondent (7200, 62 per cent administrators) was to indicate on a five-point scale how much emphasis he felt each goal received at his institution and, additionally, how much each should receive. Thus the questionnaire provided perceived and preferred goal structures.

The results of this study generally support the thesis resulting from the Institutional Character findings that there is a paucity of diversity and an excess of conformity across interest

[11] John Smith, *Value Convictions and Higher Education* (New Haven: Hazen Foundation, 1959), p. 18.

[12] In John Barth's novel, *The Floating Opera*, one of the characters, Todd Andrews, states a view that seems to hound all of Barth's heroes: "The reasons for which people assign value to things are always (not necessarily immediately) arbitrary, irrational. In short, there is no ultimate reason for calling anything important or valuable; no ultimate reason for preferring one thing to another (p. 238)."

[13] Edward Gross and Paul Grambsch, *University Goals and Academic Power* (Washington, D.C.: American Council on Education, 1968).

groups and among various types of institutions in American higher education. Gross and Grambsch found "considerable congruence" between perceived and preferred goal structures, and, by inference, a high degree of satisfaction among faculty and administrators "that goals are receiving the proper emphasis."[14] Furthermore, they found that the "larger universities in the sample pursue essentially the same goals as the smaller ones, whether bigness is measured by size of the student body or of the staff."[15] Nor did these researchers find any meaningful differences when comparing rural universities with those in urban settings. Finally, said Gross and Grambsch, "administrators and faculty tend to see eye to eye to a much greater extent than is commonly supposed,"[16] and:

> . . . the high degree of congruence that exists between perceived and preferred goals at particular institutions underscores the selective nature of our universities, their tendency to attract and keep faculty and administrators who are in basic sympathy with the goal emphases of the university.[17]

The point at which the Gross and Grambsch study seems to differ from this one comes with their distinction between the "elitist" schools and the "service" ones—the "elitist-service dichotomy." They put it this way:

> . . . with respect to the global characteristics of productivity (as measured by number of doctorates awarded and by dollar volume of contract research), prestige (as measured by ratings of quality made by a nationwide sample of faculty and administrators), and graduate emphasis (as measured by the percentage of graduate students in the student body), a clear pattern of relationships emerges, and it is similar for all three measures. Those universities ranking high on any of these measures manifest an elitist pattern of perceived goals: They emphasize developing the student's intellective and scholarly qualities; they carry on pure research; they see themselves as centers for disseminating ideas and preserving the cultural heritage. With respect to support goals, they stress those aimed at satisfying the desires and needs of the faculty, they tend to slight undergraduate instruction but to encourage graduate work, and they demon-

14 *Ibid.*, p. 110.
15 *Ibid.*, p. 111.
16 *Ibid.*, p. 115.
17 *Ibid.*, pp. 115–116.

strate a concern for position goals having to do with the top
quality of the academic program and with prestige.

Universities ranking low on these characteristics—i.e.,
those that are relatively unproductive, low in prestige, and lacking strong emphasis on graduate work—manifest a "service"
orientation in their perceived goal structures: They give relatively
great emphasis to such nonintellective student output goals as
preparing the student for a useful career and cultivating his
taste and to direct service and adaptation goals that involve
giving the surrounding community practical help and main-
taining the favor of outside agencies or groups. Each of the three
global characteristics has its own peculiarities; the pattern is
slightly different for each, but the basic antithesis is there in all
three analyses.[18]

These findings do not dislocate the presence of conformity
at the level of values in higher education. It has not been claimed
in the Institutional Character study that there are no differences
among institutions in what faculty, administrators, and students
actually do in them. That some colleges as well as universities are
service-oriented is indisputable. That the values of the people there
are predominantly congruent with what they do is the point at
question. The conclusion of this study is that administrators and
faculty at "service" institutions aspire to have institutional goals
and professional interests akin to their colleagues at the elitist universities. At the level of intention rather than practice, academics
are the same.

The crucial distinction, as Gross and Grambsch say, is not
between faculty and administrators or, perhaps, between types of
institutions. It is "between the 'outsiders' (legislators, the state
government, regents)—who though technically within the university
actually share little of its day-to-day life—and the academicians."[19]
It is the outsider who defends the service or practical goals. The
challenge for educators, then, is to take youth who have been under
societal influences that do not mesh with those prevailing on campus, especially on the intellectual and academic levels, and bring students over to the values of academics. If there be doubt that this
is the preferred goal if not the actual practice of faculty and ad-

[18] *Ibid.,* pp. 111–112.
[19] *Ibid.,* p. 115.

ministrators, consider Gross and Grambsch again: "According to our respondents, goals related to students receive relatively little emphasis at American universities today, the one exception being that of training students for scholarship, research, and creative endeavor."[20]

But can youth be changed? Can colleges and universities change the values students bring to campus? The review of the literature on the subject by Newcomb and Feldman (1968)[21] showed that the conclusion of some researchers was that the college experience does help to effect change in "college persisters," moving these students toward autonomy, independence, and a tolerance for complexity, while other researchers have stressed that individual predisposition plays the focal role in any such development. The Trent-Medsker study, *Beyond High School,* showed that youth who persisted in college were different from those who did not, but ". . . it appears that college may provide the opportunity for students to grow who are ready for this rather than foster development from the beginning."[22] It is not evident that one college is better than another in causing changes or that the college environment is responsible for changes effected.

Additionally, the changes in college persisters may have involved the substitution of one form of conformity for another. Most youth put off conformity to the values of the system out of which they came, the home and general social setting, in favor of conformity to the values of the system into which they went, that of the institution of higher education. It appears that students may put off allegiance to certification, social and professional, as defined in the societal setting, in favor of professionalism, as defined by the campus milieu.

Are college students really more autonomous or independent? To answer that question it would be necessary to test the extent to which students show autonomy or independence from the values of

[20] *Ibid.,* p. 109.
[21] Theodore Newcomb and K. Feldman, *The Impact of College upon Their Students* (New York: Carnegie Foundation for the Advancement of Teaching, 1968) (mimeographed).
[22] James Trent and L. Medsker, *Beyond High School* (Berkeley: Center for Research and Development in Higher Education, University of California), p. 215. (Also San Francisco: Jossey-Bass, 1968.)

the system within which they find themselves—the campus situation. They may change somewhat in relation to their earlier connections and loyalties, but such change does not mean that they are truly independent persons. Independence is a virtue earned in the context of available options and present influences. When students leave campus and return to the larger society the vast majority either revert to the values they brought to college or take up those of the educated power structure, that segment of the societal context into which they move at graduation. It appears that, far from being independent, students are usually dependent on the values that prevail where they find themselves.

There are colleges and universities that make a special difference with their students, in the sense of having value impact on them. They are the institutions that show substantive as well as procedural distinctiveness. In this country the perennialism of the "Great Books" tradition at St. Johns College, the ego-existentialism of Antioch, the neo-Thomist realism of some Catholic schools or the biblical orientation of evangelical Protestant colleges, even the unabashed pragmatism of certain universities, provide ideological contexts within which participants may come to grips with human categories of meaning—order and disorder, certitude and mystery, aspiration and human frailty. But it must be said that the handful of colleges unusual in values are tolerated by the established educational leadership as institutional "sports," the exceptions that prove the rule. The other less distinctive places, while acknowledged as having a certain uniqueness, are seen as providing harmless variations on approved themes. There is, generally, an absence of value diversity and a plethora of value conformity to conventional criteria of institutional excellence—to what may be called the Standard.

Dominance of Conventional Standard

One of the assumptions of the Institutional Character study was that so-called conventional criteria of institutional excellence would figure prominently in the respondents' delineation of what went into the creation of institutional character, but we were not prepared for the dominance of these criteria in various types of institutions and their authority with a variety of interest groups.

Jencks and Riesman reported in *The Academic Revolution,* a study chronicling the rise and triumph of professionalism on campus, that they saw evidence of increasingly convergent goals adhered to by ever more similar means.[23] Their book reveals, we think, a case of means become ends. The emphases of professionalism were originally intended as means to ends other than themselves. They were meant to help realize institutional objectives set by a school's philosophy of education. They were to help men become what their ideal inspired them to want to be. An ideal is impotent without its instrumentalities, even as functions always operate in the context of assumptions. Hence, the conventional criteria of institutional excellence were intended to be nothing more than forms of implemental distinctiveness. However, now those means have become ends. This happened because during the fifty years or more when the academic revolution was taking place, academics failed to give attention to assumptions and goals, to fundamental value formulations, and thereby allowed the resulting vacuum of purpose to be filled by those powerful and useful means that, taken together, are called professionalism—the means become ends.

Today, institutional character is defined and evaluated by professionalism's standard. In the colleges and universities of this study, institutional character was not set by a philosophy of education or by purposes and goals inherent to the institution, nor was institutional distinctiveness seen as the result of a commitment to innovation or experimentation. Most of the schools had institutional character of a sort, but what they had was provided by this super-institutional value orientation, professionalism. This condition was less noticeable among the newer and innovative colleges of the study but it was evident enough even there to allow the generalization to stand.

The consequences of institutions and persons being accountable to this norm are profound: It means that a school's educational philosophy as well as any efforts at innovation and change are made to support the Standard. The academic revolution of the last fifty years is now a revolution become counter-revolutionary, bent on crushing rivals and blocking further change. Deviation

[23] Christopher Jencks and D. Riesman, *The Academic Revolution* (Garden City, N.J.: Doubleday, 1968), p. 39.

from the norm is not tolerated because it would be a challenge to the supremacy of this new behemoth. The traditions of the West have for more than 2000 years favored some of monotheism—and, still, in education, our god is a jealous god.

A related consequence is that academics are caught in a one-model box. That is true of faculty in public and private institutions, large universities and small colleges. They are mesmerized by the model of the "versity," in one of its three sizes—the miniversity, the university, and the multiversity. There is not nearly so much diversity at the level of professional aspiration as is claimed.

The conventional criteria of excellence were almost as strong among faculty in the newer, innovative colleges of our sample as in the older, more traditional schools. "Teaching in the area of specialization," for example, was regarded as *very important* by over 85 per cent of faculty respondents in the Standard Bearer institutions and by 72 per cent of faculty in the Radical colleges. "Research and writing," another of the marks of commitment to the Standard, was deemed *very important* to 69 per cent of the respondents in conventional schools and to 61 per cent of the people at innovative places. Our data suggest that, lacking alternative models, as is now the case, faculties at liberal arts colleges will press their institutions into professionalism and toward success as measured by the Standard as fast as the school's resources and their own persuasiveness permit, even as the majority of faculty in innovative colleges may be expected, when things get rough as they always do in prototype situations, to revert to conventionalism.

There are other effects emanating from the dominance of professionalism today, several of which figure in present campus unrest:

1. Measuring institutional success by the criteria of the Standard—by cognitive learning, command of certain language skills, use of code words and concepts, a social style and a personal manner thought to reflect academic values—has justified the corollary of ever tightening student admissions criteria, with adverse effects for the social mix and idea exchange capability of the institution.

2. Students have been limited to a formal, even tutelary, relationship with faculty due to the hierarchical organization of edu-

cational institutions. This situation existed prior to professionalism, when patriarchialism was the style, but it has been buttressed by linear, sequential ways of measuring learning and by the status consciousness of professors in the now dominant arrangement. Organizing life on campus for the convenience of faculty and administrators, an ancillary effect of professionalism, may have improved faculty morale and helped to promote order, but it has had negative effects on student creativity and self-realization.

3. Another consequence of the dominance of the Standard, a positive one in the eyes of most faculty, has been increased emphasis on academic freedom as conventionally defined in American colleges and universities. Professionals in all fields insist on a good measure of freedom, and therefore, in education as elsewhere, the security of academic freedom, protected by tenure, has become a feature of professionalism. (The first goal, on both the perceived and preferred sides, as reported by faculty and administrators in the Gross and Grambsch study, was the protection of academic freedom.)

4. Another outcome of professionalism, a negative one, is that educational costs have soared as teaching hours were reduced to add time for research, as various local roles have been replaced by guild activities, and as other features of the Standard were emphasized. If there were alternative models that could gain respectability, perhaps many schools would not follow the present norm with its high costs for professionally oriented facilities and faculties.

5. The consequences of the Standard for the spirit of community have been negative because while the Standard provided a basis for a certain type of community (the fellowship of expertise), professionalism eventually divided campuses into compartments that fragmented the student's learning experience and confined faculty to the system's rigid categories.

Training for the professions and specific professional standards emerged out of legitimate concern for both social and educational improvement. Now, however, the rise of professionalism in education, which replaced the varied structures and functions of nineteenth-century schools, has culminated in a value orientation that makes the credentialing process more important than true professional competency, equates schooling with education, and makes cognitive skills a form of technique by which success is measured. The legitimate authority of professional skill has given over to the authoritarianism of professionalism.

The metaphor for our condition is the maypole dance. Students, faculty, and administrators today, in their varying garbs representing their several traditions, are all dancing around a common center. And as they clutch their ribbons and carry out the prescribed dizzying maneuvers, they seem blinded to the fact that they are dancing in an ever smaller circle and are reducing their individual freedom by binding themselves more and more tightly to the Standard.

Improved Prospects

As there were three conclusions dealing with institutional goals and the superinstitutional value orientation, so there are three dealing with the subject of change, more particularly with prospects for innovation and experimentation in American higher education. An awareness of the certainty of change in American life has prompted, first, a growing curiosity among all elements on campus about educational innovations and experimentation. It now seems to be established doctrine that while human nature may be changing very slowly, the culture of the people is changing more rapidly, and societal changes are coming very fast indeed. Technology is transforming society and thereby raising challenges basic to the scholar's ideas about man's nature, the meaning of western history, and the relationship of man to the natural world. Because the school, including the institution of higher education, is part and parcel of society, changes now so evident in the societal context are affecting it. Necessity may not always be the mother of invention but it can encourage a lively interest in change. Educators are much like other people—they sit tight as long as they can and show "get up and go" when they must. Today with their chairs being jerked out from under them, they are beginning to feel the urge to move. Profound changes in the emerging technetronic age will result in equally significant changes for institutions of higher education, not through the initiative of educators, but because of the institution's vulnerability to societal influences and despite the traditional conservatism of academics. Curiosity about those changes and willingness to test innovations in connection with them are emerging trends.

In the composite faculty samples drawn from the colleges and universities of this study, well over half of the respondents indicated a personal interest in the theme of innovation and in innovative practices and expressed a willingness to become personally involved on behalf of such developments. Sixty-six per cent said opportunities for innovation were *very important* to them, 28 per cent called innovation *somewhat important,* and only 4 per cent regarded such opportunities as *not important.*

Administrators interviewed showed an even stronger curiosity about change options as well as a high degree of professed commitment to effecting change. The same was true of the majority of students. What is alarming is that neither faculty nor administrators in any great numbers had knowledge of specific innovations, nor were they thinking about an appropriate strategy for change in institutions of higher education. They had no sense of the possible, no substantive acquaintance with changes being attempted elsewhere, and they were not sophisticated about the planning necessary for innovations to succeed. This condition was, predictably, more prevalent among faculty than administrators. The latter by the very nature of their work are more likely to be informed. Yet ignorance of change options and change mechanisms was a problem with both groups.

Our study supports the case made against faculty that they more than administrators are inhibitors of innovation, especially in the area of curriculum. And the reason, along with concern for vested interest and personal security, plus the inevitable dash of human perversity, is ignorance. Because faculty are unaware of what might be done, they cling to the familiar. The following item was in the faculty questionnaire: "In your opinion at what colleges and universities are the most promising innovations in undergraduate education taking place? (List not more than five schools, and try to list them in the order of your estimate of the importance of the innovation.)" Faculty were not given multiple choice response options but were presented two columns, one for the listing of institutions and the other for innovations.

Twenty-seven per cent of 577 respondents gave no reply to this question, by far the highest no response rate for any item. Of the 73 per cent who did reply, 17 per cent said straightforwardly that they did not know enough about innovative institutions to attempt an answer, 5 per cent named a school but no innovation, and another 10 per cent gave variant comments of one sort or another. Forty-one per cent met the specifications of the question and listed one or more colleges and one or more innovations, but even this group gave uneven answers; their responses were often vague, uncertain, or incorrect. After all due allowances are made—confusion and irritation with the form of the item or with the questionnaire, time pressures, indigestion, and other disabling conditions—the conclusion must be drawn that faculty left to their own devices to list innovative places and programs deserve low marks. Indeed, they flunk.

Curiosity about innovation and experimentation is matched by ignorance of change options. But information can be supplied. Changing attitudes is the hard job. Yet it may be inferred from these data that attitudes are changing. There is, for example, evidence of self-criticism and dissatisfaction with established arrangements. Faculty respondents in Standard Bearer institutions, those places we regarded as most conventional, were more inclined than faculty in Radical or innovative colleges to feel that course offerings in their institutions were too specialized and that not enough attention was being given to the unity of knowledge.

These faculty were also more likely to agree that not enough emphasis is placed in their colleges and universities on shaping the moral and ethical values of students. (The Gross and Grambsch data revealed that respondents felt the university ought to be giving more attention to developing student character and citizenship.) Faculty in Standard Bearer institutions also thought that there should be less emphasis on grades, units of credit, and rigid course requirements.

Because faculty are shaken by events on campus and off to the extent that their attitude toward change is changing, we are prepared to contend that innovation—as defined in this study—may now be possible on a broad scale.

Limitations on Change

Throughout this book the word "innovation" has been used to signify new means to established ends and "experimentation" has been used for new means to new or open ends. In the context of in-

novation, so defined, the basic values behind conventional higher
education are thought to be sound and the need is for better ways
of achieving them. In experimentation, the values underlying existing institutional arrangements are deemed to be inadequate and in
need of change. The experimental idea implies the overthrow of the
old order and the substitution of something new.

Today, neither in the schools of the Institutional Character
study nor elsewhere is there much experimentation. This is not
surprising since institutions of higher education are essentially agents
of socialization and almost never radical agents of social change.
But there is a promising future for innovation, for those changes
likely to make colleges and universities agents of social change in
the more restricted sense of refining and improving existing objectives and programs.

When the institutional samples for this project were divided
into three previously discussed categories—the independent liberal
arts colleges, called the "Libarts"; the older colleges of arts and
sciences in universities sponsoring cluster colleges, designated "Elder
Siblings"; and the new cluster colleges, or "Newcomers"—it was
possible to distinguish gradations of interest in innovation among
types of schools, although all types showed considerable interest in
the subject. For example, faculty at Newcomer colleges felt that
most of their colleagues would be willing to participate personally
in educational change efforts, representatives from the Libarts estimated that about half of their faculty contacts were so inclined, and
the sample from the Elder Siblings thought that just "some" of their
peers would do so. These differences were significant at the .01
level with a chi square test.

The picture was reversed when faculty respondents were
asked to scale their colleagues as to the proportion who were not
hostile to innovation but were unwilling to get personally involved.
The sample from the Elder Siblings said that this would be true for
about half of the faculty they knew, in the Libarts group this judgment was reduced to *some,* and in the Newcomers it was thought to
to apply to from *some* to *very few.* The Newcomers differed from
Libarts at the .05 level of significance with a chi square test while
the difference between Newcomers and Elder Siblings was at .01.

These data show that new, innovative colleges have succeeded in bringing together larger proportions of innovatively oriented faculty than was true elsewhere. But it is also noteworthy that in the liberal arts colleges, and even in the established units of the universities, there were significant elements of the faculty who were regarded by colleagues as potential participants in change activities.

Forms of Innovation

Other data from the Institutional Character study suggest that certain specific innovative proposals are viable change options now. Seven out of ten entering freshmen stated a preference for group discussions rather than lectures. Independent study also ranked high. An integrative academic program was favored by most students over a specialized one. To be sure, most respondents had only vague notions about what these innovations might mean for their future, and, after a year or two on campus, their attitudes would probably be modified by the lure of the Standard; nevertheless, the point remains that at entrance to college there was strong sentiment among students in support of discussion classes, independent study, and integrative curricula. These innovations are especially accessible beachheads for change.

It must not be inferred that the interests of entering freshmen regarding areas of viable innovation were the same as those of faculty. The faculty were more beholden to the Standard. Even the faculty in those colleges regarded as innovative, the Radicals, were on a par with faculty in the Standard Bearer institutions in the importance for them personally of an opportunity for research and writing. The only significant difference between the two groups emerged when respondents were asked to judge their colleagues on this same matter. Faculty at the Radical schools saw research and writing as *very important* for themselves but only *somewhat important* for their colleagues, while the Standard Bearers continued to maintain, in the rating of colleagues, that it was *very important*.

Another example that faculty were pretty much agreed on the conventional criteria of institutional excellence was seen in faculty attitudes, without differentiation by types of schools, toward that accepted symbol of excellence—faculty control of academic policy formulation. (At schools in the sample, students had advisory roles on administrative committees in some cases, full voting participation on student life committees in most cases, but active assignments on blue ribbon committees handling academic policy formulation in no cases.) Sixty-two per cent of faculty respondents in the composite institutional total declared that students should not be involved more in academic policy matters than they were at the time of the study.[24] Yet it is also significant that 34 per cent of the faculty respondents favored some sort of change in governance.

It is also worth noting that many of the characteristics of a valuable educational experience as perceived by students were akin to those that educators have traditionally associated with liberal education—unitary learning, the spirit of community, integrity for the individual, and human relevance in the curriculum. Given the uncertainty and general confusion that characterizes faculty thinking these days, when they seem eager for ideas that will revitalize the humanistic traditions of their institution, innovations that deal with these concerns may find a ready hearing from both faculty and students.

In this connection, perhaps the appeal for innovation should not in the future be based on faculty self-interest as has usually been the case in the past. That approach seems to have been carried to its nadir. The "soft" data gathered by project interviews and observations suggest that the educated are physically comfortable but not very happy; healthy in body but less so in mind, and still less in spirit; active, efficient, articulate, but bothered by deep anxiety about the meaning of what they do. There is need among scholars and intellectuals to think again about what men ought to live for, about assumptions, values, objectives. Perhaps the new appeal for effecting change should be the renewal of an old appeal with the added dimension of relevance, the appeal to purpose. There is reason to think that it would get an active response.

Data point also to the idealism of freshmen. These youth have an exalted notion of the nature of the institution of higher education and of what the educational experience should mean. That is important. What the student brings with him to college

---

[24] The goal of involving students in governance was at the bottom of both "is" and "ought" lists in the Gross and Grambsch study. The fact that their data were gathered in 1964–65, before the urgencies created by student unrest, may have contributed to the haughtiness of the "in" crowd.

from his past in terms of aptitudes, learning experiences, and personal attitudes, the "input factors" emphasized by Paul Heist and others at the most important variables for college success, should be balanced in research evaluation by attention to the forward looking attitudes, what a youth aspires to become (which of course is affected by his past) or what he thinks about himself, and by the school's level of expectation for him. A point of encouragement is that the youth in this study seemed to aspire at entrance to college to the achievement of individual character in a setting of an institution with character. Students believe that to learn is to change. Now colleges are learning that lesson.

Faculty in this study, while largely ignorant of change options and loyal to the Standard, also give indications of being attracted to certain innovations. For example, although team teaching failed miserably with the sample and must be regarded as an unpromising form of innovation for college level faculty tied to the Standard, respondents expressed interest in interdisciplinary teaching. Forty-one per cent of the composite total called the opportunity for such contacts and teaching *very important* to them personally, while 45 per cent regarded it as *somewhat important* and only 13 per cent marked *not important*. It is true that there was considerable attrition in enthusiasm for cross-disciplinary teaching when respondents were reporting their ideas of what colleagues thought about that proposal, with the percentages dropping to 17 per cent *very important,* 53 per cent *somewhat important,* and 21 per cent *not important*. Even so, these data encourage a prediction of success for what is called at Sussex University "relational learning"—where the disciplines are not scorned, nor are two subjects simply carried forward on parallel tracks, but where the subject matter of the disciplines is studied "in relation" and taught by specialists. The informal dynamics, if not formal structures, seem to favor it.

Faculty also showed a positive attitude toward the concept of community. Here is another point where faculty and student interests touch. To be sure, the composite faculty response, with 36 per cent declaring "community" to be *very important,* 50 per cent *somewhat important,* and 12 per cent *not important,* may have been skewed by a legacy factor—lingering sentiment for a lost tradition. Nevertheless, in a day when faculty commitment to professionalism is being countered among some students with individualism that runs off into radical subjectivism, with the consequence that standards are hardening into dogma on the one hand and settling into mush on the other, there is reason to note the leverage available to innovators who may be disposed to create new learning configurations featuring "community." There is support for a variation of a theoretical position long associated with Reinhold Niebuhr—man's potential makes community possible, man's frailty makes it necessary.

Administrators today are no less eager than faculty for viable innovations. Like everyone else, they play the referral-deferral game where declarations of interest in change are balanced by complaints about being blocked by faculty or trustees or finances, by the lack of time and the need for the propitious moment. Nevertheless, administrators know that the future will be different from the past and they are beginning to sense that they have ways of shaping it. They complain that they have no cogency, that the power to effect change resides in the departments. However, student unrest raises threats to public goodwill—a problem area in which administrators have "expertise"—and the tactics of dissident students create conditions that embarrass faculty style and interrupt faculty work. In these circumstances there may be a shift of power on campus in the direction of administrators, toward those who supposedly have the competence to deal with the trouble and who have the sociopolitical area as their domain. Faculty eagerly yield over unpleasant responsibility, but with it goes considerable power. Thus, administrators come into position to give leadership for institutional change.

It is true that the values of administrators are basically conservative. They can be expected to show interest in innovation as here defined, but not in experimentation. They will be the first to become uneasy if programs committed to change turn out to be radically different. Administrators conditioned to the administrative function, by which attention centers on continuity more than change, on harmony more than dissonance, are usually opportunists interested in diversity of means but not diversity of ends. But if they are opportunists, they now have their opportunity.

The innovation that provides the most promising opportunity today for administrators interested in promoting institutional change, is the cluster college concept whereby small semiautonomous colleges can be established within the general framework of the large university or whereby academic subunits are organized within colleges—the college within college idea. Cluster colleges offer a way to change and improve institutions of learning by giving a new twist to the ancient maxim "divide and conquer." They may divide the masses of students into groups small enough to encourage identity and participation, thereby creating, as an additional benefit, a way for the absolute size of the university to increase while the working units remain small. And more, they can help to conquer that student apathy or hostility which grows out of a sense of powerlessness by encouraging student involvement with the faculty in testing innovation, thus creating in the university a mechanism for institutional change without sacrificing order and tradition.

But more important than these reasons for establishing cluster colleges is the potential the concept has for the development and testing of holistic models that many prove appropriate for the future of higher education. While there is growing agreement that the pattern of the past will not be adequate for the future, not because the past was necessarily bad but because the future will be radically different, there is no agreement on what changes would be best. The option open is the structuring of alternative models where innovative or experimental probes may be carried out in the hope that the direction and mechanisms needed for learning in the future will thus become known.

When a few prestigious universities are setting the academic style and enforcing the Standard, the cluster college idea encourages the hope that these key institutions might now, under the developing awareness of current urgencies, spin off colleges commissioned to innovate radically. Substantive change would have a chance as the principle of growth through real diversity was applied in the centers of academic power. Two of the institutions in this study were of such stature and were, indeed, formally committed to innovation reaching to experimentation. The results of the study, where such colleges were operative, showed that the idea is a harbinger of hope. The colleges had the will to be different and were making a difference.[25]

There is no reason to conclude from these data that institutions of higher education are without resources with which to effect change. The human resources are there; interested faculty, students, and administrators comprise at least a significant minority of the whole. The hope for change is with a coterie of the concerned drawn from no one interest group but from across several of them, from students, faculty, and administrators willing to share responsibility for creating alternative models promising institutional character. Until such leadership and specific options are forthcoming, everyone will continue to live by the conventional standard of excellence and by it institutional character will be judged.

Even if the college within college idea proves valuable as a mechanism for testing specific educational options, and even if a coterie of the concerned emerge to provide leadership, there will still be the "criterion problem"—the perennial need for standards by which to evaluate organizational options and the ideas of new leadership. By what criteria shall proposals be judged, who sets them, and why—by what authority?

In this century, as has been mentioned, all aspects of the sociopolitical life of the institution of higher education have been subject to the judgment of an American orthodoxy, whose dogmas were sanctioned by the industrial-religious-educational elite. Meanwhile, life on the academic side in our colleges and universities has been under the control of professionalism and the conventional standard of excellence.

Now, however, sociopolitical orthodoxy is losing authority, especially with the young, giving way before a contextualist ethic, relevant for the individual and "validated" by the existentialist's defense of self-determination as a prerequisite to self-authentication. And academic professionalism wanes too, losing force because of the association of its emphases with a technological society and the threat of life as technique.

Certain effects of these changes are now evident. There is a

[25] See Warren Martin, *Alternative to Irrelevance: A Strategy for Reform in Higher Education* (Nashville: Abingdon Press, 1968), pp. 69–134, for more on the concept of cluster colleges.

tendency, on the sociopolitical side, to set aside college regulations supporting the concept of *in loco parentis,* to free students "to do their own thing." On the academic side, faculty still try to hold the line, insisting that conventional standards be maintained. But it is a losing battle. The outer defenses have already fallen—units of credit, time/learning equivalences, conventional grades, examinations, course prerequisites and sequences, SAT scores, IQ tests, and many other formal measurements of student potential and academic accomplishment. Challenges to the dignities of faculty and administration are no less marked, and no less successful. The old aristocratic-separatist organizational hierarchy based on titles, degrees, age, and office is coming down and opening up.

These shifts, accommodations, and adjustments are not likely to end with superficial changes. That which is happening at the surface level bespeaks change at the deep level of fundamental norms. The emergent themes feature renewed confidence in the individual, increased anti-institutionalism, and the quest for a better basis for community. Yet, at the level of values, nothing is certain except the evidence of substantive change. This is a day when the old ways are suffering the disarray of a retreat equaled only by the factionalism of the advancing new ways.

The criterion problem remains, whether the issue for the future is the validation with the young of the conventional standard of excellence or the selection of alternative guidelines. It has not been the purpose of this author to declare criteria by which the institution of higher education in the future should be evaluated, but it is possible to state a conceptual framework within which to evaluate assumptions, values, and goals. It is a framework with two sides, one acknowledging the inevitability of value judgments for individuals and institutions, and the other emphasizing the provisional nature of all value judgments. To posit the inevitability of value judgments, and to proceed to establish certitudes, gives a basis for action and character. Coupling that process with the admission of the provisional nature of all value judgments keeps certitudes from hardening into absolute certainties, and keeps the institution open to change.

This approach should also help to overcome the problem confronting those colleges which in the past have found that their distinctiveness tended to become dogmatized, thus blocking further change. The very success of an effort can lead to its downfall. Mechanisms erected to protect the results of change can become barriers to criticism and obstructions to further innovation. The human tendency to absolutize achievements and assure their continuation by rules frequently transforms means into ends, as happened with professionalism.[26]

But the tentative nature of all value commitments, institutional as well as individual, would be a defense against the premature solidification of gains. Commitments would be understood to be real and obligating, but they would not be unchangeable. Criticism and creativity would have legitimate functions as the concept of process and the practice of change were institutionalized. In this way colleges and universities could have character even as they change and could make change a dimension of their distinctiveness.

---

[26] Robert K. Merton has described this development as "the familiar process of displacement of goals whereby an instrumental value becomes a terminal value." R. Merton, "Bureaucratic Structure and Personality," A. Etzioni (ed.), *Complex Organizations* (New York: Holt, Rinehart and Winston, 1961), pp. 53 ff.

BIBLIOGRAPHY

ALLPORT, G. W., VERNON, P. E., AND LINDZEY, G. *Study of values,* revised edition. Cambridge: Houghton Mifflin, 1951.

ALTBACH, P. "The student movement and the American university." *Phi Delta Kappan,* 1966.

ARGYRIS, C. *Organization and innovation.* Homewood, Ill.: Dorsey Press, 1965.

ASHLEY, E. *Technology and the academics.* London: Macmillan, 1958.

ASTIN, A. W. *Who goes where to college.* Chicago: Science Research Associates, 1965.

ASTIN, A. W. *The college environment.* Washington, D.C.: American Council of Education, 1968.

ASTIN, A. W. "Undergraduate achievement and institutional quality." In *Inventory of current research on higher education, 1968.* New York: McGraw-Hill, 1968.

ASTIN, A., AND HOLLAND, J. "The distribution of wealth in higher education." *College and University,* Winter, 1962.

AXELROD, J. "New organizational patterns in American colleges and universities." In Logan Wilson (ed.), *Autonomy and inter-*

243

dependence: Emerging systems in higher education. Washington, D.C.: American Council on Education, 1964.

AXELROD, J. "An experimental college model." *Educational Record,* Fall, 1967.

AXELROD, J. *New patterns in undergraduate education: Emerging curriculum models for the American college.* New Dimensions in Higher Education series. Washington, D.C.: U.S. Office of Education, 1967.

AXELROD, J. "New patterns in internal organizations." In L. B. Mayhew (ed.), *Higher education in the revolutionary decade.* Berkeley: McCutchan, 1968.

AVERILL, L. J. *A strategy for the Protestant college.* Philadelphia: Westminster, 1966.

AYRES, L. P. "History and present status of education measurements." *Seventeenth Yearbook* of the National Society for the Study of Education, Part II. Bloomington, Ind.: Public School Publishing, 1918.

AXELROD, J., et al. *Search for Relevance: The Campus in Crisis.* San Francisco: Jossey-Bass, 1969.

BARNARD, C. *The functions of the executive.* Cambridge: Harvard University Press, 1942.

BARRETT, H. G. *Innovation: The basis of cultural change.* New York: McGraw-Hill, 1953.

BARRETT, W. *Irrational man.* Garden City, N.J.: Doubleday, 1962.

BARTH, J. *Giles goat-boy.* Garden City, N.J.: Doubleday, 1966.

BARTH, J. *The floating opera.* New York: Avon, 1956.

BARTON, A. *Studying the effects of college education: A methodological examination of changing values in college.* New Haven: Hazen Foundation, 1959.

BARTON, A. *Organizational measurement and its bearing on the study of college environments.* New York: College Entrance Examination Board, 1961.

BARTON, A. *The college as a social organization.* New York: Columbia University Bureau of Applied Social Research, 1963.

BARZUN, J. *Teacher in America.* New York: Doubleday, 1953.

BAY, C. "A social theory of higher education." In N. Sanford (ed.), *The American college.* New York: Wiley, 1962.

BASKIN, S. (ed.). *Higher education: Some newer developments.* New York: McGraw-Hill, 1965.

BECKER, E. *Beyond alienation: A philosophy of education for the crisis of democracy.* New York: Braziller, 1967.

BELL, D. *The reforming of general education.* New York: Columbia University Press, 1966.

BINET-SIMON. *A method of measuring the development of the intelli-*

gence of young children, third edition. Chicago: Medical Book 1915.

BLOCK, J., HAHN, N., AND SMITH, B. "Activism and apathy in contemporary adolescents." In J. F. Adams (ed.), *Understanding adolescence.* Boston: Allyn and Bacon, 1968.

BLOOM, B. S. *Stability and change in human characteristics.* New York: Wiley, 1964.

BLUM, R. H., et al. *Students and drugs.* San Francisco: Jossey-Bass, 1969.

BOLMAN, F. *How college presidents are chosen.* Washington, D.C.: American Council on Education, 1965.

BOOCOCK, S. "Toward a sociology of learning: A selective review of existing research." *Sociology of Education,* 1966, *39*(1).

BOOTH, W. *The knowledge most worth having.* Chicago: University of Chicago Press, 1966.

BOROFF, D. "Status seeking in academe." *Saturday Review,* December 19, 1964.

BOULDING, K. E. "Evidences for an administrative science." *Administrative Science Quarterly,* 1958, *3*(1).

BOULDING, K. E. *The impact of the social sciences.* New Brunswick: Rutgers University Press, 1966.

BRAMELD, T., AND ELAN, S. (eds.). *Values in American education.* Bloomington, Ind.: Phi Delta Kappa, 1964.

BRONOWSKI, J. *Science and human values.* New York: Harper, 1965.

BRONOWSKI, J., et al. *Imagination and the university.* Toronto: University of Toronto Press, 1963.

BRUBACHER, J. S. *Bases for policy in higher education.* New York: McGraw-Hill, 1965.

BUBER, M. *Between man and man.* Boston: Beacon Press, 1955.

BURNS, G. P. *Trustees in higher education.* New York: Independent College Fund, 1966.

BURNS, T., AND STALKER, G. W. *The management of innovation.* Chicago: Quadrangle, 1961.

BUSWELL, G., et al. *Training for educational research.* Berkeley: Center for the Study of Higher Education, 1966.

BUTTERFIELD, E. W. "The plenary inspiration of the dotted line." *Educational Review,* 1925, *68*(2).

BUTZ, O. (ed.). *To make a difference; A student look at America.* New York: Harper, 1967.

BUXTON, C. E. *A guide to college teaching.* New York: Harcourt, Brace, 1956.

CAPEN, S. P. *The management of universities.* Buffalo: Stewart and Foster, 1953.

CAPLOW, T., AND MCGEE, R. J. *The academic marketplace.* New York: Basic Books, 1958.

CARLSON, R. O. *Adoption of educational innovations.* Eugene: University of Oregon Press, 1965.

CARTTER, A. M. *An assessment of quality in graduate education.* Washington, D.C.: American Council on Education, 1966.

CENTER FOR RESEARCH AND DEVELOPMENT IN HIGHER EDUCATION. *Omnibus personality inventory: Research manual.* Berkeley: Center for Research and Development in Higher Education, 1967.

CERNMAGER, H., MCEWEN, R., AND BLANCHARD, B. *Education in a free society, II.* Pittsburgh: University of Pittsburgh Press, 1960.

"CHANGING CONCEPTS OF HUMAN NATURE." *American Scholar,* Winter, 1968–69.

CHICKERING, A. W. *Education and identity.* San Francisco: Jossey-Bass, 1968.

CHICKERING, A. W., et al. *Research and action: A project on student development at selected small colleges.* Washington, D.C.: Council for the Advancement of Small Colleges, 1968.

Chronicle of Higher Education, December 21, 1967, 2(8).

CLARK, B. R. "The cooling out function in higher education." *American Journal of Sociology,* 1960, 5(65).

CLARK, B. R. *The open door college.* New York: McGraw-Hill, 1960.

CLARK, B. R. *Educating the expert society.* San Francisco: Chandler, 1962.

CLARK, B. R. "The character of colleges: Some case studies." In R. J. Ingham (ed.), *Institutional backgrounds of adult education: Dynamics of change in the modern university.* Boston: Center for the Study of Liberal Education for Adults, 1966.

CLARK, B. R., AND TROW, M. A. "Determinants of college subculture." In T. M. Newcomb and E. K. Wilson (eds.), *The study of college peer groups.* Chicago: Aldine, 1966.

COLE, C. C., JR., AND LEWIS, L. G. *Flexibility in the undergraduate curriculum.* New Dimensions in Higher Education, No. 13, Washington, D.C.: U.S. Government Printing Office, 1962.

COLUMBIA UNIVERSITY TEACHERS COLLEGE. *Character of education inquiry: Studies in the nature of character,* three volumes. New York: Macmillan, 1928.

CONANT, J. B. *Shaping educational policy.* New York: McGraw-Hill, 1964.

CORSON, J. J. *Governance of colleges and universities.* New York: McGraw-Hill, 1960.

COWLEY, W. H. "Some myths about professors, presidents and trustees." *Teachers College Record,* 1962, 64.

CRANE, R. S. *The idea of the humanities,* Vol. I. Chicago: University of Chicago Press, 1967.

CROSS, K. P. "Student values revisited." *Research Reporter,* 1968, *3*(1).

CURTI, M., AND NASH, R. *Philanthropy in the shaping of American higher education.* New Brunswick: Rutgers University Press, 1965.

DAVIS, J. "What college teachers value in students." *College Board Review,* Spring, 1965.

DENNIS, L. E., AND JACOB, R. M. (eds.). *The arts in higher education.* San Francisco: Jossey-Bass, 1968.

DENNIS, L. E., AND KAUFFMAN, J. F. *The college and the student.* Washington, D.C.: American Council on Education, 1966.

DEVANE, W. C. *Higher education in twentieth-century America.* Cambridge: Harvard University Press, 1965.

DEWEY, J. "Control of universities." *School and Society,* 1915, 2.

DODD, H. *The academic president—educator or caretaker?* New York: McGraw-Hill, 1962.

DOSTOEVSKY, F. *The brothers Karamazov.* New York: Modern Library, 1950.

DRESSEL, P. L. "Factors involved in changing the values of college students." *Educational Record,* 1965, *46*(2).

DRESSEL, P. L., AND LEHMAN, I. J. "The impact of higher education in student attitudes, values, and critical thinking abilities." *Educational Record,* 1965, *46*(3).

DRESSEL, P. L., AND LORIMER, M. *Attitudes of liberal arts faculty members toward liberal and professional education.* New York: Teachers College, Columbia University, 1960.

DRESSEL, P. L., et al. *Evaluation in higher education.* Boston: Houghton Mifflin, 1961.

DURANT, W. *The story of philosophy.* New York: Simon and Schuster, 1926.

EDDY, E. E. *The college influence on student character.* Washington, D.C.: American Council on Education, 1959.

ELLUL, J. *The technological society.* New York: Knopf, 1965.

ERIKSON, E. H. *Childhood and society,* second edition. New York: Norton, 1963.

ERIKSON, E. (ed.). *The challenge of youth.* Garden City: Doubleday, 1965.

ETZIONI, A. "Authority structure and organizational effectiveness." *Administrative Science Quarterly,* 1959, 6.

ETZIONI, A. (ed.). *Complex organizations.* New York: Holt, 1961.

EVANS, R. I., AND LEPPMANN, P. K. *Resistance to innovation in higher education.* San Francisco: Jossey-Bass, 1968.

FELDMAN, K. A., AND NEWCOMB, T. M. *The impact of college on students.* San Francisco: Jossey-Bass, 1969.

FEUER, L. "The decline of freedom at Berkeley." *Atlantic Monthly,* 1966, 218.

FLETCHER, J. *Situation ethics.* Philadelphia: Westminster, 1966.

FLEXNER, A. *Medical education in the United States and Canada.* New York: Carnegie Foundation for the Advancement of Teaching, 1910.

FOOTE, C., et al. *The culture of the university: Governance and education.* San Francisco: Jossey-Bass, 1968.

FRANKE, P. R., AND DAVIS, R. A. "Changing tendencies in educational research." *Journal of Educational Research,* 1931, *23.*

FRANKL, V. "Dynamics, existence and values." *Journal of Existential Psychiatry,* Summer, 1961.

FRANKL, V. *Man's search for meaning.* New York: Washington Square Press, 1963.

FREEDMAN, M. B. *Impact of college.* Washington, D.C.: U.S. Office of Education, 1960.

FREEDMAN, M. B. "Changes in six decades of some attitudes and values held by educated women." *Journal of Social Issues,* 1961, *17*(1).

FREEDMAN, M. B. "Personality growth in the college years." *College Board Review,* 1965, *56.*

FREEDMAN, M. B. *The college experience.* San Francisco: Jossey-Bass, 1967.

FRIEDENBERG, E. Z. *The vanishing adolescent.* Boston: Beacon Press, 1959.

GAFF, J. *Innovations and consequence: A study of Raymond College, University of the Pacific.* Berkeley: Center for Research and Development in Higher Education, 1967.

GARDNER, J. W. *Self-renewal.* New York: Harper, 1964.

GARDNER, J. W. *Agenda for the colleges and universities: Higher education in the innovative society.* New York: Academy for Educational Development, 1965.

GARNSWORTH, I. *Psychiatry, education, and the young adult.* Springfield, Ill.: Thomas, 1966.

GLENNY, L. A. *Autonomy of public colleges: The challenge of coordination.* New York: McGraw-Hill, 1969.

GOOD, C. V. "Organized research in education: foundations, commissions, and committees." *Review of Educational Research,* 1939, *9*(5).

GOODMAN, P. *Compulsory miseducation and the community of scholars.* New York: Vintage, 1964.

GOULD, S. B. *Knowledge is not enough.* Yellow Springs, Ohio: Antioch College Press, 1959.

GOULDNER, A. W. "Cosmopolitans and locals: Toward an analysis of latent social roles." *Administrative Science Quarterly,* 1958, *2*(4).

GREELEY, A. M. "The teaching of moral wisdom." In G. K. Smith (ed.), *Stress and campus response: Current issues in higher education*. San Francisco: Jossey-Bass, 1968.

GRIFFITHS, D. C. "Administrative theory and change in organizations." In M. B. Miles (ed.), *Innovations in education*. New York: Teachers College, Columbia University, 1964.

GRIFFITHS, D. E. "Research and theory in educational administration." In *Perspectives on educational administration and the behavioral sciences*. Eugene, Oregon: Center for the Advanced Study of Educational Administration, 1967.

GROSS, E., AND GRAMBSCH, P. V. *University goals and academic power*. Washington, D.C.: American Council on Education, 1968.

GROSS, N. "Organizational lag in American universities." *Harvard Education Review*, 1963, 33.

GUMPERZ, E. *The internationalizing of American higher education: Innovation and structural change*. Berkeley: Center for Research and Development in Higher Education, in press.

GUSFIELD, J., AND RIESMAN, D. "Faculty culture and academic careers: Some sources of innovation in higher education." *Sociology of Education*, 1964, Summer(4).

GUSFIELD, J., AND RIESMAN, D. "Innovation in higher education: Notes on student and faculty encounters in three new colleges." In H. Becker, et al. (eds.), *Institutions and the person: Essays in honor of E. C. Hughes*. Chicago: Aldine, 1968.

GUSTAD, J. W. "Community, consensus, and conflict." *Educational Record*, Fall, 1966.

HARRIS, C. W. (ed.). *Encyclopedia of educational research*. New York: Macmillan, 1960.

HARRIS, S. E., et al. (eds.). *Challenge and change in American education*. Berkeley: McCutchan, 1965.

HARVARD UNIVERSITY COMMITTEE. *General education in a free society*. Cambridge: Harvard University Press, 1945.

HASSENGER, R. (ed.). *The shape of Catholic higher education*. Chicago: University of Chicago Press, 1967.

HASWELL, H. A., AND LINDQUIST, C. B. *Undergraduate curriculum patterns*. Washington, D.C.: U.S. Office of Education, 1965.

HATCH, W. R. *What standards do we raise?* New Dimensions in Higher Education, No. 12. Washington, D.C.: U.S. Office of Education, 1965.

HEATH, D. H. *Growing up in college*. San Francisco: Jossey-Bass, 1968.

HEATH, R. *The Reasonable Adventurer*. Pittsburgh: University of Pittsburgh Press, 1964.

HECKMAN, D., AND MARTIN, W. *Inventory of current research on higher education*. New York: McGraw-Hill, 1968.

HEILBRONER, R. L. *The future as history*. New York: Grove Press, 1961.

HEIST, P. "Intellect and commitment: the faces of discontent." In O. A. Knorr and W. J. Minter (eds.), *Order and freedom on the campus: The rights and responsibilities of faculty and students.* Boulder, Colo.: Western Interstate Commission for Higher Education, 1965.

HEIST, P. "Higher education and human potentialities." In H. A. Otto (ed.), *Explanations in human potentialities.* Springfield, Ill.: Thomas, 1966.

HEIST, P. "Creative students: college transients." In P. Heist (ed.), *The creative college student: An unmet challenge.* San Francisco: Jossey-Bass, 1968.

HEIST, P. "Personality and social theory basic to student development during the college years." Berkeley: Educational Testing Service and Center for Research and Development in Higher Education, 1968 (mimeographed).

HENDERSON, A. D. "The desired influence: Improving communication between administration and faculty." *Journal of Higher Education,* June 1967.

HENDERSON, A. D. "Effective models of university governance." In G. K. Smith (ed.), *In search of leaders: Current issues in higher education.* Washington, D.C.: American Association of Higher Education, 1967.

HENMAN, V. A. C. "The function, value and future of educational research in college and universities." *Journal of Educational Research,* March 1934, 27.

HODGKINSON, H. L. *Education, interaction and social change.* Englewood Cliffs, N.J.: Prentice-Hall, 1967.

HODGKINSON, H. L. "Students and an intellectual community." *Educational Record,* 1968, 49(4).

HOFSTADTER, R., AND HARDY, C. *The development and scope of higher education in the United States.* New York: Columbia University Press, 1952.

HOFSTADTER, R. AND METZGER, W. *The development of academic freedom in the United States.* New York: Columbia University Press, 1955.

HOLLAND, J. L. "Undergraduate origins of American scientists." *Science,* 1957 (126).

HOWARD, V., AND WARRINGTON, W. "Inventory of beliefs: changes in beliefs and attitudes and academic success prediction." *Personnel Guidance Journal,* 1958, 27.

HOWES, R. F. (ed.). *Vision and purpose in higher education.* Washington, D.C.: American Council on Education, 1962.

HOYT, D. "The relationship between college grades and adult achievement: A review of the literature." *American College Testing Research Reports,* No. 7. Iowa City, 1965.

HUGHES, E., et al. "Student culture and academic effort." In N. Sanford (ed.), *The American college*. New York: Wiley, 1962.

HUNGATE, T. L. *Management in higher education*. New York: Teachers College, Columbia University, 1964.

HUTCHINS, R. *The university of utopia*. Chicago: University of Chicago Press, 1953.

HYMAN, H. "The value systems of different classes." In R. Bendix and M. Lipset (eds.), *Class, status and power: A reader in social stratification*. Glencoe, Ill.: Free Press, 1953.

INGRAHAM, M. H. *The mirror of brass: The compensation and working conditions of college and university administrators*. Madison: University of Wisconsin Press, 1968.

JACOB, P. E. *Changing values in college*. New York: Harper, 1957.

JACOBS, P. AND LANDAU, S. (eds.). *The new radicals*. New York: Vintage, 1966.

JASPERS, I. *The idea of the university*. Boston: Beacon Press, 1959.

JENCKS, C. "Social stratification and higher education." *Harvard Educational Review*, 1968, *38*(2).

JENCKS, C., AND RIESMAN, D. *The academic revolution*. Garden City, N.Y.: Doubleday, 1968.

JOHNSON, S. W. "Progressive changes in students' values, needs and educational objectives." Reports 1–6. Plattsburgh, N.Y.: State University College, June 1962–June 1963.

KATZ, J. *Growth and constraint in college students*. Stanford: Institute for the Study of Human Problems, 1967.

KATZ, J., et al. *No time for youth*. San Francisco: Jossey-Bass, 1968.

KAUFMAN, W. "Educational development and normative philosophy." *Harvard Educational Review*, Summer, 1966.

KEETON, M. "The climate of learning in college." *College and University Bulletin*. Washington, D.C.: Association for Higher Education, November 15, 1962.

KEETON, M. "Future of the liberal arts college study." Yellow Springs, Ohio: Antioch College Press, 1967 (mimeographed).

KEETON, M. "Governance study." Occasional papers. Yellow Springs, Ohio: Antioch College Press, 1968.

KELLY, F. J. "Contributions of research to higher education." In *Thirty-Seventh Yearbook of the National Society for the Study of Education, Part II*. 1930.

KENISTON, K. *The uncommitted*. New York: Harcourt, Brace, 1965.

KERR, C. *The uses of the university*. Cambridge: Harvard University Press, 1963.

KLOTSCHE, J. M. *The urban university—and the future of our cities*. New York: Harper, 1966.

KNAPP, R. H., AND GOODRICH, H. B. *Origins of American scientists*. New York: Russell and Russell, 1952.

KNAPP, R. H., AND GREENBAUM, J. J. *The younger American scholar: His collegiate origins.* Chicago: University of Chicago Press, 1953.

KNIGHT, D. M. "The college as a community." *The Christian Scholar,* 1957, *40*(2).

KOOS, L. V., AND CRAWFORD, C. C. "College aims past and present." *School and Society,* 1921, *14*.

LAZARSFELD, P. F., AND SIEBER, S. D. *Organizing educational research.* Englewood Cliffs, N.J.: Prentice-Hall, 1964.

LAZARSFELD, P. F., AND THIELENS, W. *The academic mind.* Glencoe, Ill.: Free Press, 1958.

LEARNED, W. S., AND WOOD, B. D. *The student and his knowledge.* New York: Carnegie Foundation for the Advancement of Teaching, Bulletin 29, 1938.

LEE, C. B. T. (ed.). *Improving college teaching.* Washington, D.C.: American Council on Education, 1967.

LEHMANN, I. H. "Yardsticks for gauging values." *University College Quarterly,* 1966, *1*.

LEHMANN, I. J., AND PAYNE, I. K. "An explanation of attitude and value changes in college freshmen." *Personnel Guidance Journal,* 1963, *41*.

LENSKI, G. *The religious factor: A sociological study of religious impact on politics, economics and family life.* New York: Doubleday, 1961.

LIKERT, R. *New patterns of management.* New York: McGraw-Hill, 1961.

LIPSET, S. M. *Political man.* Garden City, N.J.: Doubleday, 1960.

LIPSET, S. M. (ed.). *Student politics.* New York: Basic Books, 1967.

LUNSFORD, T. F. (ed.). *The study of academic administration.* Boulder, Colo.: Western Interstate Council on Higher Education, 1963.

LUNSFORD, T. F. "Authority and ideology in the administered university." *The American Behavioral Scientist,* 1968, *11*(5).

LYND, L. "The new radicals and participatory democracy." *Dissent,* 1965, *12*.

LYND, R. S. *Knowledge for What?* New York: Grove Press, 1939.

MADGE, J. *The tools of social science.* Garden City, N.J.: Doubleday, 1965.

MALLERY, D. *Ferment on the campus: An encounter with the new college generation.* New York: Harper, 1966.

MARCH, J. D., AND SIMON, H. A. *Organizations.* New York: Wiley, 1958.

MARCUSE, H. *Eros and civilization.* New York: Vintage, 1955.

MARCUSE, H. *One-dimensional man.* Boston: Beacon Press, 1964.

MARTIN, W. B. "The chance for educational change." *Fordham Magazine,* 1968, *3*(1).

MARTIN, W. B. *Alternative to irrelevance: A strategy for reform in higher education.* Nashville: Abingdon Press, 1968.

MARTIN, W. B. "Education as intervention." *Educational Record,* 1969, *50*(1).

MARTIN, W., AND HECKMAN, D. *Inventory of current research on higher education.* New York: McGraw-Hill, 1968.

MASLOW, A. H. *New knowledge in human values.* New York: Harper, 1959.

MASLOW, A. H. *Toward a psychology of being.* Princeton, N.J.: Van Nostrand, 1962.

MAYHEW, L. B. *The smaller liberal arts college.* New York: Teachers College, Columbia University, 1964.

MAYHEW, L. B. *Colleges today and tomorrow.* San Francisco: Jossey-Bass, 1969.

MCCONNELL, T. R. "The attainment of individuality." In K. McFarland (ed.), *Urbanization and the college student: The social psychology of the future state metropolitan campus.* Minneapolis: University of Minnesota Press, 1966.

MCCONNELL, T. R. *A general pattern for American public higher education.* New York: McGraw-Hill, 1962.

MCCONNELL, T. R. "The function of leadership in academic institutions." *Educational Record,* 1968, *49*(2).

MCCONNELL, T. R., AND HEIST, P. "Do students make the college?" *College and University,* 1959, *34*(4).

MCCONNELL, T. R., AND HEIST, P. "The diverse college student population." In N. Sanford (ed.), *The American college.* New York: Wiley, 1962.

MCGRATH, E. J. "Control of higher education in America." *Educational Record,* 1936, *17*.

MCGRATH, E. J. *The liberal arts college and the emergent caste system.* New York: Teachers College, Columbia University, 1966.

MCGRATH, E. J. *Universal higher education.* New York: McGraw-Hill, 1966.

MCGRATH, E. J., AND HEFFERLIN, L. *Study of institutional vitality.* New York: Teachers College, Columbia University, 1968 (mimeographed).

MCGREE, R. "The function of institutional inbreeding." *American Journal of Sociology,* 1960(65).

MCGREGOR, D. *Leadership and motivation.* Cambridge: Massachusetts Institute of Technology, 1966.

MCKEACHIE, W. J. *New developments in teaching.* In New Dimensions in Higher Education, No. 16. Washington, D.C.: U.S. Office of Education, 1967 (mimeographed).

MEDSKER, L. L. *The junior college: Progress and prospect.* New York: McGraw-Hill, 1960.

MEIKLEJOHN, A. *Freedom and the college.* New York: Century, 1923.

MEYERSON, M. "The ethos of the American college student: Beyond the protests." In R. Morrison (ed.), *The American university.* Boston: Houghton Mifflin, 1966.

MILES, M. B. (ed.). *Innovation in education.* New York: Teachers College, Columbia University, 1964.

MILLETT, J. D. *The academic community.* New York: McGraw-Hill, 1962.

MILLS, C. W. *The power elite.* Oxford: Oxford University Press, 1956.

MINER, J. B. "Conformity among university professors and business executives." *Administrative Science Quarterly,* 1962, June (7).

MINTER, J., AND THOMPSON, I. *Colleges and universities as agents of social change.* Boulder, Colo.: Western Interstate Commission for Higher Education, 1968.

MOBERLY, SIR W. *The crisis in the university.* London: SCM Press, 1949.

MONROE, W. S., et al. *Ten years of educational research, 1918–1927.* Urbana: University of Illinois Press, 1928.

MOONEY, R. L. "A problem of leadership in the university." *Harvard Education Review,* 1963, Winter (33).

MORRIS, C. W. *Varieties of human value.* Chicago: University of Chicago Press, 1956.

MORRISON, J. C. "The role of research in educational reconstruction." In *The Forty-Fourth Yearbook,* Part II, *Structured reorganization.* Chicago: University of Chicago Press, 1945.

MUSCATINE, C. (Chairman), *Education at Berkeley.* Berkeley: Select Committee on Education, University of California, 1966.

NESBIT, R. *The sociological tradition.* New York: Basic Books, 1966.

NEVINS, A. *The state universities and democracy.* Urbana: University of Illinois Press, 1962.

NEWCOMB, T. M. *Personality and social change: Attitude formation in a student community.* New York: Dryden, 1943.

NEWCOMB, T. M., et al. *Persistence and change.* New York: Wiley, 1967.

NEWCOMB, T. M., AND FELDMAN, K. A. *The impacts of colleges upon their students.* New York: Carnegie Foundation for the Advancement of Teaching, 1968 (mimeographed).

NEWCOMB, T. M., AND WILSON, E. (eds.). *College peer groups.* Chicago: Aldine, 1966.

NEWFIELD, J. *A prophetic minority.* New York: New American Library, 1966.

NEWMAN, J. H. *Idea of the university.* New York and London: Longmans, Green, 1927.

NIEBUHR, R. *Man's nature and his communities.* New York: Scribners, 1965.

"Organization and administration." In *Encyclopedia of education research*, third edition. New York: Macmillan, 1960.

ORTEGA Y GASSET, J. *Mission of the university.* Princeton, N.J.: Princeton University Press, 1944.

PACE, C. R. "Five college environments." *College Board Review,* 1960 (41).

PACE, C. R. "Implications of differences in campus atmosphere for evaluation and planning of college programs." In R. L. Sutherland, et al. (eds.), *Personality factors on the college campus.* Austin: University of Texas Press, 1962.

PACE, C. R. "Methods in describing college cultures." *Teachers College Record,* 1962, January(63).

PACE, C. R., AND STERN, G. G. "An approach to the measurement of psychological characteristics of college environments." *Journal of Educational Psychology,* 1958, 49.

PACE, C. R., AND STERN, G. G. *A criterion study of college environment.* Syracuse, N.Y.: Psychological Research Center, Syracuse University, 1958.

PARKINSON, C. N. *Parkinson's law and other studies in administration.* Cambridge: Harvard University Press, 1957.

PARSONS, T. "The problems of the theory of change." In W. Bennis, K. Berne, and R. Chin (eds.), *The planning of change.* New York: Holt, 1961.

PARSONS, T., AND PLATT, G. *The academic profession: A pilot study.* Cambridge: Harvard University, 1968 (mimeographed).

PATILLO, M. M., AND MACKENZIE, D. M. *Church-sponsored higher education in the United States.* Washington, D.C.: American Council on Education, 1967.

PATTERSON, F., AND LONGWORTH, C. L. *The making of a college: Plans for a new departure in higher education.* Cambridge: Massachusetts Institute of Technology, 1966.

PERKINS, J. A. *The university in transition.* Princeton, N.J.: Princeton University Press, 1966.

PETERSON, R. E. *The scope of organized student protest in 1967–1968.* Princeton, N.J.: Educational Testing Service, 1968.

PFEIFFER, J. *New look at education: Systems analysis in our schools and colleges.* New York: Odyssey, 1968.

Phi Delta Kappa. *Research studies in education.* Bloomington, Ind.: Phi Delta Kappa, 1962.

President's Commission on Higher Education. *Higher education for American democracy,* Vol. I, *Establishing the goals.* Washington, D.C.: U.S. Government Printing Office, 1947.

President's Committee on Education Beyond the High School. *Second report to the President.* Washington, D.C.: U.S. Government Printing Office, 1957.

PRESTHUS, R. *The organizational society.* New York: Vintage, 1965.

RAUSHENBUSH, E. *The student and his studies.* Middletown, Conn.: Wesleyan University Press, 1965.

REEVES, M. *Eighteen plus: Unity and diversity in higher education.* London: Faber and Faber, 1965.

RICE, J. M. "The futility of the spelling grind." *Forum,* 1897(23).

RIESMAN, D. *Individualism reconsidered.* Glencoe, Ill.: Free Press, 1954.

RIESMAN, D. *Constraint and variety in American education.* Lincoln: University of Nebraska Press, 1958.

RIESMAN, D. "Notes on new universities: British and American." *Universities Quarterly,* March, 1966.

RIESMAN, D., AND JENCKS, C. "The viability of the American college." In N. Sanford (ed.), *The American college.* New York: Wiley, 1962.

ROGERS, E. M. *Diffusion of innovation.* New York: Free Press, 1962.

ROHMAN, G. "Justin Morrill College, Michigan State University." In W. Hamlin and L. Porter (eds.), *Dimensions of changes in higher education.* Yellow Springs, Ohio: Union for Research and Experimentation in Higher Education, 1967 (mimeographed).

ROKEACH, M. (ed.). *The open and closed mind.* New York: Basic Books, 1960.

ROSE, P. I. "The myth of unanimity: Student opinions on critical issues." *Sociology of Education,* 1964(37).

ROSENBERG, M. *Occupations and values.* Glencoe, Ill.: Free Press, 1957.

ROSSI, P. H. "Researchers, scholars and polity-makers." *Daedalus,* Fall, 1964.

ROURKE, F. E., AND BROOKS, G. E. *The managerial revolution in higher education.* Baltimore: Johns Hopkins Press, 1966.

RUDOLPH, F. *The American college and university.* New York: Knopf, 1962.

SANFORD, N. "Theories of higher education and the experimental college." In S. E. Harris (ed.), *Higher education in the United States: The economic problems.* Cambridge: Harvard University Press, 1960.

SANFORD, N. "Research and policy in higher education." In N. Sanford (ed.), *The American college.* New York: Wiley, 1962.

SANFORD, N. (ed.). *The American college.* New York: Wiley, 1962.

SANFORD, N. *Where colleges fail: A study of the student as a person.* San Francisco: Jossey-Bass, 1967.

SARTRE, J. P. *Existentialism and human emotion.* New York: Philosophical Library, 1957.

SCHEIN, E. H., AND BENNIS, W. G. *Personal and organizational change.* New York: Wiley, 1965.

SCHIFF, A. L. "Innovation and administrative decision-making: A study of the conservation of land resources." *Administrative Science Quarterly,* 1966, 2(1).

SCHON, D. *Technology and change.* New York: Delta, 1967.

SELDEN, W. K. *Accreditation: The struggle over standards in higher education.* New York: Harper, 1960.

SHERIF, C. W., SHERIF, M., AND NEBERGALL, R. E. *Attitude and attitude change.* Philadelphia: Saunders, 1965.

SMELSEN, N. J. *Theory of collective behavior.* New York: Free Press, 1963.

SMITH, G. K. (ed.). *Stress and campus response: Current issues in higher education.* San Francisco: Jossey-Bass, 1968.

SMITH, H. *The purposes of higher education.* New York: Harper, 1955.

SMITH, J. E. *Value convictions and higher education.* New Haven: Hazen Foundation, 1959.

SNOW, C. P. *The masters.* New York: Macmillan, 1951.

SOROKIN, P. *Social and cultural dynamics* (One volume edition). Boston: Porter Sargent, 1957.

STARR, R. *The beginnings of graduate education in the United States.* Chicago: University of Chicago Press, 1953.

STERN, G. G. *Scoring instructions and college norms: Activities index, college characteristics index.* Syracuse, N.Y.: Psychological Research Center, 1963.

STICKLER, W. H. (ed.). *Experimental colleges: Their role in American higher education.* Tallahassee: Florida State University, 1964.

STECKLEIN, J. E. "Research on faculty recruitment and motivation." In L. Wilson, et. al. (eds.), *Studies of college faculty.* Boulder, Colo.: Western Interstate Commission on Higher Education, 1961.

STOKE, H. *The American college president.* New York: Harper, 1959.

STONE, J. C. *Breakthrough in teacher education.* San Francisco: Jossey-Bass, 1968.

STROUP, H. *Bureaucracy in higher education.* New York: Free Press, 1966.

"Students and politics." *Daedalus,* 1968, 97(1).

Students for a Democratic Society. *The Port Huron statement.* New York: Students for a Democratic Society, 1964.

SWANSON, J. W. "The counter-university movement: In defense of the system." *Journal of Higher Education,* 1966, 57(7).

THOMPSON, V. A. "Bureaucracy and innovation." *Administrative Science Quarterly,* 1965, June(10).

THOMSON, F. A. "College and university surveys." *School and Society,* June 23, 1917, 5.

THORNDIKE, E. L., et al. *The measurement of intelligence.* New York: Teachers College, Columbia University, 1927.

THORNTON, J. W. *The community junior college.* New York: Wiley, 1966.

TRENT, J. W. *Catholics in college: Religious commitment and the intellectual life.* Chicago: University of Chicago Press, 1967. "Tradition and change." *Daedalus,* 1966, *95*(3).

TRENT, J. W., AND CRAISE, J. L. "Commitment and conformity in the American college. *Journal of Social Issues,* 1967, *23*(3).

TRENT, J. W., AND MEDSKER, L. L. *Beyond high school.* San Francisco: Jossey-Bass, 1968.

TROW, M. "Social research and educational policy." In *Research in higher education.* New York: College Entrance Examination Board, 1964.

UNIVERSITY OF GEORGIA, *Journal of research and development in higher education: USOE-funded R and D centers.* Athens: University of Georgia, 1968.

VAN DOREN, M. *Liberal education.* Boston: Beacon Press, 1959.

VEYSEY, L. R. *The emergence of the American university.* Chicago: University of Chicago Press, 1965.

VOLLMER, H. M., AND MILLS, D. L. (eds.). *Professionalization.* Englewood Cliffs, N.J.: Prentice-Hall, 1966.

WATSON, G. "Utopia and rebellion: The new college experiment." In M. B. Miles (ed.), *Innovation in education.* New York: Teachers College, Columbia University, 1964.

WATTS, W. A., AND WHITTAKER, D. "Some sociological differences between highly committed members of the Free Speech Movement and the student population at Berkeley." *Journal of Applied Behavioral Science,* January–March, 1965, *33.*

WEBSTER, H., FREEDMAN, M. B., AND HEIST, P. "Personality changes in college students." In N. Sanford (ed.), *The American college.* New York: Wiley, 1962.

WEISS, J. "The university as corporation." *New University Thought,* Summer, 1965, (4).

WESTLEY, W. A., AND EPSTEIN, N. B. *The silent majority: Families of emotionally healthy college students.* San Francisco: Jossey-Bass, 1969.

WHALEY, R. M. *Study of new and/or emerging institutions.* Washington, D.C.: American Council on Education, 1968 (mimeographed).

WHITEHEAD, A. N. *The aims of education.* New York: American Library, 1929, 1963.

WHITELY, P. L. "The consistency of personal values." *Journal of Abnormal Social Psychology,* 1938, *33.*

WHYTE, W. H., JR. *The organization man.* New York: Simon and Schuster, 1956.

WILLIAMS, R. L. *The administration of academic affairs.* Ann Arbor: University of Michigan Press, 1965.

WILLIAMSON, E. G. *Student personnel services in colleges and universities.* New York: McGraw-Hill, 1961.

WILSON, J., WILLIAMS, N., AND SUGARMAN, B. *Introduction of moral education.* Baltimore: Penguin, 1967.

WILSON, L. *Basic premises for a national policy in higher education.* Washington, D.C.: American Council on Education, 1963.

WILSON, L. *Academic man.* New York: Octagon, 1964.

WILSON, L. "Form and function in American higher education." *Educational Record,* 1964, 45(2).

WILSON, L. (ed.). *Emerging patterns in American higher education.* Washington, D.C.: American Council on Education, 1965.

WILSON, R., AND GAFF, J. *Studies of faculty characteristics and faculty influence on students.* Berkeley: Center for Research and Development in Higher Education (in press).

WINTHROP, H. "Phenomenological and existential considerations surrounding the problem of values." *Journal of Existential Psychiatry,* Fall, 1961.

WISE, G. "Integrated education in a dis-integrated world." *Teachers College Record,* 1966, 67(6).

WISE, M. *They come for the best of reasons: College students today.* Washington, D.C.: American Council on Education, 1958.

WRIGHTMAN, L. S. *Bibliography of research on the philosophies of human nature scales,* Revised edition. Nashville: George Peabody College, 1968 (mimeographed).

WRISTON, H. M. *Academic procession: Reflections of a college president.* New York: Columbia University Press, 1959.

YOUNG, M. *The rise of the meritocracy, 1870–2033.* New York: Random House, 1959.

"Youth 1967—the challenge of change." *American Scholar,* 1967, 36(4).

ZWEIG, M. *The idea of a world university.* Carbondale: Southern Illinois University Press, 1967.

INDEX

A

Academic community (*see* Community, academic)

Academic freedom, 35

Administrators: attitudes toward innovations, 144–145, 151–152, 232, 238–239; conventional criteria for, 97; coteries of, 59; educational perspectives, 104–106, 172; job description, 13; recasting responsibilities of, 129–130

ALLEN, W. H., xiii

Antioch College, 227

ASHBY, E., 13

Assumptions, educational and societal, 10–11

Athletics, intercollegiate, 125

AYERS, L. P., x

B

BARTH, J., 223n

BAY, C., 212

Black power, 8–9, 77, 134–135, 182–183

BOULDING, K., xiii, 214

BUBER, M., xx

Budgets, educational, 5, 28, 36, 105–106

BUSWELL, G. T., viii

BUTTERFIELD, E. W., xii–xiii

C

California, University of, 1–2, 26; Berkeley, 128, 158; Santa Cruz, 132

CARTER, L. F., xii

Center for the Study of Democratic Institutions, 88

L